The Great Flip

"Fraser is a patient educator, while never showing bias, which is crucial. Importantly, the book is not a stuffy academic text reciting streams of dates and names and sequential events that compose some overarching thesis; *Fraser is a consummate storyteller*, bringing the past into sharp focus, and drawing conclusions about human nature and the American way that will resonate for readers in every corner of this country, regardless of political allegiance. Instead of a political tract, this is an objective exploration of individualism and republicanism, which can be appreciated by both sides of the aisle."

—Self-Publishing Review ★★★★★

"Fraser offers a new history of seismic ideological changes in the American Democratic and Republican Parties . . . The author's primary aim is to demonstrate the many ways that liberals and conservatives have, over the long sweep of American history, swapped positions on that central role of energetic government . . . All of this is popular history done very, very well. *Fraser is uniformly excellent at breaking down complex subjects into readable, comprehensive narratives*—a godsend considering the intricacies of the material he's covering. [The author] strikes a *welcomingly nonpartisan tone* while discussing social and political subjects that have become radioactively divisive in the 21st century."

—Kirkus Reviews

"Fraser's use of research is mostly inspired, refreshing readers' faded recollections of long-ago history lessons with surprising facts . . . Anyone interested in gaining perspective on America's current, apparently impassable political impasse should find food for thought in Fraser's original approach."

—blueink Review

"In today's political landscape, terms like 'liberal' and 'conservative' seem like fixed absolutes. . . historian Donald J. Fraser challenges this assumption . . . The rivalry between Thomas Jefferson and Alexander Hamilton embodies the conflict between two fundamental perspectives on the role of government—whether government should take an active part in ensuring its people's welfare and equality, or whether it should instead defend liberty and self-government . . . Thoroughly researched and supported with numerous citations, [the book] is an *incisive, compellingly readable work that offers a welcome refresher on the nuanced, often paradoxical development of American political thought.*"

—Indie Reader 4.8 stars (out of 5)

". . . for much of the country's history, Fraser notes, conservatives believed that the government should intervene so that an elite few could prevent the self-interested masses from descending into chaos, while liberals believed in the ability of the people to govern themselves, independent of oversight. Through engaging, informative prose, Fraser reveals that it was only with the rise of powerful monopolies and increasing income inequality that liberals embraced active government as a way of protecting average citizens—while business minded conservatives came to oppose such measures."

—Foreword Reviews ★★★★★

The
GREAT FLIP

The GREAT FLIP

The Shifting Views of Liberals and Conservatives on Active Government

DONALD J. FRASER

FRASER & ASSOCIATES
ROSEVILLE, CA

For information contact:
Fraser & Associates
Roseville, California
www.perspectiveshistory.com

978-0-9970805-4-4 (paperback)
978-0-9970805-5-1 (e-book)

Library of Congress Control Number: 2023914647

Book Design by Dotti Albertine
Democratic/Republican Illustration by Chris Fraser

Printed in the United States of America

COVER IMAGES:
Portrait of Thomas Jefferson: By Rembrandt Peale - https://www.whitehousehistory.org/galleries/presidential-portraits, Public Domain, https://commons.wikimedia.org/

Portrait of Alexander Hamilton: By John Trumbull (1756-1843), Google Art Project, National Portrait Gallery, Public Domain, https://commons.wikimedia.org/

Herbert Hoover's official White House portrait: By Elmer Wesley Greene, Public Domain, https://commons.wikimedia.org/, Colorization by: https://pin.it/5EpFJzk

Photograph of Franklin D. Roosevelt: By Rembrandt Peale - https://www.whitehousehistory.org/galleries/presidential-portraits, Public Domain, https://commons.wikimedia.org

To my parents,
in loving memory

I own, I am not a friend to a very energetic government. It is always oppressive.
    —Thomas Jefferson

For out of this modern civilization economic royalists carved new dynasties. Against economic tyranny such as this, the American citizen could appeal only to the organized power of government.
    —Franklin Delano Roosevelt

Energy in government is essential to that security against external and internal danger and to the prompt and salutary execution of the laws which enter into the very definition of good government.
    —Alexander Hamilton

Every step of bureaucratizing of the business of our country poisons the very roots of liberalism. . . . It is the road not to more liberty, but to less liberty.
    —Herbert Hoover

CONTENTS

CONTENTS

The idea for this book came from a lecture I was giving to one of my history classes at the Osher Lifelong Learning Institute at UC Davis. I was explaining how the Whig Party led by Henry Clay was generally conservative, but they supported activist government to implement Clay's American System. The Democratic Party at that time, led by Andrew Jackson, was liberal but opposed an energetic government. Given how different this was from our politics today, it confused my students. So, I decided to write a book that traced why liberals and conservatives eventually changed positions on the role of government in American society.

I want to thank all of those involved in making this book a reality. First to my editor, Brittany Dowdle, who has made this volume immeasurably better through her keen eye for detail and pointing out those places where I was unclear (or in some cases simply wrong factually on something). To Dotti Albertine, who is working on her third book with me. Her expertise in compiling this book and in preparing the covers brings a true measure of professionalism to this endeavor. Finally, to Ælfwine Mischler for her expertise in preparing the index.

Language is constantly evolving, as I learned in writing this book. There are numerous places where I have quoted other authors or historians who have written important works in the past when different words were considered acceptable. I have included their critical insights in their own words, but I have used current best practices in my own writing to honor the diverse experiences and dignity of all Americans.

INTRODUCTION

*In the future days, which we seek to make secure, we look
forward to a world founded upon four essential human
freedoms.*

— Franklin Delano Roosevelt, State of the Union Address, January 6, 1941

Franklin Delano Roosevelt leaned back in his chair and began to dictate. He was in a meeting with his main speechwriters, Harry Hopkins, Samuel Rosenman, and Robert Sherwood. On the fourth draft of his soon-to-be-delivered State of the Union address, FDR was looking for a fitting ending for a speech designed to lay out the dangers that the United States and the rest of the world faced from fascism and communism. Suddenly, Roosevelt said to his stenographer: "Dorothy, take a law."[1]

Roosevelt may have been thinking back to a press conference from the previous summer when he had discussed what a postwar world might look like if the forces of totalitarianism were defeated by the democracies. Keep in mind, this was before Pearl Harbor, and FDR was still struggling with how to get the American people to support involvement in another European war. "Slowly the President had listed [his objectives]: freedom of information and religion and of self-expression and freedom from fear," the historian James MacGregor

Burns writes. A reporter questioned whether there was another one, freedom from want. FDR replied that he had inadvertently forgotten that one and that it indeed was a part of the four important freedoms. He had also been thinking about and cataloging ideas for an economic bill of rights related to freedom from want.[2]

Later when he stood before Congress on January 6, 1941, Roosevelt laid out his ideas for the Four Freedoms. The act of standing was quite a feat for FDR, who had contracted polio at the age of thirty-nine, a disease which had paralyzed him below the waist. Though he had been an athletic young man who enjoyed tennis, golf, and sailing, standing for Roosevelt was now excruciating. "It was as if he braced his body for a bullet," the journalist Eliot Janeway once wrote. FDR had also hidden the fact of his paralysis from the American public, during a time when reporters did not reveal every detail they knew. "The public had no idea that their president could stand only for short periods of time, that he could walk only when pushed along by the momentum of another person, that he had to be carried up and down steps and helped into bed at night by his valet," Doris Kearns Goodwin has written. Yet polio had also made Roosevelt a better man. Once a bit of a dilettante, FDR emerged from polio "completely warm hearted with new humility," according to his Labor Secretary Frances Perkins, who described him as a man who "came to empathize with the poor and underprivileged."[3]

The State of the Union address was largely devoted to the need for the United States to prepare itself for "meeting this foreign peril" from Germany and Japan. But as he ended the speech, he began to talk about the "foundations of a healthy and strong democracy" that would ensure equality of opportunity and jobs for those who needed them. He then launched into his Four Freedoms:

The first is the freedom of speech and expression—everywhere in the world.

The second is freedom of every person to worship God in his own way—everywhere in the world.

The third is freedom from want—which translated into world terms, means economic understandings which will secure to every nation a healthy peacetime life for its inhabitants—everywhere in the world.

The fourth is freedom from fear—which, translated into world terms, means a world-wide reduction of armaments to such a point and in such thorough fashion that no nation will be in position to commit an act of physical aggression against any neighbor—anywhere in the world.[4]

While parts of FDR's Four Freedoms were uncontroversial, rooted in the Declaration of Independence and the Constitution, freedom from want embodied "principles associated with the New Deal," the historian Eric Foner argues. Roosevelt had been elected in 1932 at the height of the Great Depression, which had begun with the stock market crash of 1929. Unemployment stood at close to 25 percent, the banking system had collapsed, and economic activity had dropped precipitously. In response, Roosevelt had announced a "New Deal for the American people" in his acceptance speech at the Democratic National Convention. In his first one hundred days in office, FDR began a series of improvised policies that placed the federal government at the center of ending the Great Depression. Now Roosevelt, with the announcement of his Four Freedoms, was establishing that governmental activism and responsibility for the welfare of the people should be adopted worldwide.[5]

By 1944, the president's announcement of freedom from want became a call for an economic bill of rights. "We have come to a clear realization of the fact that true individual freedom cannot exist without economic security and independence," Roosevelt argued. Henceforth, the forces of liberalism would be aligned with government policies designed to ensure people had a job and "a decent standard of living, medical care, education, and adequate protection from the ravages of old age, sickness, accident, and unemployment," Foner writes.[6]

FDR's proposals did not go unnoticed by his conservative political opponents, who attacked his use of government for such purposes. Edith N. Rogers, a Republican from Massachusetts, had declined to criticize Roosevelt directly, but instead indicated that "Freedom of Private Enterprise" should be the fifth freedom, since the four would be meaningless in the absence of the American free enterprise system. As liberals became ever more supportive of active government, one of the prime opposition spokesmen became Friedrich A. Hayek, an Austrian-born economist who published *The Road to Serfdom* in 1944. "Hayek claimed that even the best-intentioned government efforts to direct the economy posed a threat to individual liberty," Foner writes. Hayek's critique was in part grounded in the classical liberal argument that liberty was "freedom from coercion." Hayek's criticism would become central to conservative efforts in the future to roll back the role of government in the life of Americans.[7]

All of this should be quite familiar to the modern reader, with liberals supporting an active role for government in the economy and society to promote the twin goals of liberty and equality. Modern conservatives, on the other hand, see government as a threat to liberty and see inequality as the natural outcome of differing talents and skills that people possess. What may not be so well-known is that the position of modern liberals for active government is diametrically opposed to that of the founder of the Democratic Party, Thomas Jefferson. In his day, the party was originally called the Republican or Democratic-Republican Party, which eventually became the Democratic Party under Andrew Jackson. And active government was supported by the conservative Alexander Hamilton during the founding era.

In a letter to James Madison in 1787, Jefferson told him: "I own, I am not a friend to a very energetic government. It is always oppressive." Madison was attempting to get his friend to support the new federal constitution, which proposed to strengthen the hand of the federal government and create one nation out of thirteen separate sovereign states. Jefferson would equivocate on the new constitution, and eventually support it. He was not opposed to all government, but rather feared placing too much power in the federal government. Part of his opposition to an active government was grounded in his optimistic view of human nature. Man was a social creature who naturally got along with other people and could act with virtue "in doing good to others," as he once wrote to John Adams. Jefferson subscribed to the theory that "virtue flowed from the citizen's participation in society, not in government, which the liberal minded increasingly saw as the source of the evils of the world," Gordon Wood has written.[8]

Hamilton, on the other hand, had a more negative view of human nature. Government needed sufficient power to control man's baser instincts in Hamilton's worldview. He especially supported a strong and "energetic" executive. "Energy in the executive is a leading character in the definition of good government," Hamilton writes in *Federalist* No. 70. Hamilton had an abiding fear of disorder due to the evil that existed in human nature. Government was needed "because the passions of men will not conform to the dictates of reason and justice without constraint." He also saw that men were capable of good, but that the capacity to act with virtue was largely found in society's elite, which made him distrust democracy.[9]

The way in which liberals and conservatives have switched positions on the role of government is the core subject of this book. Why did this occur? In addition to the brief outline above, what were the major reasons that liberals like Jefferson feared a strong and active government, and conservatives like Hamilton supported strong governmental actions? What changed over the course of American history that led Franklin D. Roosevelt, the inheritor of the party of Jefferson, to support an active role for government in the lives of the American people? What caused conservatives to adopt Jefferson's worldview on limited government? These are some of the questions that this book explores.

Individualism and Communitarianism

Another underlying theme of this book is the role that two distinct ideologies have played in how historical actors have viewed the role of government. One is the importance of the individual, the other the importance of the group. These two can be boiled down to an *I* approach to societal problems versus a *we* approach.

Individualism was an outgrowth, at least in part, of Enlightenment thinking on the part of men like Thomas Hobbes and John Locke. While both men were interested in the individual, they drew different conclusions from their work. Hobbes saw humankind as essentially selfish and unsocial, in pursuit of self-interest. Only an autocratic government could rein in man's baser instincts and avoid a "war of every man against every man." Locke thought that man had a moral core, and that all men were free and equal in a state of nature. In Locke's view, the individual gives up part of their freedom to the government to secure certain rights, including "life, liberty and estate." Lockean liberalism, sometimes referred to as *classical liberalism*, is based on the idea that government is grounded in the consent of the governed.[10]

Individualism has much to commend it. It implicitly requires that the equal dignity of each person be respected. It opens a world in which individuals are free to pursue their own interests and to succeed in society to the maximum extent of their abilities. It also calls for each person to have a role in their government, and for laws designed to protect the rights of the individual. But individualism has its limitations as well, especially in the economic sphere, where unbridled individualism can lead to greed and unsustainable levels of wealth inequality.

The founding generation would have been surprised at the idea of unbridled individualism since they also subscribed to a more communitarian view, sometimes referred to as classical republicanism. They believed that self-government needed to be grounded in public virtue, in the willingness of the individual to place the common good above self-interest.

Equality was the glue that held together both individualism and communitarianism during our early history. "Many leaders of the Revolution seem to the modern eye simultaneously republican (in their concern for the public good and citizens' obligations to the polity) and liberal (in their preoccupation with individual rights)" historian Eric Foner has written. Jefferson, who is often seen as a Lockean liberal, also espoused republican ideals, most famously that "all men are created equal." Even Locke believed in equality in a state of nature, and he would not completely understand the use that some have made of individualism, a term he did not use. The political scientist Ruth Grant has argued that "the opposite of Locke's political individualism is not community but hierarchy" and that his views were not incompatible with "the importance of communal ties" but rather were opposed to any form of "natural or divinely ordained hierarchy" among people.[11]

By the 1830s Tocqueville would observe how Americans had reconciled individualism with the public good, and how equality played a role in this. He thought that "it is possible to imagine an extreme point at which freedom and equality meet and blend together" at some point in the future. But he also worried that excessive individualism could be a danger to public virtue and the public interest. Tocqueville thought that individualism and self-interest in America were sometimes misunderstood. "Americans . . . are delighted to explain almost all the acts of their life in the light of self-interest properly understood. They are quite willing to show how enlightened self-love continually leads them to help one another," and to make "great and sincere sacrifices for the common good," he wrote.[12]

Roosevelt would, in fact, change the definition of what a liberal was, from an opponent to a supporter of active government. In doing this, he was building a bridge between the classical liberal and classical republican ideas, between the individual and the community. The reader will note that FDR called his proposal the Four Freedoms, tying them to the classical liberal concern with liberty. Yet freedom from want is an attempt to ensure the public good is served by promoting economic equality.

Over time, individualism and communitarianism would often find themselves in conflict, and one side or the other would become predominant. This would have an important impact on liberal and conservative views on the role of government.

The Problem of Income Inequality

In this book we will examine how liberal support for small government was initially grounded in the view that the United States should remain a largely rural and farming-based society. In such a society, there were not large disparities of wealth, and so income inequality was not a major problem. Concerns about inequality were tied to the desire to develop a more democratic society, one in which the common white man was treated with equal dignity as the rich and powerful, and where individual rights were protected. However, such rights did not extend to women, Black people, or Native Americans. Those who followed Jefferson and his Democratic-Republican Party believed that a democracy could only survive in a society of independent property owners. Inequality was considered to occur because of outside structural forces at work, especially the use of the power of government to reward one group over another, which many thought corrupted republican society.

Conservative support for active government was grounded in the need for economic change. Led by Alexander Hamilton, conservative leaders wanted to create an industrial base to ensure that the United States became a powerful and independent nation on the world stage. Support for banking, tariffs, infrastructure, and corporate charters were all integral to achieve this goal. While both sides supported equality of opportunity and equality under the law, conservatives were less concerned about inequality of wealth, believing it was a natural outgrowth of the differing skills and abilities of people.

Ultimately, the Hamiltonian vision of the United States as a powerful industrial nation would gradually become a reality, especially in the aftermath of the Civil War. The resulting problem of income inequality presented liberals with a dilemma: retain a commitment to small government and watch society become ever more unequal—or become supporters of activist government. By the time of the election of Franklin D. Roosevelt in 1932, the transformation of the Democratic Party would be complete. The party would ultimately use Hamiltonian means (active government) to achieve Jeffersonian ends (a more equal society). Meanwhile conservative antipathy to government, as represented by the modern Republican Party, would grow over time.

Endnotes

1   James MacGregor Burns, *Roosevelt: Soldier of Freedom* (New York: Harcourt Brace Jovanovich, 1970), p. 33.

2   Burns, p. 33.

3   Doris Kearns Goodwin, *No Ordinary Time: Franklin and Eleanor Roosevelt: The Home Front in World War II* (New York: Simon & Schuster, 1994), p. 16–17, and p. 586.

4   Roosevelt's State of the Union speech from January 6, 1941.

5   Eric Foner, *Story of American Freedom* (New York: W. W. Norton, 1998), p. 223; the statistics on the Great Depression were retrieved July 11, 2019, from the FDR Presidential Library & Museum at https://www.fdrlibrary.org/iw/great-depression-facts.

6   Foner, p. 234.

7   Foner, p. 235–236.

8   The quote from the letter to James Madison dated December 20, 1787, are from Adrienne Koch and William Peden, eds. *The Life and Selected Writings of Thomas Jefferson* (New York: Modern Library, 1972), p. 440; the quote from the letter to Adams is from Garrett Ward Sheldon, *The Political Philosophy of Thomas Jefferson* (Baltimore: The Johns Hopkins Press, 1991), p. 58. Richard K. Matthews, *The Radical Politics of Thomas Jefferson: A Revisionist View* (Lawrence: University Press of Kansas, 1984), p. 53; Gordon Wood, *Revolutionary Characters: What Made the Founders Different* (New York: Penguin Press, 2006), p. 106.

9   The quote is from the edition of *The Federalist Papers:* Alexander Hamilton, *James Madison, John Jay* with an introduction by Clinton Rossiter (New York: New American Library, 1961), p. 110. All quotes footnoted based on the primary author and page number. Michael P. Federici, *The Political Philosophy of Alexander Hamilton* (Baltimore: Johns Hopkins University Press, 2012), p. 62 and p. 64.

10 Stanley M. Honer and Thomas C. Hunt, *Invitation to Philosophy: Issues and Options* (Belmont: Wadsworth Publishing Company, 1973), p. 167 and 179.

11 Ruth W. Grant, "Locke's Political Anthropology and Lockean Individualism," *The Journal of Politics*, vol. 50, no. 1 February 1988, p. 51; Foner, p. 8.

12 Alexis de Tocqueville and Arthur Goldhammer, *Democracy in America* (New York: Library of America, 2003), chapters 1–4.

CHAPTER 1

The Impact of the American Revolution on Government and Society

We have it in our power to begin the world over again.
—THOMAS PAINE, *COMMON SENSE*

The American Revolution unleashed the forces of modernization in the thirteen colonies and upset the hierarchical world that existed in the late seventeenth century. There was little distinction between private and public spheres prior to the revolution, whereas afterward there was, which had an impact on how people viewed the role of government. In the years after declaring independence, the fear of centralized governmental power, which the British Empire represented, caused the creation of a very weak government under the Articles of Confederation. While the Constitution strengthened the federal government, it also institutionalized the debate over the role that government should play in American society.

The Colonial World

The colonial world was monarchical and hierarchical, even though the colonies were lightly ruled by Great Britain. Unlike the mother country, colonial America did not have ranks or titles, such as prince, duke, or earl. Instead, the colonial world was divided into the gentry, or gentlemen, and commoners. The gentry saw themselves as the natural rulers of society. "Social honors, social distinctions, perquisites of office, business contracts, privileges and monopolies, even excessive property and wealth of various sorts . . . in fact seemed to flow from connections to government, in the end from connections to monarchical authority," according to Gordon Wood. Government was on the side of the gentleman in society, not the common person.[1]

Common people were disparaged as inferior and were often blocked from attempting to move out of their dependent role in society as farmers or laborers. The consumption of luxury goods was considered the domain of the gentry. To the extent that commoners consumed too much, "they would become idle, begin to act like aristocrats, and thus confound all social distinctions," Wood writes. Inequality was considered the norm in the colonial world, with the gentry born to their superior position in society. Yet inequality was less about wealth, since the colonies were far more equal than our society is today or compared to England or Western Europe at the time. The richest 1 percent in the colonies had 8.5 percent of total income in 1774, compared to 45 percent in Great Britain. Inequality in the colonies was about social rank and attitude, not wealth.[2]

Still, unlike in Great Britain or Europe, there was a route to break out of the role of a commoner, and that was through a combination of unique skills, hard work, and most importantly, the patronage of a member of the gentry. Benjamin Franklin was able to start his own print shop when he was only twenty years old due to the help of powerful friends he had made. George Washington was assisted in his rise through his relationship with Lord Fairfax. Alexander Hamilton came to American from the Caribbean by catching the eye of powerful men on the island of Saint Croix. Upward mobility was built into the world of colonial America, even if it partly depended on relationships.[3]

However, the colonial world did not begin as a structured hierarchy. Virginia, for example, was established in 1606 as a proprietary colony, a private venture called the Virginia Company. In 1619, the same year that enslaved Africans were first brought to Virginia, a local elected assembly met specifically to represent most settlers, not just the rich. Virginia was to be a commonwealth, "founded on the well-being of the people as a whole, not the few," writes James Horn of the Jamestown Rediscovery Foundation. Disparities of wealth soon began to emerge as tobacco became the dominant crop, and the wealthy argued "that poor people's lack of independence, property, and education disqualified them from prominent roles in society," Horn writes. Within a few years, the larger and wealthier planters would come to dominate the government of Virginia.[4]

The British found that they needed to share authority in running their colonies in both Virginia and Maryland with the wealthy planters, who would not pay taxes without having some say in how the colonies were run. Taxation was initially regressive, with the poor paying as much as the rich, who also reaped the reward of holding political offices that were highly compensated. Wealthy planters came to dominate throughout the South, including the Carolinas and Georgia, building their great wealth on the backs of slave labor. The slave system helped to foster ever more concentrations of wealth in the hands of fewer and fewer men who owned large plantations. "Virginia had become an aristocracy . . . not more than a hundred families controlled the wealth and government of the colony" by the middle of the seventeenth century, the historian Daniel J. Boorstin has written.[5]

By the eighteenth century, Virginia's Southern gentry had begun to oppose higher taxes for their poorer brethren. They did this not out of altruism but to curry favor with the voters, since approximately 60 percent of white men could vote. To get elected to the local assembly, the gentry needed to cultivate support among these small planters, by plying them with food and alcohol before they voted and by helping to advance their interests. Thus, even in the highly structured environment of Virginia, there were the early beginnings of self-government. "Less burdened by taxes . . . eighteenth-century common planters began to regard their wealthy neighbors as powerful protectors of their common interests," historian Alan Taylor writes.[6]

But it wasn't just the need to get elected that caused the gentry to cater to the small planters. So too did the need to control enslaved people. Bacon's Rebellion, which occurred in 1676, saw "poor farmers, including former slaves and servants," march on Jamestown, the then capital. In the aftermath of that incident, the gentry began to "split the lower classes apart along racial lines," according to historian Heather Cox Richardson. Edmund Morgan, who wrote the definitive account of the link between slavery and freedom, has written that this was done was through racism in order "to separate dangerous free whites from dangerous slave [B]lacks by a screen of racial contempt." Thus, at the heart of the early American experiment was this dangerous paradox—that liberty and equality for some meant that others must be enslaved. It would have important implications for the future use of governmental powers.[7]

In contrast to the experience of the Southern colonies, New England represents a very different experience, yet it too had its share of hierarchy. The New England colonies started as religious settlements by the Puritans, who came to establish a shining city on a hill, as John Winthrop told his small group of migrants on the *Arbella* in 1630. These colonies were quite independent of Great Britain, and they quickly established republics, "where the propertied men elected their governors and councils, as well as their assemblies, and where much decision making was dispersed to the many small towns," according to Taylor. The Puritans were in many ways intolerant, having banished Roger William to Rhode Island because of his dissident views. A hierarchical society was natural to the Puritans, "who commanded their wives, controlled their adult sons and daughters, and kept out any deviants who might spoil the harmony of their peaceable kingdoms," Joyce Appleby has written. There were numerous attempts by Great Britain to exert greater control in New England, but they eventually settled into a structure where royal governors shared power with locally elected assemblies that tended to be dominated by rich property owners.[8]

Despite the hierarchical nature of colonial society, land ownership and voting were widespread in New England. Much of government took place at the town level, where men gathered at town hall meetings to elect representatives and set tax rates. "The main business of the town concerned roads and bridges, schools, and the poor," one historian writes of the town of Concord. While large numbers of men were eligible to vote, once that occurred, governing was restricted to the gentry. "The upper orders were to rule, the lower to follow," according to historian Robert A. Gross.[9]

The Impact of the American Revolution

The hierarchical world of the colonies would be shaken over the next fifty years due to the American Revolution and the debate over the future of the newly independent United States. There were also certain countervailing trends present that would aid in the transition toward republican governments. One was the public's experience with self-government. The colonial governments had legislative bodies that were elected by property owners. Since property ownership was widespread in many of the colonies, or voting laws were liberal, participation in elections was widespread by the standards of the society of the time. As historian James T. Kloppenberg has written, "the idea of popular sovereignty grew from the colonial experience of self-government."[10]

Second, as members of the British Empire, the colonists viewed themselves as the inheritors of British liberty. Eric Foner writes that "British freedom celebrated the rule of law, the right to live under legislation to which one's community had consented, restraints on the arbitrary exercise of political authority, and the rights like trial by jury enshrined in the common law." A series of British actions would cause the colonists to believe that their rights as British citizens, especially their liberty, were being endangered in the run-up to independence.[11]

In the aftermath of Great Britain's victory in the French and Indian War in 1763, King George III and his ministers took a series of steps designed to rationalize the administration of their colonies. The actions were designed to rein in the independence of the colonies and to raise revenue to pay off the debt that had accumulated during the war with France. In 1765, the British approved the Stamp Act, which led to a series of colonial protests, with the British finally removing the tax in 1766. While the colonial elite protested through peaceful means by filing grievance petitions with the king and Parliament, the common people would sometimes turn to violent protests. The dispute had opened a major question in the relationship between Great Britain and its colonies: who controlled their internal administration, especially the imposition of taxes? The king and Parliament maintained that they had the sole right to legislate for the colonies "in all cases whatsoever." The colonists maintained "that it is inseparable to the freedom of a people, and the undoubted right of Englishmen, that no taxes should be imposed upon them, but with their consent." Since the colonists were not represented in Parliament, they should not be taxed.[12]

Disputes over taxation and representation continued over the next thirteen years. Great Britain would impose a tax, the colonists would protest, and the tax would be removed. Then another tax would be imposed and trigger a similar round of disputes. Finally, the Tea Act of 1773 led to the Boston Tea Party, in which colonial leaders, poorly disguised as members of the Mohawk tribe, dumped tea into the harbor. The British overreacted, responding with the Coercive or Intolerable, Acts, which suspended the Massachusetts charter (essentially disbanding their colonial government) and placed the colony under a military governor. Soon thereafter, the colonies sent delegates to a Continental Congress so that they could take concerted action in response to the British. By early 1775, the dispute had turned violent, with the two sides engaging in open warfare in the Massachusetts towns of Lexington and Concord. By the summer of 1776, the Americans declared independence, and the Revolutionary War began.[13]

The colonial protests were accompanied by the development of two key contrasting perspectives that would impact the colonists' views toward government. The first was a fear of concentrated power. The second, and opposing, view was that united action between the colonies was needed to confront the British Empire.

Both ideologies shared a fear that concentrated power, such as that represented by the British system of government, was dangerous to liberty and could lead to tyranny. In a series of writings and pamphlets that began to appear in the late 1760s and early 1770s, the colonists asserted that the British Constitution had come under the control of a corrupt and despotic form of ministerial government. The balance that had been contained in the British Constitution between the one (the king), the few (the aristocracy), and the many (the commons) had become unhinged. The colonists greatly feared that the wealthy few had gained too much power and control over Great Britain, with the result that liberty would be extinguished, not only in England but also in the North American colonies. Liberty and power were viewed as two opposing ends of the spectrum. "Power is by its nature aggressive, encroaching, unstable; liberty is passive, exposed, subvertible," as historians Stanley Elkins and Eric McKitrick write. Once one element of the British system became too powerful, in this case the ministers that made up the king's cabinet, they would eradicate liberty. This emerging ideology would have grave implications for the creation of one American nation after independence, since the colonists would initially oppose the establishment of a new and powerful national government, looking at it as simply a replacement for the central control of the English. The fear of concentrated power would continue to affect the way that governmental power was viewed by many in the United States.[14]

While the ideology of the revolution would reflect a fear of strong central power, especially that of an executive, the reality of confronting the British Empire required a united response. Both the First and Second Continental Congress were organized to provide the colonists with a means to coordinate a joint response to the actions of the British, but it was a unity that was born from the press of events. The tension between the need to unite to defeat the British and the founders' fear of centralized power would be one of the fundamental reasons why the formation of an American nation proved difficult.

This tension was at the very core of the American drive for independence and has cast a long shadow on the legitimacy of the actions of the federal governmental ever since. The debates that ensued can be seen in various guises throughout our history.

There were also three other ideas, sometimes complementary and sometimes in conflict, that impacted the way people viewed the role of government in society. One—liberalism—dealt with the role of the individual and the importance of liberty; republicanism dealt with the role of the group in promoting the general welfare of the society. The final idea was equality, which could act as a bridge linking the individual to the group.

Classical Liberalism and Republicanism

George Will, in his 2019 book *The Conservative Sensibility*, writes that "liberalism championed individualism and the rights of the individual against those forces of enforced order," or government. It is a succinct description of classical liberalism. At the heart of classical liberalism is the idea of liberty—that everyone has a right to personal freedom, so long as they don't injure others. Government's main role, in some sense its sole role, is to protect each individual's natural rights, especially their freedom "to use their bodies, labor, and justly acquired property as they see fit, as long as they respect the equal freedom of others," as the scholar George H. Smith writes. A system of limited government is a core element of classical liberalism, since liberty is viewed as being advanced by removing governmental restraints.[15]

The individual is at the center of the liberal world view, rather than "a family, a tribe, a nation, or some other type of social group," political scientist Francis Fukuyama writes. People act to advance their own self-interest, and only cooperate because they believe it advances their interests. Much of modern economics is built around the theory of the individual—that we are all "rational utility maximizers." The theory of liberalism "begins with the claim that we are separate, individual persons, each with our own aims, interests, and conceptions of the good life," political philosopher Michael J. Sandel has observed. Liberalism also meant that everyone should be treated with equal respect and dignity.[16]

Yet classical liberalism was just one strain of thought that existed at the founding. Classical republicanism was in some ways complementary to the liberal tradition, but in other ways contradictory, providing a more social, or group, approach to American life than the individualism of liberalism. Thus, from the birth of the United States, both individualism and communitarianism were built into the American experience, both a desire for freedom from governmental interference and the use of government to advance the public good. James T. Kloppenberg has written that the American founding was one in which "arguments for freedom and arguments for community have jostled against each other."[17]

One of the core values of republicanism was the importance of public virtue. In a republic, each individual must "sacrifice his private interests for the good of the community," Wood writes. Compliance with the demands and laws of government were enforced using fear in monarchies, but this was anathema in a republic where the people consent to be governed. If not fear, then what would motivate compliance with the law? For John Adams and others of the period, the answer would be found in public virtue. Adams, in a letter to Mercy Warren, described it this way: "Public virtue cannot exist in a Nation without private (virtue), and public virtue is the only foundation of Republics. There must be a positive passion for the public good, public interest . . . established in the minds of the people, or there can be no Republican government, nor any real liberty: and the public passion must be superior to all private passions." Public virtue was related to public, or political, liberty in republican thought, which considered virtue to be essential so that the people could participate in their government and make wise decisions. "Political liberty meant the right to participate in public affairs," as Eric Foner writes.[18]

Historians have tended to see either classical liberalism or classical republicanism as exclusively being at the core of the American founding, but both were present. Kloppenberg has written the following, which summarizes succinctly the pragmatism of our founding generation: Americans have always drawn upon a variety of sources to fashion the arguments they want to make. At times those arguments have been "republican," if we must characterize invocations of virtuous citizens and the public good as republican. At times they have been "liberal," if we must characterize invocations of individual freedom and rights as liberal. . . . But almost always they have been hybrids of these and other languages and traditions.[19]

During the founding era there was a fear that public officials would act in a corrupt manner, since power tended to corrupt. Today we view corruption most egregiously as attempts to bribe public officials, or more subtly through actions to influence politicians by providing large campaign donations or through lobbying efforts in which private interests are chosen over the public's interest. Perhaps the most basic form of corruption, the one that persists to this day, is that a public official will use the power of their office to advance their own personal interests at the expense of the public's interest. This concern led the Founding Fathers to include the power of impeachment in the Constitution for the president and other executive-branch officials.

During the founding era, there were also concerns that public officials would use the power of government to favor certain groups in society, and that those groups would in turn sustain them in power. Additionally, there was a fear that public officials would corrupt private persons. The most important way this was done was by using government power to charter private corporations, who were seen as receiving a public benefit not available to everyone. Many feared that the power of government would be used to advance the interests of the already rich and powerful, which caused men like Jefferson to oppose active government.[20]

Equality

While classical liberalism and classical republicanism formed two legs of the ideological stool, the third leg was equality.

When Lincoln gave the Gettysburg Address in 1863, he exalted Jefferson's assertion in the Declaration of Independence that the United States was "conceived in liberty and dedicated to the proposition that all men are created equal." Equality wed together both classical liberalism and classical republicanism. Locke had written "that all men were born equal" in a state of nature. By 1766, John Adams agreed, writing "all men are born equal." Equality was also at the heart of republicanism, with the idea that a government grounded in the will of the people required an independent and virtuous citizenry that treated each other as equals.[21]

This belief in equality dovetailed with the revolution, which unleashed criticism of hierarchy. A society grounded in natural rights meant that those "rights imply equality in the instances to which they belong and must be treated without respect to the dignity of the persons concerned in them," one revolutionary leader wrote. As with republicanism, equality had many different meanings. For some it meant equality under the law. For others, social equality—that no man should be considered better than any other because of wealth, family connections, or social status. Another meaning was civic equality—that all should have a role in participating in politics.[22]

Calls for equality ultimately led to a sense that opportunity should be open to all people. Success in society would be based on skills, talents, and abilities, not bloodlines. This was what Jefferson viewed as the natural aristocracy. After he had left the presidency and taken up communications with John Adams once again in 1813, Jefferson wrote: "The natural aristocracy I consider as the most precious gift of nature, for the instruction, the trusts, and government of society." Jefferson differentiated between the natural aristocracy, made up of those with "virtue and talent" and an artificial aristocracy "founded on wealth and birth."[23]

Better opportunity and a more fluid and open system for upward mobility would lead to a rough equality of condition. Many thought "that a society could not long remain republican if only a tiny minority controlled most of the wealth and the bulk of the population remained dependent servants or landless laborers," Wood writes. Those that were dependent on others would be unable to act independently and could be manipulated by the rich and powerful. It wasn't that economic inequality would be completely eliminated, but rather that it would be lessened, that everyone would have "a minimum degree of property," as political scientist Clement Fatovic frames it.[24]

This was why Jefferson wanted the United States to remain a largely rural nation populated by yeoman farmers who owned land. Jefferson believed in a "rough equality of condition for a republican society—with every man an independent property owner." Jefferson, although no friend to energetic government, proposed governmental policies to deal with the problem of wealth concentration, in part by the elimination of primogeniture, which could reduce inequality caused by passing wealth from one generation to another. By eliminating primogeniture, Jefferson was attempting to eliminate an aristocracy of inherited wealth. Jefferson also proposed policies in the Virginia Constitution of 1776 that provided for the distribution of land to "every person of full age," which would include women as well as men. This proposal was not approved, indicating that policies involving redistribution may have been as controversial during the revolutionary period as they are today.[25]

Jefferson, while serving in France, saw the problems with the extreme concentration of wealth, and wrote to Madison about his concerns with a society in which "property is absolutely concentrated in a very few hands." He went on to say, "I am conscious that an equal division of property is impracticable. But the consequences of this enormous inequality producing so much misery to the bulk of mankind, legislators cannot invent too many devices for subdividing property." Jefferson believed that "another means of lessening the inequality of property is to exempt all from taxation below a certain point, and to tax the higher portions of property in geometrical progression as they rise."[26]

During the founding era, debates over economic equality would play an important role in support for or opposition to active government. Then, as today, there were liberals (not to be mistaken for classical liberalism), conservatives, and moderates who disagreed over the best way to organize the flow of authority in society (whether top down or bottom up), the role of change versus tradition, views toward outsiders, and views about equality. Liberals tend to "believe in the innate, inner equality of all people, [and] attribute the world's inequalities to outer, structural injustices," according to the evolutionary anthropologist Avi Tuschman. Liberals want to break down differences that occur because of power relationships, believing this will lead to a more just world. Thomas Jefferson, perhaps more than any other member of the founding generation, represented this point of view. Jefferson believed that a better world could be created if the privileges bestowed on the few by government were removed. To the extent that overarching authority could be removed, men would once again live in harmony. That was in large part why he supported limited government.

Conservatives believe that "hierarchies reflect inner, individual capabilities," and that inequalities "reveal the worth of the powerful and the weak," which makes them more tolerant of inequalities, Tuschman writes. Alexander Hamilton reflected this point of view. So too did John Adams, who told Jefferson that his views on the "natural and artificial aristocracy" were not well founded. Adams thought that there would always be the few and the many, the rich and the poor: "Inequalities of Mind and Body are established by God Almighty . . . no policy can ever plain them down to a level." The battles that would occur in the 1790s after the adoption of the Constitution would reflect the views of the founders over the role of government in society and its impact on equality.[27]

Liberty, Equality, or Slavery?

Fundamental rights like liberty, equality, and justice were denied to a wide swath of American society at the time of the revolution, including women, Native Americans, and, most glaringly, enslaved people. In 1750, there were over 250,000 enslaved Africans in the colonies, with over 80 percent of them found in the South. Many of the patriots described the imposition of British taxation measures as a way to enslave the colonists. Washington wrote that the British "will make us the tame and abject slaves as the [B]lacks we rule over with such arbitrary sway." The Virginians were leaders of the revolution, which caused the historian Daniel J. Boorstin to write that "the value they placed on their individual liberties [had been increased] by the sharp contrast with the slavery they saw about them." At least part of the ideology of the revolution was grounded in the importance of the protection of private property, "which suggested that it would be an infringement of liberty to relieve a man of his property (including slave property) without his consent," Foner writes.[28]

Still, it was Jefferson's immortal words in the Declaration of Independence—that all men have certain inalienable rights—that called into question whether slavery could exist in a society dedicated to such ideals. The gradual elimination of slavery was particularly strong in the North and the upper South during the revolutionary period. By 1774, Rhode Island and Connecticut prohibited new enslaved people from being brought into their colonies. Vermont abolished slavery in 1777. Pennsylvania began the process of gradual abolition in 1780, and in 1783 the Massachusetts Supreme Court found that slavery was unconstitutional. Other New England states soon followed suit with their own plans for gradual elimination. New York and New Jersey took much longer, in large part because they had a greater number of enslaved people. But by the early 1800s, they too adopted plans for the gradual elimination of slavery.[29]

In the upper South, including Virginia and Maryland, those who held enslaved people questioned its compatibility with their own ideology. Not only Jefferson, but Washington, Madison, Mason, and other leaders of the revolution found it difficult to square their support of liberty and equality with owning human beings. While many of those in the upper South saw the pernicious impact of slavery, they could not find a way to be free of the system without bringing financial ruin on themselves and the economy of their states. The leadership of South Carolina and Georgia were the great defenders of slavery. Their ancestors had come from Barbados, where enslaved people were treated brutally. At least some of the concern over too much centralized power in government came from those who defended slavery.[30]

The Constitution

The revolution had begun to break down the hierarchical order in colonial America, but this was the beginning, not the end, of that process. Life in a complex society does not move from hierarchy to democracy in a linear fashion. Many of society's elite had very real concerns that America was becoming too democratic and egalitarian, that the people themselves were beginning to act in a despotic manner. The movement to adopt a new Constitution was partly motivated by these concerns, and also by a need to create a republic that could thrive on a national scale.

There are many ways to tell the story of how the United States abandoned its first constitution under the Articles of Confederation for the Constitution. In the *Emergence of One American Nation*, I primarily tell the story from the perspective of building one nation out of thirteen disparate states. The central government under the Articles was too weak to govern, and this caused substantial problems in the areas of finance, administration, trade, and foreign policy. Those who feared centralized government had carried the day under the Articles of Confederation, placing most of the power in the individual states, which were recognized as sovereign. To its supporters, the decentralized political system under the Articles represented the true spirit of 1776.

Those who pushed for a new governmental structure looked at the original founding as incomplete. The central government under the Articles had no power to tax; it could only requisition money from the states. When the states refused to comply, the central government lacked the ability to enforce their requests. In addition, the Articles had not provided for an executive to implement congressional policies. The lack of an executive reflected the fear of centralized power—that liberty would be threatened by one man's tyranny. The state governments that had been formed after the Declaration had severely weakened the role that governors played. So "corrupting was the power of ruling that an elected magistrate was actually no less to be dreaded than [a] hereditary one," like the king of England, as Wood writes. Pennsylvania went the furthest, replacing the role of governor with an executive council.[31]

These deficiencies led to serious problems with national finances, causing major hardships in the everyday lives of average people and in providing supplies and pay to the army during the war. Since the government had no taxing power, its ability to borrow money was limited. Much of the war effort was funded by printing excessive amounts of paper money, which caused inflation. By the end of the war, the debt owed to the public amounted to over $43 million, which did not include moneys owed to foreign governments, nor the debts of the states. Alexander Hamilton would later place the total debt of the United States at over $77 million. Attempts to amend the Articles to provide Congress with the power to tax faltered, since all thirteen states were required to approve such an amendment. By 1785 Congress failed to make interest payments on loans owed to France.[32]

Foreign policy problems also mounted, and the Confederation Congress lacked the resources and authority to deal with them. Trade problems between the states were a further source of tensions in the

1780s. Each state not only issued its own currency, causing problems with exchange rates, but states levied tariffs on the products of neighboring states.[33]

Many elites were concerned that the United States would soon break into multiple confederacies if something wasn't done to strengthen the central government. In 1786, Madison undertook a systematic analysis entitled *Of Ancient and Modern Confederacies*. He reached the conclusion that "weak unions courted disaster," as his biographer Ralph Ketcham writes. "Ancient and modern [confederacies] all tended to fly apart for lack of a supreme authority," Madison wrote. Elites' fears were further exacerbated by Shays's Rebellion in western Massachusetts, when a small group of farmers shut down local courts to stop property foreclosures for taxes that had not been paid. Washington responded to Shays's Rebellion with a continuing refrain, that the federal union was too weak to deal with such disturbances. "What stronger evidence can be given of the want of energy in our governments than these disorders? . . . Thirteen Sovereignties pulling against each other, and all pulling at the federal head, will soon bring ruin on the whole."[34]

Another element in the buildup to the Constitutional Convention was a sense that the states had become too democratic, that average people had gained too much control over state governments. In this context, the crafting of the new Constitution can be seen as a counter-revolution on the part of elites to rein in democracy. This was certainly the sentiment on the part of some of the delegates who attended the convention, which opened on May 25, 1787, in Philadelphia. Edmund Randolph, who introduced the Virginia Plan at the opening of the convention, thought that problems in the state governments arose "from the democratic parts of our constitutions" and that those state constitutions had failed to provide "sufficient checks against democracy." Randolph was not alone in his skeptical view on the subject. Elbridge Gerry believed "the evils we experience flow from the excess of democracy." Roger Sherman hoped that "the people . . . have as little to do as may be about the government." Hamilton wanted the new government to be structured to protect against the "imprudence of democracy."[35]

James Madison, of all the participants at the Constitutional Convention, combined concerns over the weakness of the national government with a fear that the majority in a republic can sometimes trample on the rights of the minority. Madison was also concerned about how to advance the republican notion of the common good with liberal ideas for the protection of the individual. As Jack Rakove frames it, Madison judged political decisions by "asking whether they satisfied both the public good and private rights." Unlike some of his colleagues, Madison also had a healthy respect for the people's need to participate in government, writing that "the fundamental principle of republican Government [is] that majority who rule in such Governments, are the safest Guardians both of public Good and private rights."[36]

During the 1780s, Madison had become disillusioned with the way state governments operated, due to his experience serving in the Virginia legislature. He had become convinced that there was a need to control factions, particularly majority factions. He saw that an overreliance on the legislative branch and its direct dependence on the public had led to a series of bad laws. "Madison's suspicion . . . [of government power] was based on his fear that the elected officials were only too representative, only too expressive of the passions of the people who had elected them," according to Gordon Wood. He saw the Virginia legislators as "parochial, illiberal, [and] small minded," as a group that only served a "particular interest." He was especially concerned in the 1780s with state laws that favored debtors over creditors through the issuance of paper money, which he feared would lead to inflation, as it had during the Revolutionary War. His solution was to shift more power to the central government as a check on the state governments.[37]

Madison thought that a national government operating over an extended sphere could reduce the concern that government would become nothing but an arena where the most powerful interests, or factions, prevailed, in opposition to the public good. Madison recognized that factions were endemic in a republic, that they were sewn into the nature of man. As he wrote in *Federalist* No. 10, "the most common and durable source of faction has been the various and unequal distribution of property. Those who hold and those who are without property have ever formed distinct interests in society." Madison did not think it prudent to eliminate self-interest, or faction, as he called it, because that would be a remedy "worse than the disease," since factions were the price for living in a free society. Instead, by extending the sphere of the republic, by creating a truly national government, one could control the deleterious impacts of factions. "Extend the sphere and you take in a greater variety of parties and interests; you make it less probable that a majority of the whole will have a common motive to invade the rights of other citizens," Madison wrote in *Federalist* No. 10.[38]

Madison also shared the view of his Federalist brethren that legislators should act in a disinterested fashion, and that only a few in society could act this way. Madison was attempting to find a way to balance the need for disinterestedness on the part of legislators with a society and economy that was increasingly focused on promoting self-interest and the profit motive. *Disinterestedness* was "used as a synonym for the classic conception of civic virtue," Wood writes, to describe a person "not influenced by private profit." The advantage of a large-scale republic was that it would result in the election of men of independent judgment, those who were disinterested, due to the benefit of larger legislative districts. "In the next place, as each representative will be chosen by a greater number of citizens in the large than in the small republic, it will be more difficult for unworthy candidates to practise with success the viscous arts by which elections are too often carried; and the suffrages of the people being more free, will be more likely to center on men who possess the most attractive merit and the most diffusive and established characters." During the Virginia ratifying convention, Madison stated that "I go on this great republican principle, that the people will have virtue and intelligence to select men of virtue and wisdom." All of this was grounded in the civic virtue of the people. "Is there no virtue among us? If there be not, we are in a wretched situation. . . . to suppose that any form of government will secure liberty or happiness without any virtue in the people is a chimerical idea."[39]

For Madison, being a legislator was similar to acting in a semi-judicial role, and he wanted to see elected officials act with independent judgment. "Madison thought that government should be essentially arbitrative, with neutral umpires weighing competing interests, to strike a just balance," the historian Garry Wills has written. "This meant separating the officials, in some measure, from their local ties, freeing them to be impartial." The union to be established would not only protect liberty, but also result in the election of more able representatives.[40]

In order to do this, the Constitution would eventually give elected officials longer terms in office than those provided for under the state constitutions of the time, remove the power of recall, and eliminate term limits—all to ensure that elected officials could act in as disinterested a fashion as possible.[41] Madison was grappling with the age-old problem in democratic governments of whether elected officials should act purely as delegates who simply follow the wishes of their constituents, or whether they should exercise independent judgment, voting based on their conscience. Madison clearly preferred the latter, although all politicians must, in fact, balance both of these approaches.

The movement for a new constitution was elitist. Unlike the drive for independence, where mobs formed to demand action against the British, there was no groundswell among the public to strengthen the central government. Joseph J. Ellis has written that "the very weakness of the federal government under the Articles of Confederation [was] the ideal expression of revolutionary intentions." The pursuit of a new and stronger central government was a top-down movement, led primarily by Madison and Hamilton, who were able to elicit Washington's support in this effort. Although Washington was a strong nationalist, he was initially reticent to participate in the Constitutional Convention for a variety of reasons. In part, he did not want to go back on his commitment to the American people that he had retired from public life in the aftermath of the war. He also feared that the convention would be unsuccessful. Still, Madison and Hamilton continued their lobbying efforts, and soon the threesome set off to "expand the meaning of the American Revolution so that it could function on a larger, indeed national scale," Ellis has written.[42]

Over the summer of 1787, the delegates to the Constitutional Convention hammered out a new and stronger federal government. Behind closed doors, exceeding the mandate granted by the

Confederation Congress to propose amendments to the Articles, they reached a series of compromises on a wholly new government. The key compromise was over congressional representation, with the large states winning membership in the House of Representatives based on population and the small states obtaining an equal vote in the Senate. The South received protections for slavery, without which they would not have entered into a stronger union, while the North received the authorization to implement navigation acts (items like tariffs) with a majority vote. The new Constitution would operate directly on the people of the United States, and so the government consisted of a series of finely crafted institutional arrangements to check abuses of power. There would be three branches of government: a bicameral legislature, a strong executive, and a judiciary. Many of the compromises caused some of the most ardent nationalists, men like Madison and Washington, to consider whether they should support the new Constitution, which they ultimately did. Ratification was extremely close in many of the states, but all states eventually joined the new union.

They were indeed successful in their efforts to create a stronger government, which allowed the arguments over democracy—and over the protection of individual rights, equality, and the public good—to eventually occur on a national scale. In part their success was a result of concessions they made over the division of sovereignty between the states and the new national government at the convention. The antifederalists, those opposed to the Constitution during ratification, argued that the states would be eviscerated because they were losing sovereignty and would be replaced by a consolidated government. At the Pennsylvania Ratification Convention, James Wilson provided an ingenious response, arguing that in fact sovereignty was not in the state governments or the national government, but rather was vested in the people. As such, the people "can delegate it in such proportions, to such bodies, on such terms, and under such limitations, as they think proper." Essentially the supporters of the Constitution, now dubbed Federalists, were forced to ground their proposal for a new government in the will of the people, despite the reservations many of them had about democracy. Early in the republic, a debate would occur on a national scale over the new union, with the liberal side committed to limited government, while the conservative side preferred an activist government.[43]

Endnotes

1   Gordon Wood, *The Radicalism of the American Revolution* (New York: Alfred A. Knopf, 1992), p. 5 for the quote and p. 11–32 for a fuller discussion of the hierarchical nature of the colonial world. Also see Robert E. Shalhope, *The Roots of Democracy: American Thought and Culture 1760–1800* (Lanham: Rowman and Littlefield, 1990), p. 1–9.

2   Wood, *Radicalism*, p. 32–36; Peter H. Lindert and Jeffrey G. Williamson, *Unequal Gains: American Growth and Inequality Since 1700* (Princeton: Princeton University Press, 2016), p. 37; Gary J. Kornblith and John Murrin, "The Dilemmas of Ruling Elites in Revolutionary America," in Steve Fraser and Gary Gerstle, eds., *Ruling America: A History of Power in a Democracy* (Cambridge: Harvard University Press, 2005), p. 29.

3   Wood, p. 74–76.

4   James Horn, *1619 Jamestown and the Forging of American Democracy* (New York: Basic Books, 2018), p. 8.

5   Alan Taylor, *American Colonies: The Settling of North America* (New York: Penguin, 2001), p. 140, p. 147, p. 226; Daniel J. Boorstin, *The American: The Colonial Experience* (New York: Random House, 1958), p. 103.

6   Taylor, p. 151–153.

7   Heather Cox Richardson, *How the South Won the Civil War* (New York: Oxford University Press, 2020), p. 18–22; Edmund S. Morgan, *American Slavery, American Freedom* (New York: W.W. Norton, 1975), p. 328.

8   Taylor, p. 247 and p. 285; Joyce Appleby, *Capitalism and a New Social Order: The Republican Vision of the 1790s* (New York: New York University Press, 1984), p. 7.

9   Robert A. Gross, *The Minutemen and Their World* (New York: Hill and Wang, 1976), p. 10–12.

10   James T. Kloppenberg, *The Virtues of Liberalism* (New York: Oxford University Press, 1998), p. 30.

11   Eric Foner, *The Story of American Freedom* (New York: W.W. Norton, 1998), p. 5.

12   Donald J. Fraser, *The Emergence of One American Nation: The Revolution, the Founders and the Constitution* (Roseville: Fraser & Associates, 2015), p. 33–37; Kornblith and Murrin, p. 34.

13   Fraser, chapter 3.

14   This is one of the underlying themes of my first book, *The Emergence of One American Nation.* The quote is from Stanley Elkins and Eric McKitrick, *The Age of Federalism: The Early American Republic, 1788–1800* (New York: Oxford University Press, 1993), p. 6.

15   George F. Will, *The Conservative Sensibility* (New York: Hachette Books, 2019), p. xxiv; George H. Smith, *The System of Liberty: Themes in the History of Classical Liberalism* (Washington, DC: Cambridge University Press 2013), p. 2.

16   Francis Fukuyama, *Identity: The Demand for Dignity and the Politics of Resentment* (New York: Farrar, Straus and Giroux, 2018), p. 12–13 and p. 22; Michael J. Sandel, *Democracy's Discontent: America in Search of a Political Philosophy* (Cambridge: Belknap Press, 1996), p. 11.

17   Quotes in E. J. Dione Jr., *Our Divided Political Heart: The Battle for the American Idea in an Age of Discontent* (New York: Bloomsbury, 2012), p. 74.

18   Gordon Wood, *The Creation of the American Republic: 1776–1787,* (Chapel Hill: University of North Carolina Press, 1998), p. 68; Wood, *Radicalism,* p. 104; Eric Foner, *The Story of American Freedom* (New York: W.W. Norton, 1998), p. 6–7.

19   Kloppenberg, p. 68; during the 1950s, historians argued that American history was grounded in liberalism. The classic statement in this regard is Louis Hartz, *The Liberal Tradition in America* (San Diego: Harcourt Brace & Co., 1955). By the 1960s and 1970s, historian like Bernard Bailyn (see footnote 30), Gordon Wood (footnote 24), and J. G. A. Pocock, *The Machiavellian Moment, Florentine Political Thought and the Atlantic Republican Tradition* (Princeton: Princeton University Press, 1975), had established the importance of republicanism to the exclusion of liberal thought. Some balance has been brought back by Kloppenberg and Joyce Appleby, *Liberalism and Republicanism in the Historical Imagination* (Cambridge: Harvard University Press, 1992), who have shown the importance of both the liberal and republican traditions.

20   John Joseph Wallis, "The Concept of Systematic Corruption in American and Political and Economic History," retrieved from https://nber.org/papers/w10952.

21 Wood, *Radicalism*, p. 236–237.

22 Bernard Bailyn, *The Ideological Origins of the American Revolution* (Cambridge: Belknap Press, 1992), p. 306–309; Wood, *Radicalism*, p. 232–233.

23 Adrienne Koch and William Peden, eds., *The Life and Writings of Thomas Jefferson* (New York: Modern Library, 1944), p. 633.

24 Wood, *Radicalism*, p. 234; Clement Fatovic, *America's Founding and the Struggle Over Economic Inequality* (Lawrence: University Press of Kansas, 2015), p. 10.

25 Jack Rakove, *Revolutionaries: A New History of the Invention of America* (Boston: Mariner Books, 2011), p. 305–307.

26 Thomas Jefferson letter to James Madison, October 28, 1785, retrieved from http:// press-pubs.uchicago.edu/founders/print_documents/v1ch15s32.html.

27 Avi Tuschman, *Our Political Nature: The Evolutionary Origins of What Divides Us* (Amherst: Prometheus Books, 2013), p. 250–251; the quotes from John Adams come from Joseph J. Ellis, *American Sphinx: The Character of Thomas Jefferson* (New York: Vintage Books, 1996), p. 297–298.

28 The statistics on slavery were retrieved on September 16, 2019, from https://faculty. weber.edu/kmackay/statistics_on_slavery.htm; Fraser, p. 59 and p. 70; Foner, p. 33.

29 Gordon Wood, *Empire of Liberty: A History of the Early Republic, 1789–1815* (Oxford: Oxford University Press, 2009), p. 517–520; Joseph J. Ellis, *Founding Brothers: The Revolutionary Generation* (New York: Vintage Books, 2000), p. 88–90.

30 Fraser, p. 58, p. 187 and p. 304 for the quotes; Wood, *Empire*, p. 522; Taylor, p. 224.

31 Wood, *Creation*, p. 135–137.

32 Fraser, p. 133–139 and p. 175.

33 Fraser, p. 176–178.

34 Ralph Ketcham, *James Madison: A Biography* (Charlottesville: University Press of Virginia, 1994), p. 184; Jeff Broadwater, *Jefferson, Madison, and the Making of the Constitution* (Chapel Hill: University of North Carolina Press, 2019), p. 128; Fraser, p. 179 and 195.

35 The quotes are from Richard Beeman, *Plain, Honest Men: The Making of the American Constitution* (New York: Random House, 2009), p. 89; Winton Solberg, ed., *The Federal Convention and the Formation of the Union of the American States* (Indianapolis: Bobbs-Merrill Company, 1976), p. 85; Richard Hofstadter, *The American Political Tradition* (New York: Knopf, 1948), p. 4; and John Ferling, *A Leap in the Dark: The Struggle to Create the American Republic* (Oxford: Oxford University Press, 2003), p. 290.

36 Jack N. Rakove, *A Politician Thinking: The Creative Mind of James Madison* (Norman: University of Oklahoma Press, 2017), p. 11 and 16.

37 Gordon Wood, *Revolutionary Characters: What Made the Founders Different* (New York: Penguin, 2006), p. 145 and 148.

38 The quotes from *Federalist* No. 10 are from the edition of *The Federalist Papers* with an introduction by Clinton Rossiter (New York: New American Library, 1961). All quotes footnoted based on the primary author and page number. The quote from Madison is from p. 77–80.

39 Gordon Wood, *The Idea of America: Reflections on the Birth of the United States* (New York: Penguin, 2011), p. 142; Madison's quote from the Virginia ratifying convention is from James T. Kloppenberg, *The Virtues of Liberalism*, p. 33.

40 Madison, p. 82; Garry Wills, *James Madison* (New York: Times Books, 2002), p. 33.

41 This point on the need for independent judgment is from Wills, *Madison*, p. 33.

42 Joseph J. Ellis, *His Excellency: George Washington* (New York: Vintage Books, 2004), p. 169, and *The Quartet: Orchestrating the Second American Revolution: 1788:1789* (New York: Alfred A. Knopf, 2015), p. xv. See also Fraser, p. 180–182, which shows that my thinking on this issue has been heavily influenced by Ellis.

43 Fraser, p. 361.

CHAPTER 2

Government and the Founders: Hamilton versus Jefferson

Those who labor in the earth are the chosen people of God . . .
—THOMAS JEFFERSON, NOTES ON THE STATE OF VIRGINIA

The Secretary of the Treasury . . . has applied his attention . . .
to the subject of Manufactures . . .
—ALEXANDER HAMILTON, REPORT ON THE SUBJECT OF MANUFACTURES

*I*t is but a slight exaggeration, a bit of hyperbole, that never in American history have there been two men so different in background and outlook competing to define the future course of the American experiment as Alexander Hamilton and Thomas Jefferson. The gulf that existed between the two was both political, dealing with how democratic the new nation would be, and economic, influencing whether the United States would remain largely agricultural or have a mixed economy that also included industry. Both the political and economic were inseparable.

Background on Jefferson and Hamilton

Thomas Jefferson was born in Virginia on April 13, 1743, the eldest son of a prosperous family that "dined with silver, danced with grace, entertained constantly," as historian Jon Meacham has written. The Jeffersons were part of the Virginia gentry, but Thomas would become one of the main proponents of the rights of the common man, despite his holding enslaved people for his entire life. Trained as lawyer, Jefferson joined the revolutionary cause and made quite a stir in July of 1774 when he released a *Summary View of the Rights of British America*. In it, Jefferson explained many of his core beliefs: that people are bestowed with certain natural rights, that the legislature is the supreme repository of power, and that sovereignty rests in the will of the majority.[1]

Jefferson and John Adams, the cantankerous delegate to the Second Continental Congress from Massachusetts, became fast friends in the heady days of the revolution in 1776. It was Adams who asked Jefferson to write the draft of the Declaration of Independence, telling him that he (Jefferson) "can write ten times better that I can." Jefferson would craft a document whose preamble would go on to become the American Creed, exalting equality, liberty, self-government, and the pursuit of happiness.[2]

Both Jefferson and Adams would spend a good deal of time in Europe in the years after independence. The two men's relationship strengthened, and later Adams would write that his son John Quincy "appeared to me as much your boy as mine." Both men were gone during the difficult days under the Articles of Confederation, when the weak union just about came apart. Jefferson was initially lukewarm toward the new Constitution, while Adams was quite complementary. Jefferson's other good friend, James Madison, had helped craft the document and was ultimately able to convince him to support it. Jefferson's true feelings toward a strong central government were made plain in 1787 when he wrote the following to Madison: "I own, I am not a friend to a very energetic government. It is always oppressive."[3]

Once the Constitution was ratified, George Washington was elected the first president, with Adams his vice president. Washington wanted to fill his cabinet with the best men, and so he selected Jefferson to serve as the first secretary of state. He and Hamilton, who did not yet know each other, would now serve in the same cabinet. It did not go well. Jefferson was the "Aristocrat as Democrat," as Richard Hofstadter titled a chapter in his book *The American Political Tradition*. Alexander Hamilton, on the other hand, started with nothing and became not only extraordinarily successful but also a great defender of the elite in society.

Born in Nevis, in the British West Indies, in 1755, Hamilton was the illegitimate son of James Hamilton, a ne'er-do-well. Fortunately for Alexander, he inherited his brains from his mother, Rachel Fawcett Lavine. Abandoned by his father, his mother died in the bed next to him when he was thirteen. But so talented was the young Hamilton that he caught the eye of some powerful patrons, who helped him get to America. Landing in New York, he attended King's College and then he too became involved in the revolution. After joining the New York militia, Hamilton stood out for his bravery during the battle of New York in 1776. A small man, he was described by one soldier during the retreat from New York as a "youth, a mere stripling." But his extraordinary ability was recognized by General Washington, who made Hamilton his aide-de-camp. He had an uncanny ability to read Washington, becoming "his alter ego, able to capture his tone on paper or in person," Ron Chernow writes.[4]

From his position on Washington's staff, Hamilton was able to pursue the beautiful Eliza Schuyler, daughter of one of New York's first families. Once Hamilton married into the powerful Schuyler family, he joined the elite world of New York society. Near the end of the war, he earned a law degree and was elected to the Confederation Congress, becoming one of the prime adherents of the need to strengthen the federal government. He teamed with Madison to help bring about the Constitutional Convention, and the two combined to write most of the *Federalist Papers*, designed to promote ratification of the Constitution.

When Washington needed a treasury secretary, he turned to Hamilton. He and Jefferson would now serve together and would soon become like "two cocks in a pit," as Jefferson framed it. The men would disagree over Hamilton's approach to economics and the impact those policies would have on the future of democracy in the nation.

Hamiltonian Economics

On December 5, 1791, Hamilton submitted to the House of Representatives his *Report on the Subject of Manufactures*. Building on work already done by Assistant Treasury Secretary Tench Coxe, who had written a book on the subject, Hamilton put forward a plan that tied together all of his economic policies. His goal was to convert the United States into a powerful and independent nation on the world stage. To do this, he would utilize an activist federal government. Both he and Washington shared a fear that the country was too dependent on foreign industry to survive another war. Washington had told Congress that America should "promote such manufactories as tend to render them independent [of] others for essential, particularly for military supplies."[5]

In the report, Hamilton recognized that agriculture "has *intrinsically a strong claim to pre-eminence over every other kind of industry,*" but that it should not have an "exclusive predilection." As Hamilton indicated, the United States had already established some industrial capacity, but it was in its infancy. Fortunately for the country, it now had access to capital, not only from foreign investment but also due to the other policies that he had designed and implemented, including a funded debt and a national bank.[6]

Dealing with the debt that was left over from the Revolutionary War was Hamilton's first task as treasury secretary. It stood at over $79 million, which included both state and federal debt. Hamilton referred to the debt in his *First Report on the Public Credit* as the "price of liberty," a remnant from the pursuit of independence. He proposed that the federal government assume the entire debt and refinance it into new and lower interest rate securities. Both the assumption of state debts and his decision to pay off the existing debt at face value to the current holders proved controversial.[7]

Those states that had little debt, or had already paid off their debts, were opposed to that part of the plan. The proposal to pay off the current holders of the debt at face value also elicited opposition. James Madison, among others, opposed both proposals. Much of the debt had been acquired from the original holders by speculators, sometimes at pennies on the dollar, and Madison opposed rewarding what he called the "stockjobbers." He preferred a policy of discrimination in which the original owners and the speculators would share in the profit, but it was unworkable. Madison's plan "entailed insuperable problems of locating original owners, determining the prices at which they had sold their shares, and distinguishing the ones who had sold on account of genuine necessity from those who had sold more opportunistically," historian H. W. Brands has written.[8]

The House voted down Madison's proposal and passed that part of Hamilton's plan. Still, Madison was able to bottle up Hamilton's debt-assumption proposal. Hamilton was surprised by Madison's opposition, since the two had become friends and collaborators in bringing about the Constitution. When Madison first arrived in New

York to take his seat in Congress, Hamilton had come to visit him and to seek his advice on securing approval of his plan. But he and Madison, who had agreed wholeheartedly on the need to strengthen the federal government, disagreed just as vociferously over economics. Hamilton saw the debt as a "national blessing" because it would provide a ready supply of currency. Since the owner of the debt could sell it in the secondary market, it would serve as a substitute for hard currency, which was in short supply in America. Hamilton's plan was akin to adding oil to a car, since it would serve as a lubricant for economic activity. It would also tie the wealthy in society to the new federal government. For Madison, the debt was a "public evil" and represented the type of corruption that so worried those committed to republicanism. Here was a very real example of a public official using the power of his office and governmental power to favor one group (investors) over everyone else. "So acute was his dismay that Hamilton declared that if he had known Madison was to oppose him, he would not have accepted the post of Secretary Treasury," historian John C. Miller has written. It was the first of many friendships that would soon begin to dissolve over political disagreements.[9]

Jefferson helped to break the logjam. Recently returned from France to assume the position of secretary of state, Jefferson was on the way to visit the president when he came upon Hamilton, "who was in despair" over his inability to get Congress to pass his plan for the assumption of state debts. He asked if Jefferson "would appeal . . . to the judgment and discretion of some of my [Jefferson's] friends" to change their vote. Jefferson, fearful that the union would collapse in its infancy without action, subsequently hosted a dinner that Madison also attended in which a compromise was struck. Madison would remove his opposition, but not vote for the bill, and in return Hamilton would use his influence to help locate the national capital in Virginia. Jefferson would later claim he did not understand the financial issues fully and regretted his decision, seeing it as a step toward an aristocratic and ultimately a monarchical government in the United States modeled after Great Britain. He would later write that "Hamilton was not only a monarchist, but for a monarchy bottomed on corruption." Jefferson thought that Hamilton was "so bewitched and perverted by the British example, as to be under thorough conviction that corruption was essential to government of a nation." Corruption would be fostered by an executive branch, which through patronage and financial enticements, like bank stock, would control the legislative branch. He was joined in this view by many others. Benjamin Rush from Pennsylvania, an ally of Madison, thought that Hamilton's debt policy was "fundamentally unjust . . . [and would] . . . lay the foundation of an aristocracy in our country."[10]

The second major component of Hamilton's plan was banking. "The introduction of Banks has . . . a powerful tendency to extend the active Capital of a Country," he wrote in the *Report on Manufactures*. In December of 1790 he proposed that Congress charter the First Bank of the United States. The bank would be responsible for managing the debt of the country, produce a stable money supply in an "economy traditionally short of specie," and be a source of lending to larger commercial enterprises. The bank would issue notes that would be restricted, because those holding the notes could redeem them for gold or silver. This would create a liquid source of capital and avoid the rapid inflation that had occurred during the war.[11]

The bank elicited major opposition from both Madison and Jefferson, this time on constitutional grounds. Both men maintained that the Constitution did not include a specific provision for the creation of a bank by Congress, which, while true, reflected a strict constructionist view. Hamilton then put forward what one of his biographers has called "the most brilliant argument for a broad interpretation of the Constitution in American political literature." Hamilton posited that the necessary and proper clause gave Congress the means to carry out all of its ends, even if the specific power was not listed in the document. Ultimately, Washington sided with Hamilton, in large measure because he was as much a supporter of a strong central government as Hamilton was. Shortly thereafter, Jefferson and Madison set off on a journey north to gauge the level of discontent with the policies of Hamilton, which would lead to the creation of an opposition political party to the Federalists.[12]

The *Report on Manufactures* was Hamilton's third major report to be provided, and as previously mentioned, it brought together all his plans under one roof. In the report, Hamilton once again envisioned the active use of government to promote manufacturing and industry in the United States. The federal government would protect infant industries from foreign competition by implementing tariffs. There would be "pecuniary bounties," or what we would refer to as subsidies, for specific businesses. The federal government would invest in "good roads, canals, and navigable rivers" in order to facilitate "the transportation of commodities." The power of the federal government would even be used to regulate and inspect "manufactured commodities."[13]

It was indeed an audacious plan. While Hamilton generally supported a free market approach to the economy, writing that "human enterprise ought doubtless to be left free in the main," he recognized that newly emerging economies "may be beneficially stimulated by prudent aids and encouragements on the part of the government." Hamilton's economic and political views consistently blended together. He saw human nature as basically competitive and driven by self-interest. Hamilton believed that only the elite in society could break through their own self-interest and act from "more worthy motives," from a disinterested perspective. In this regard, he thought authority in society needed to flow down from the elites, and not up from the masses, as Jefferson believed. He did not support the establishment of a monarchy in America, nor the creation of a hereditary aristocracy, a charge that Jefferson and the Republicans (Democratic-Republicans) would repeatedly level against him. But he was also not concerned with great concentrations of wealth, which his policies would ultimately help to foster. Unlike later uses of government by liberals, Hamilton intended to use the power of government to advance the wealthy, who would then invest in the American economy. By doing this, he believed he was also advancing the interests of the overall society. It was an issue that Jefferson and his Republican Party vociferously disagreed with.[14]

Hamilton's plan for manufacturing went nowhere, but his debt and bank plans stabilized the American economy, which began a period of sustained growth in the 1790s. Still, Hamilton's economic plans stirred substantial opposition and led to the formation of the first political party in the United States, the Republicans, led by Jefferson.

Jeffersonian Economics

Jefferson's vision for the future of America was that it should remain rural, with an economy largely agricultural in nature. "Those who labor in the earth are the chosen people of God," he wrote in *Notes on the State of Virginia*. He subscribed to the view that industrialization and urbanization were not progress but decay, a dialogue that had been ongoing in the late eighteenth century. While David Hume (along with Hamilton) celebrated industry as the next phase forward, Rousseau, among other theorists, believed that industrial societies created major inequalities and placed workers under the power of the owners of capital. It was a view shared by both Jefferson and Madison. So long as the United States remained largely rural, then an active government, which in Jefferson's view was "always oppressive," could be avoided. The danger, for Jefferson, occurs "when we get piled upon one another in large cities, as in Europe," which would lead to corruption of the people and their dependence on the business class. Jefferson's view on economics was the exact opposite of Hamilton's.[15]

For Jefferson and the Republicans, there was a strong connection between the economy and democracy—or a republic, as they would call it. The only way a republic could survive was in a system without major inequalities of wealth, in which there was a widespread distribution of property. Jefferson was committed to the expansion of democracy, of political participation for ordinary men—at least ordinary white men. For such a political system to work, the Jeffersonian Republicans believed that the economy of the United States would need to be decentralized and grounded in a community of independent yeoman farmers endowed with a high degree of equality. For Jefferson, power should flow up from the people, not down from the rulers.[16]

The Republican Party view was that the consolidation of economic power in the hands of the few would also lead to the introduction of an aristocratic government in the United States, which is why the Republicans sometimes referred to Hamilton and his Federalist Party as the monocrats. They justified this view by claiming that the Federalist program was attempting to replicate the British system of a funded debt, the creation of a national bank, and the movement toward an industrial society. The Republicans charged that Hamilton's program had led to a government that favored a small group of moneyed men, the so-called stockjobbers, some of whom were members of Congress. This gave the treasury secretary too much control over the legislature, which would no longer be able to act independently in the public interest. To the Jeffersonian Republicans, this was the height of corruption in the political system of the United States. Madison, in a 1792 essay in the *National Gazette*, argued that the Federalists "wish to point the measures of government less to the interest of the many [than] of a few" which would lead the government into "[a] hereditary form."[17]

Jefferson and Madison did not oppose all industry or commerce in America. Rather, they felt that the country should have the right types of manufacturing. Industry should support an agricultural economy and provide basic goods that could be supplied through home industries and artisan production, without the need for large-scale industrial production. Later in life, particularly after the War of 1812, Jefferson began to accept that some level of manufacturing was needed to ensure the economic independence of the United States. Madison too would once again make a major swing in his views, adopting a quasi-Hamiltonian view of the economy near the end of his second term as president, based on lessons learned in the War of 1812.

Two Views of Capitalism

Was Hamilton the capitalist and Jefferson the democrat? To some extent this is true, but reality is never so simple. Hamilton and Jefferson were a mix of both, and our nation blends both men in its DNA, as historian John Ferling has written.

It is true that Hamilton and the Federalists were not fans of an extensive democracy, sometimes equating it with mob rule. This view became even more pronounced in the aftermath of the Reign of Terror during the French Revolution. Hamilton certainly cut a poor figure at the Constitutional Convention, arguing for lifetime appointments for both the Senate and the president. But he also proposed that the people elect house members for three-year terms. He and Madison both shared a concern about direct democracy, and so he put his faith in representative democracy, where "the people ruled indirectly through their representatives," political scientist Michael P. Federici writes. In 1792 Hamilton wrote, "I am *affectionately* attached to the republican theory. I desire *above all things* to see the *equality* of political rights, exclusive of all *hereditary* distinction, firmly established by a practical demonstration of it being consistent with the order and happiness of society."[18]

For some historians, Jefferson is characterized as a capitalist, while others disagree. Much depends on the definition one uses for *capitalism*, a word that was not used in the 1790s, although *capitalist* was. The economist John Kenneth Galbraith has summarized a capitalist system as emerging from classical liberalism, with self-interest, competition, and minimal state regulation as its hallmarks. Another economist, Robert Heilbroner, notes that "it is surprisingly difficult to find a succinct definition of capitalism," but that it usually involves private ownership of property and a free market system for distribution. Political scientist Ellen Meiksins, in her book *The Origin of Capitalism*, argues that "it is a system in which the bulk of society's work is done by the propertyless labourers . . . in exchange for a wage." Historian Michael Merrill goes so far as to say that "capitalism is an economy run by or in the interests of capitalists."[19]

Given the lack of a clear definition of capitalism, it is perhaps better to take the various characteristics of these different definitions, plus other elements of an emerging market economy, and compare the Federalists and the Republicans.

Elements of a Market Economy

Characteristic	Federalist *Hamilton*	Republican *Jefferson*
1. Support for private ownership of property	Yes	Yes
2. Distribution through market mechanisms	Yes	Yes
3. Profit motive	Yes	Yes
4. Support for wage labor	Yes	No
5. Support of banking and credit/debt	Yes	No
6. Control of government and economy by moneyed class	Yes	No

The last three characteristics are the reason that the Republicans favored limited government during this era. They believed that so long as property was widely held, a republic/democracy could be sustained, and small government was possible. But once wealth became highly concentrated in an industrial society, with most people becoming wage earners, later liberals would gradually begin to shift in their attitudes toward government and advocate for the use of public means to equalize wealth and power in society.

The concerns of the Republicans of the era can be seen in correspondence between Madison and Jefferson in the early 1790s. Madison had grave concerns that the many were taking advantage of the few during the 1780s through paper money issuance and debtor relief laws, so this was part of the reason he supported strengthening the union under the Constitution. Yet he had not envisioned how far Hamilton would go through his debt and banking plans to favor the already wealthy under the Constitution. "The true difference seems to be that in the former the few were the victims to the many; by the latter the many to the few," as Noah Feldman frames it. Madison now feared "that private capital would come to run the entire system," overturning a system of "government by the people," for one run by private capital.[20]

Some historians, like Merrill, have argued that capitalism is limited to just those systems controlled by the moneyed interests. This is certainly one form of capitalism, and the United States has featured it at various times during its history. But there is another version that attempts to bridge the divide between democracy and capitalism. Historian Richard White calls this "utopian capitalism," in which a free market economy is able to "sustain rather than threaten democratic societies." He attributes this version of capitalism to both Jefferson and later Andrew Jackson, who "imagined a world of small producers in which the paradoxical combination of a free market and local control over the economy produced a roughly egalitarian world of white men."[21]

Both Jefferson and Jackson tried to implement a version of capitalism that was compatible with democracy by limiting certain features of the system, such as banking, industry, and wage labor. They ultimately failed at this. Over time, liberals would realize that the only method to achieve the best of the capitalist system, which can defeat scarcity and famine, and yet protect democratic government, was to turn to the use of active government. This is what the Progressives would do at the turn of the twentieth century, and later what Franklin D. Roosevelt would implement with the New Deal in the 1930s.

Jefferson's version of capitalism is also most closely tied to classical liberalism in terms of promoting individualism and liberty. Joyce Appleby, in her classic study *Capitalism and a New Social Order*, writes about how Jefferson and the Republicans had reconciled the "tension between individual self-interest and the welfare of the community" by believing that "the rights of the whole can be no more than the sum of the rights of individuals," as Jefferson observed. The Republicans had turned self-interest into a leveling mechanism in society, "raising ordinary people to the level of competence and autonomy while reducing the rich, the able, and the well-born to equality." Or at least so long as industrial society did not overwhelm the rural nature of American society.[22]

In the election of 1800, the Republicans would emerge victorious when Thomas Jefferson was elected the third president of the United States. He would usher in a more democratic era, but a period of one-party rule would ensue as the Federalists began to shrink into a regional party only found in New England. Yet Hamilton's ideas on the economy did not go away; they in fact continued to hold sway as well. "By reason of its amazing variety of resources, the versatility of its native and immigrant populations, and its strategic location, the United States was destined to develop a far more complex and diversified economy than Jefferson had foreseen," economic historian E. A. Johnson has written. Hamilton's ideas would get an assist from an unusual source—none other than James Madison.[23]

The Madisonian Platform

James Madison had come full circle. He had been a staunch nationalist in the 1780s, and an ally of Hamilton in the march to strengthen the federal government through the framing and ratification of the Constitution. Yet Hamilton's economic program had thrown Madison into opposition. He helped Jefferson form the first and oldest political party in the world, ironic since he thought that the Constitution had eliminated the need for parties. The hallmark of the Republicans (later the Democrats under Andrew Jackson) was minimal government at the federal level and a states-rights-based view of where power should reside. After eight years as secretary of state to Jefferson and another eight years as the fourth president, during which the United States barely survived the War of 1812, Madison the nationalist reemerged.

Jefferson's two terms as president, beginning in 1801, were, much like the man, a bundle of contradictions. On the one hand, he "eliminated domestic taxes, reduced the national debt, and shrank the size of the civil service," Appleby has written. But Jefferson was unable to fully eliminate Hamilton's financial system. "The English half-lettered ideas of Hamilton" had caused the United States to move away from "true principles," Jefferson wrote to Pierre-Samuel du Pont de Nemours in early 1802. While "we can pay off his debt in 15 years we can never get rid of his financial system." Perhaps Jefferson felt this way because he had needed to compromise with the Federalists in 1801 to break the tie between himself and Aaron Burr, and part of that compromise was to maintain major parts of Hamilton's financial system.[24]

Jefferson also expanded the power of the presidency to achieve his objectives. He viewed the expansion of the boundaries of the nation as essential to the preservation of republican government since it would provide open space and land for agricultural uses. When the opportunity arose to acquire the Louisiana Territory from France, he moved forward quickly despite his own reservations that he lacked the authority to do so, and that the Constitution should be amended to provide for the purchase. Acquisition of land would allow the United States to continue to maintain a rural-based farming economy, as Jefferson's "Empire of Liberty" continued to expand westward. The embargo that he and Madison engineered primarily against Great Britain in 1807 was largely a failure, causing Jefferson to extensively use executive power to implement it. Jon Meacham has written that "it is not too much to say that Jefferson used Hamiltonian means to pursue Jeffersonian ends."[25]

It was the Republicans' small-government orthodoxy that would come back to haunt Madison during the War of 1812.[26] In March of 1811, the charter for the Bank of the United States ended. Madison now supported renewal of the bank, arguing that its long-term existence "amounted to the requisite evidence of the national judgement and intention" that a national bank was constitutional. But due to his prior opposition, and his belief that the executive should defer to the legislature, Madison did not lobby for the renewal of the bank charter, and it failed to receive the required votes in Congress. The United States thus entered the war without one of the major tools needed to fight a war—the ability to borrow money. The Republicans had also spent the past decade reducing military spending, leaving the country little ability to defend itself. At one point Madison was forced to flee the White House and watch as the British burned it and the Capitol to the ground. Madison was fortunate the nation survived the War of 1812 intact.

Yet Madison had learned some valuable lessons from the failures of Republican orthodoxy. He and other Republicans began to rethink their commitment to America as a purely agrarian society of small yeoman farmers that lacked a military, operated under a weak central government, and eschewed banking. Madison made this clear in his last State of the Union message, which was submitted in writing to Congress in December of 1815. Four things stood out in his address. The first was the importance of military preparedness, given the American experience during the War of 1812. While the state militias were still considered important, the training of professional military officers was also needed "through the enlargement of the Military Academy," as well as the "completion of the works of defense" including naval ships. The second element in his address was a commitment to a new national bank. In addition, a tariff should be continued to protect infant industries needed for "public defense or connected with the primary wants of individuals." Finally, "roads and canals" should be built "under the national authority" and a constitutional amendment should be pursued to provide Congress with the authority to do this. These proposals became known as the Madisonian Platform.[27]

Reaction to the Madisonian Platform was not uniformly positive. The old-line Republicans, led by John Randolph, condemned the program and stated that Madison now "[out-Hamiltons] Alexander Hamilton." However, this was a distinctly minority view, and even

Jefferson now supported the new nationalist vision, at least in terms of the need for the United States to be independent "for the comforts of life" by placing "the manufacturer by the side of the agriculturist."[28]

The elements of the Madisonian Platform would form the basis for a faction of the Republican Party to split off and become known as the National Republicans. They would do battle over these measures and would eventually form the Whig Party, which would oppose the policies of Andrew Jackson, the leader of the other Republican faction, which would become known as the Democrats.

The Anomaly of Slavery

The Republicans were the party of the common man. They supported the importance of equality in American society and wanted to continue to break down the hierarchy that had existed during the colonial period. Yet, the strength of the party lay in the South among wealthy enslavers whose small-government philosophy was in many ways a justification to protect slavery. The Federalists, whose greatest strength lay in New England and who generally supported a more hierarchical view of society, were antislavery.

Republican inconsistencies were best encapsulated in their leader, Thomas Jefferson. He was a lifelong opponent of slavery, seeing it as distinctly evil, yet he was also a enslaver who was dependent on it for his economic survival. He viewed Black people as inferior to whites yet had a long-term relationship with his wife's enslaved half sister, Sally Hemings, who bore him six children. Jefferson never believed that white and Black people could live together in a racially mixed society, and so he proposed numerous schemes for the colonization of Black people somewhere else upon their emancipation. As he grew older, he kept pushing out the date for ending slavery, from his own generation to future generations. Most egregiously, he refused to lead on the issue of slavery, fearing (probably correctly) that it would end his political career.

The great strength of the Republican Party lay in the South. In the Fourth Congress that met between 1795 and 1797, 80 percent of the Federalists were from the North, while almost 70 percent of the Republicans came from the South. At least some of the Republican opposition to Hamilton's economic policies, including his broad interpretation of the Constitution and activist government policies, was grounded in the fear that the North would interfere with slavery in the South. Nathaniel Macon of Virginia expressed this fear in 1818. "Tell me if Congress can establish banks, make roads and canals, whether they can free all the Slaves in the United States." So at least some of the small-government / states' rights policies of the Republicans were rooted in the "realization that, once the federal government assumed control over domestic policy, slavery was doomed," as historian Joseph J. Ellis frames it.[29]

Yet the Republican Party only came to dominate politics because it also had an appeal, a strength in the middle states grounded in their support of greater social and political equality. "In the North, however, the Republican party was the political expression of new egalitarian-minded social forces released and intensified by the Revolution," Gordon Wood has written. As we have seen, equality and democracy also appealed to aristocratic enslavers, who "condemned the privileges of rich speculators and moneyed men and celebrated the character of the ordinary yeoman farmer," as Wood goes on to write, even if they were part of the wealthy Southern elite. It was a potent mix and led both Pennsylvania and New York to support Jefferson in the 1800 election. It would later be Northern Democrats that would split from their Southern brethren over the issue of whether new territory added from the outcome of the Mexican-American War would be free or slave states.[30]

For his part, Hamilton had always carried an "antipathy to slavery," in the words of Ron Chernow. During the Revolutionary War, Hamilton had supported his good friend John Laurens in his proposal to free those enslaved people who fought for the American revolutionaries. Laurens, whose family owned a plantation in South Carolina, shared with Hamilton a sense that the "emancipation of the slaves was an inseparable part of the struggle for freedom," which the revolution represented. Hamilton would become a member of the New York Manumission Society, which pushed for the end of slavery in that state. Hamilton's hands may not have been completely clean, either, when it came to slavery. When Hamilton married into the wealthy Schuyler family, he also may have come to hold one or two enslaved people.[31]

The North had begun the movement to emancipate their enslaved persons during and immediately after the American Revolution. Many of the leaders of that movement from the North viewed slavery with contempt. As early as 1761, James Otis had written that "the colonists [of Massachusetts] are by the law of nature free born, as indeed all men are white and [B]lack." John Adams was a lifelong opponent of slavery, calling it a "foul contagion on the human character." His son John Quincy Adams would go on to be one of the foremost figures in the antislavery movement in the 1830s and 1840s.[32]

Endnotes

1   Donald J. Fraser, *The Emergence of One American Nation: The Revolution, the Founders, and the Constitution* (Roseville: Fraser & Associates, 2015), p. 95–100; Jon Meacham, *Thomas Jefferson, The Art of Power* (New York: Random House, 2012), p. 8.

2   Fraser, p. 100–102.

3   Donald J. Fraser, *The Growth and Collapse of One American Nation: The Early Republic 1790–1861* (Roseville: Fraser & Associates, 2020), *p. 51;* Fraser, *Emergence*, p. 373.

4   Fraser, *Emergence*, p. 166–168; John Ferling, *Jefferson and Hamilton: The Rivalry That Forged a Nation* (New York: Bloomsbury Press, 2013). The quote about the stripling is from the pictures after page 218. Ron Chernow, *Alexander Hamilton* (New York: Penguin, 2004), p. 150.

5   Ron Chernow, *Alexander Hamilton*, p. 374.

6   John C. Miller, *Alexander Hamilton: Portrait in Paradox* (New York: Harper & Row, 1959), p. 283; *The Report on the Subject of Manufactures* was retrieved on March 18, 2020, from https://founders.archives.gov/documents/Hamilton/01-10-02-0001-0007, from which the quotes in this section are drawn. Noah Feldman, *The Three Lives of James Madison: Genius, Partisan,* President (New York: Random House, 2017), p. 286.

7   Alexander Hamilton, *First Report on the Public Credit*, from https://wwnorton.com/college/history/archive/resources/documents/ch08_02.htm.

8   H. W. Brands, *The Money Men: Capitalism, Democracy, and the Hundred Years' War over the American Dollar* (New York: W.W. Norton & Company, 2006), p. 43.

9   Fraser, *Growth*, p. 20–23 and 26; H. W. Brands, *The Money Men: Capitalism, Democracy, and the Hundred Years' War over the American Dollar* (New York: W.W. Norton, 2006), p. 43; Miller, p. 239.

10 Adrienne Koch and William Peden, eds., *The Life and Selected Writing of Thomas Jefferson* (New York, 1944), p. 123–124 and 126–127; Feldman, p. 294.

11 Chernow, p. 348; Miller, p. 259.

12 The biographer mentioned is Jacob E. Cooke, and the quote is found in Chernow, *Hamilton*, p. 352. See also Ferling, p. 220–221, for the quote from Hamilton's opinion. Ferling also makes the point that Washington and Hamilton shared a similar perspective on the need for a strong national government.

13 *The Report on Manufactures*, p. 18 and 21.

14 Fraser, *Growth*, p. 16–18.

15 Fraser, *Growth*, p. 30–31; Koch and Peden, p. 280 and p. 440–441, from Jefferson's letter to Madison on December 20, 1787.

16 Fraser, *Growth*, p. 31–32.

17 Fraser, *Growth*, p. 34; James Madison, *Writings* (New York: Library of America, 1999), p. 531.

18 Michael P. Federici, *The Political Philosophy of Alexander Hamilton* (Baltimore: Johns Hopkins University Press, 2012), p. 76–77; Fraser, Growth, p. 17.

19 John Kenneth Galbraith and Nicole Salinger, *Almost Everyone's Guide to Economics* (Boston: *Houghton Mifflin*, 1978), p. 14–15; Robert L. Heilbroner, *The Making of Economic Society* (New Jersey: *Prentice Hall*, 1972), p. 244–245; Ellen Meiksins, *The Origin of Capitalism* (Brooklyn: Verso, 2017), p. 3; Michael Merrill, "The Anticapitalist Origins of the United States," *Review (Fernand Braudel Center)* vol. 13, no. 4, Fall 1990, p. 465–497. Merrill argues that Jefferson and the Republicans did not want the United

States to be capitalist. For a counterpoint to this, see Joyce Appleby, *Capitalism and a New Social Order: The Republican Vision of the 1790s* (New York: New York University Press, 1984). She argues that "capitalism figured prominently in the Jeffersonian social vision." It would be based on "an expanding commercial agricultural base."

20 Feldman, p. 332–333.

21 Richard White, "Utopian Capitalism" in Sven Beckert and Christin Desan, eds., *American Capitalism: New Histories* (New York: Columbia University Press, 2018), p. 121–122.

22 Appleby, p. 97.

23 E. A. J. Johnson, *The Foundations of American Economic Freedom* (Minneapolis: University of Minnesota Press, 1973), p. 21.

24 Jefferson's letter to Pierre-Samuel du Pont de Nemours, dated January 18, 1802, was retrieved April 19, 2020, from https://founders.archives.gov/documents/ Jefferson/01-36-02-0242; on the possibility of a deal between Jefferson and the Federalists, see *Fraser, Growth and Collapse*, p. 81–83. The historical record is unclear on whether any deal was reached.

25 Joyce Appleby, *Thomas Jefferson* (New York: Times Books, 2003), p. 32; Jon Meacham, *Thomas Jefferson: The Art of Power* (New York: Random House, 2012), p. 352.

26 The balance of this section is a summary from *Growth and Collapse*, chapter 4 and p. 173–175.

27 Fraser, *Growth*, p. 174.

28 Fraser, *Growth*, p. 174.

29 Robin L. Einhorn, *American Taxation American Slavery* (Chicago: University of Chicago Press, 2006), p. 186, for the composition of Congress; Joseph J. Ellis, *American Creation: Triumphs and Tragedies at the Founding of the Republic* (New York: Alfred A. Knopf, 2007), p. 175.

30 Gordon Wood, *Empire of Liberty: A History of the Early Republic, 1789–1815* (Oxford: Oxford University Press, 2009), p. 166–167.

31 Chernow, p. 121 and p. 215; Ferling, p. 173.

32 David McCullough, *John Adams* (New York: Simon & Schuster, 2001), p. 132; Chernow, p. 212.

CHAPTER 3

Government during the
Antebellum Period

It is to be regretted that the rich and powerful too often bend the acts of government to their selfish purposes.
—ANDREW JACKSON, BANK VETO MESSAGE

The transformation of the condition of the country from gloom and distress to brightness and prosperity, has been mainly the work of American legislation fostering American industry . . .
—HENRY CLAY, ON THE AMERICAN SYSTEM

It turns out both Jefferson and Hamilton were right and wrong. Democracy did indeed grow and flourish following the War of 1812, fulfilling Jefferson's dream. But so too did industrialization, driven by innovation and governmental action, as Hamilton foresaw. Yet just as the Republicans feared, this growth was accompanied by a rapid increase in inequality.

Jefferson's Republican Party, now the Democratic-Republicans (and soon to be called the Democrats under Andrew Jackson), continued to support their small-government philosophy, preferring to overturn policies that they believed provided an unfair advantage to the wealthy—especially corporate charters for banking. Liberals saw continued westward expansion as the great safety valve, an alternative to the growth of cities and industry. The more conservative Democratic-Republicans, soon to be identified with the Whig Party, pushed for active government policies to support industry, and placed their hope in fighting inequality through upward mobility. No one was more important in this regard than Henry Clay, Jackson's great rival for power, who promoted his American System.

Underlying all these issues was the future fate of slavery.

The Growth of American Democracy

There is no precise point at which the United States moved from a republic to a democratic republic, although the election of Andrew Jackson as president in 1828 is as good a place as any to mark this transition. Jackson brought to the presidency, and to American elections, a frontier quality, and a raucous sense of the outsider as leader. Born in the backcountry of the Carolinas in 1767, a descendant of the Scotch Irish, Jackson was the ultimate self-made man. He earned his national reputation through his ability to fight, first against American Indians in the South and then against superior British forces at the Battle of New Orleans near the end of the War of 1812, where he won a startling victory.

Elections continued to become more democratic, with ever greater participation among commoners as the age of Jackson unfolded. During the founding era "a republic was meant to secure the common good through the ministration of the most worthy, enlightened men," according to historian Sean Wilentz. But that was increasingly becoming an untenable position, too elitist for the tenor of the times. By 1824, eighteen of the twenty-four states assigned presidential electors based on the popular vote. By 1828, that had increased to twenty-two states. The number of people that voted increased from 350,000 in

1824 to almost 1.2 million in 1828. The method for selecting the presidential candidates had also moved from the legislative caucus to the more democratic party convention. "When new states entered the Union . . . they abolished property requirements for voting," Jill Lepore writes, placing pressure on the older states to follow suit. By 1821, only three states (of the twenty-four) still maintained property requirements for voting.[1]

But Jacksonian democracy was limited in its application to white men only. Women, free Black people, and American Indians were all excluded. Jackson enslaved people and was "blinded by the prejudice of his age" and could not see "that all are created equal," Jon Meacham argues. He was an opponent of both the abolitionist movement and those like Lincoln who were antislavery. Once he became president, he supported a bill for the removal of American Indian tribes in the South. In his relationship with his beloved wife, Rachel, one can see his paternalistic view of women. Historian Harry L. Watson succinctly describes Jackson and his followers as "advocates of democracy [that] opposed inequalities of economic class but embraced inequalities of race and gender."[2]

In 1824, Jackson was one of six candidates who ran for president. He was depicted as the outsider who would clean up "the Giant Augean Stable at Washington" that was awash in corruption. The election occurred during a period with a distinct hangover from the 1819 Panic, giving an outsider a chance to be the change agent. Jackson was able to establish himself in this role before his more distinguished competitors recognized what a threat he was. Jackson won the popular vote and had the most electors, but he fell short of the majority he needed. John Quincy Adams, the eldest son of the second president, ran just behind Jackson and emerged as the president in the House of Representatives when Henry Clay threw his support behind Adams. When Adams named Clay his secretary of state, Jackson saw further proof of corruption at the highest levels. "So you see, the Judas of the West [Clay] has closed the contract . . . was there ever witnessed such a bare faced corruption in any country before," Jackson observed.

John Quincy Adams, in his first address to Congress in 1825, put forward a future-oriented and broad vision of what government could accomplish. The government's role was not just to make physical improvements, but also extended to "moral, political, [and] intellectual" improvements. Adams may have been the first president to conceive of the notion of positive liberty, the idea that government could advance the freedom of individuals within society. Negative liberty is typically associated with placing "strong limitations on the activities of the state," as our Bill of Rights generally does. Adams's view of the use of government power was at odds with that of Jackson and his supporters, who thought that an active federal government was a "danger to liberty." Unfortunately for Adams, the notion of an activist federal government led by elites was losing favor "and the Democratic belief in limited government was definitely in the ascendancy," according to Eric Foner.[3]

Jackson bided his time, and then in 1828 he ran a sophisticated campaign in the rematch against Adams. Messages were relayed from Jackson headquarters in Tennessee to state campaign organizations. The Jackson campaign engaged in organized fundraising efforts, and numerous pro-Jackson newspapers arose to carry his message to the public to return the "government to Jeffersonian first principles and [halt] the new Federalist revival," Wilentz writes. The Jacksonians wanted to halt the use of an activist government that was first promoted by Hamilton, then later taken up by National Republicans in the Madisonian Platform, and then advanced by Adams and Clay.[4]

It was an ugly election, nothing new for the politics of the day. While some, like the Jackson supporter Martin Van Buren, had hoped for a principled campaign, "a great contest between the aristocracy and democracy of America," it soon descended into a war of slander between the two sides. Such is the dark side of an ever-expanding democracy. Ultimately, Jackson emerged the winner, capturing 56 percent of the popular vote and an Electoral College victory of 178–83.

Jackson's win was accompanied by a mob scene in the aftermath of his inaugural on March 4, 1829. The White House was thrown open for all to visit, and was soon overrun by job seekers and well-wishers. One justice of the Supreme Court said that the "reign of 'King Mob' seemed triumphant." Not everyone was happy with such a strong turn toward democracy. Even Jefferson was purported to have said that Jackson was "one of the most unfit men I know for such a place [the presidency]." This may have in fact been apocryphal, since it was a secondhand account relayed by one of Jackson's opponents, Daniel Webster. One of Jefferson's grandchildren would later say he doubted the account, although his grandfather may well have had concerns that a "military chieftain" should become president of the United States.[5]

Still, there were some very real concerns, then as now, that a demagogue could get elected to the top office in the land. The Framers of the Constitution certainly had such fears, and that was in part the reason they had created the Electoral College, to stand between the people and the president. "A small number of persons, selected by their fellow-citizens from the general mass, will be most likely to possess the information and discernment requisite to so complicated an investigation" as selecting a president, Alexander Hamilton wrote in *Federalist* No. 68. It never quite worked that way. Perhaps the last nail in the coffin of the independence of electors to select a president occurred in 2020 when the Supreme Court ruled that states can adopt laws that require electors to vote for the person they indicated when they stood for election.[6]

Both John Adams and John Quincy Adams worried about a cult of personality that could form around popular politicians like Jefferson and Jackson. They feared that "the people are not always right, can be misled, and will arrive at conclusions with insufficient information," historians Nancy Isenberg and Andrew Burstein have written. Research in political science in the aftermath of the 2016 election seems to affirm that the concerns expressed by the Adamses cannot lightly be dismissed. While there is much to admire in an expanding democracy, just like all human contrivances, the system has its flaws. Churchill's oft-quoted remark comes to mind: "Indeed, it has been said that democracy is the worst form of Government except for all of those other forms that have been tried from time to time . . ."[7]

Populist democracy, the idea that one side represents the people and the other the elite, also brought with it a certain disdain for expertise in government. Jackson believed that it was a simple matter to administer the government. "The duties of all public offices are, or at least admit being so plain and simple that men of intelligence may readily qualify themselves for their performance," he said in his first address to Congress. Garry Wills has written that there are a set of values that recur "whenever government is opposed: a belief that government, as a necessary evil, should be kept at a minimum . . . and should be provincial, amateur . . . popular . . . and rotational." On the other side are those who view government as "a positive good, and that it should be cosmopolitan, expert, authoritative . . . progressive [and] elite." Jackson's approach to rotation in office would soon morph into the "spoils system" in which many government jobs were given out based on loyalty to a political party rather than to expertise in the management of public affairs.[8]

Government and the Economy

The American economy began a remarkable transition during and in the aftermath of the War of 1812. As Hamilton envisioned, the United States modeled its economy after the British, who had been the first to industrialize. New inventions spurred ever greater economic growth. One of the most important was steam power, which revolutionized the production of goods. "No longer would society be dependent on doing work on the muscle power of humans and animals," according to Michael Lind. In New England, textile plants emerged that used cotton from Southern slave plantations as raw material and employed young women as laborers. Gradually the world of the artisan and craftsperson began to change in the North. Many found themselves employed as wage laborers in factories rather than artisans working in shops they owned. Inventions continued to transform the economy, including the beginning of railroads and ships driven by steam power. There were also corresponding improvements in the means of communication, highlighted by the invention of the telegraph in 1844. "What hath God wrought?" Morse had typed out when he sent the first message by the new machine. The "Market Revolution," as many historians have come to call the period, brought "more sophisticated technology, faster transportation and communications, more efficient business institutions, and a better-educated work force to the processes of economic development," historian Harry L. Watson has written.[9]

Most people continued to make a living through farming, but the number of farmers was gradually decreasing as a percentage of the labor force. In 1800, 83 percent of the labor force was engaged in farming, which shrunk to 53 percent by 1860. The revolution in the modes of transportation also began to pull agriculture into the market economy. No longer would farmers solely grow crops and raise animals for their own consumption, but they would increasingly sell their surplus in the market, which helped feed those who lived in cities. The invention of the cotton gin in the 1790s, along with the use of steamboats, allowed for the expansion of cotton production the South. It also led to the increasing use of slave labor, as lands in the western parts of Georgia and the Carolinas, along with Mississippi (added in 1817) and Alabama (added in 1819), began to convert to cotton production. Still, compared to the North, most Southerners remained largely outside of the market economy, other than for plantation owners, who enslaved large numbers of people and sold cotton to mills in the North and in England. The rise in cotton production fueled both exports from the United States as well as the initial phase of industrial production in the North that was tied to the textile industries.[10]

Did the Market Revolution mean that individualism and laissez-faire economic policy now triumphed? This was the position that Louis Hartz had taken in *The Liberal Tradition in America*, originally published in 1955. Hartz believed that American political ideology unfolded around Lockean liberalism and individualism. As the journalist Tom Wicker wrote in the introduction to Hartz's book, Americans believed in "liberty, equality, and capitalism" and also that "the human marketplace, where a person succeeds or fails by his or her own efforts or ability, [w]as the proper testing ground of achievement." But Hartz overgeneralized, seeing a consensus around liberalism and individualism that ignored the communitarian impulses in America. During the age of Jackson, it was the conservative side that believed that an active government should direct and assist the market economy. As we shall see later in this chapter, both the Democrats (formerly the Democratic-Republicans) and the Whigs (now representing Federalist ideals) had elements of liberalism and republicanism within their ideologies, much as the founding generation did.[11]

Disputes over the role that government should play in promoting the growth of the market economy predominated during the presidency of Andrew Jackson. He and his party, now called the Democrats, supported the small-government philosophy of Jefferson. His main rival, Henry Clay, believed in an active government. Clay formed the Whig Party during Jackson's second term as a counterweight to Jackson's use of executive power. Clay espoused policies that included (1) a protective tariff for domestic industry; (2) federal funding for internal improvements; (3) maintaining the Second Bank of the United States; and (4) the sale of public lands at a high price to fund infrastructure. Each of these policies, which Clay packaged as his American System, were controversial.

Tariffs

Under the Articles of Confederation, Congress had not been given the power to tax, and attempts to amend the Articles to allow for this through an impost (a tax on imported goods) had failed. When the new Congress met under the Constitution, the impost was quickly converted into tariffs designed to protect domestic industry. Tariffs soon became the main revenue source for the federal government during the antebellum period, equaling approximately 90 percent of federal revenue. There was little disagreement over the need to generate revenue from the tariff—the question was whether the rates should be set at a level to protect domestic industry. Clay thought that a protective tariff would "prevent well-established foreign producers from underselling their American rivals" and thus provide a measure of protection "to novice American manufacturers," according to Watson. Clay was engaged in every major dispute over tariff levels that occurred on and off from 1828 through 1850.[12]

Jackson straddled the fence on tariff policy. To win support in Northern states like Pennsylvania in 1824, Jackson had claimed he supported "fair protection" that "would place [A]merican labour in fair competition with that of [E]urope." But to an opponent of the tariff from the South, he said he favored a "judicious examination and revision" of the tariff if needed. Yet his votes while in the Senate were in support of a protectionist tariff. In 1828 he continued to allow "men of different views to imagine that his sympathies lay with them." Part of the reason Jackson was able to gain significant support in the North in 1828 was due to the adoption of extremely high tariff rates by Congress in the months leading up to the election.[13]

The disputes over the protective tariff were not just between Clay and Jackson, nor their respective parties, but rather between the North and the South. In the aftermath of the 1828 tariff, referred to as the Tariff of Abominations in the South, South Carolina began to consider the nullification of federal law. Jefferson had considered nullification when the Federalists adopted the Alien and Sedition Acts in the late 1790s. He was finally convinced to remove the language from his Kentucky resolutions, but most politicians were aware of Jefferson's original draft of the resolutions.

One of the leaders in South Carolina was John C. Calhoun, a formerly nationalist politician, who had been elected Jackson's vice president in 1828. As politics changed in South Carolina, so too did Calhoun, and he became the most ardent supporter of states' rights and a staunch defender of slavery. Calhoun's theory of the Union differed little from the governmental structure of the United States under the Articles of Confederation, in which each state was considered sovereign. Calhoun went so far as to doubt that the United States was truly one nation rather than a league of sovereign states. One of the core elements of Calhoun's nullification theory was that states had the final authority to judge the constitutionality of federal laws. Essentially, according to Calhoun's reading of the Constitution, a vote of three-quarters of the states would be required to condone the federal law in question by amending the Constitution, in which case the action of the state in nullifying federal law would be overturned. Calhoun wrote that "should the other members undertake to grant the power nullified," then that state would have the power to secede from the union.[14]

In November of 1832, South Carolina voted to nullify the tariffs of 1828 as amended in 1832. Jackson, who had grown to despise Calhoun for any number of reasons, would later regret that he had not marched the army south and hung Calhoun for his role in the crisis. Instead, Jackson issued his Nullification Proclamation, a ringing endorsement of the idea that the United States is one nation, and a complete repudiation of nullification and secession. Jackson refused to compromise on the issue of nullification, but he was willing to compromise over tariff rates, which were eventually reduced when Henry Clay forged a compromise. In return, South Carolina rescinded its Ordinance of Nullification. Disaster was averted for the time being, although secession would remain a continuing threat to the Union.[15]

Internal Improvements

There was an obvious need for infrastructure to knit the American nation together and to allow for economic expansion. The Constitution had included a provision for the establishment of post offices and post roads. In the 1790s Hamilton had recommended the funding of internal improvements in his *Report on Manufactures*. Yet the idea of federal funding for internal improvements was also controversial. Many believed that the Constitution would need to be amended to allow the federal government to fund such improvements.

In 1796 Thomas Jefferson had opposed "federal funding for a survey of a national post road that ran from Georgia to Maine," historian Brian Balogh writes, even though it was sponsored by Madison. Yet as president, Jefferson was much more pragmatic, supporting the construction of the Cumberland Road from Maryland to Ohio. In 1802 Congress devoted public land sales in Ohio to build the National Road. Jefferson was also willing to support an amendment to the Constitution to allow for federal funding of internal improvements, seeing it as a way to strengthen the bonds of union. "New channels of communication will be opened between the States, the lines of separation will disappear . . . and their union cemented by new and indissoluble ties," Jefferson wrote in his 1806 message to Congress.[16]

In 1817, the Second Bank of the United States was required to pay $1.5 million to the federal government for its charter. Henry Clay and John C. Calhoun (who was still in his nationalist phase) proposed to use the money for internal improvements. "Let us, then, bind the republic together with a perfect system of roads and canals," Calhoun argued. "Let us conquer space." Madison vetoed the bill on constitutional grounds on his last day in office. This caused the state of New York to abandon any hope for federal assistance with the Erie Canal, which ran from Albany on the Hudson River to Buffalo on Lake Erie. "The Erie Canal represented the first step in the transportation revolution that would turn an aggregate of local economies into a nationwide market economy," historian Daniel Walker Howe has written.[17]

Disputes over the federal government's authority to build infrastructure continued during the Monroe administration, as well as that of John Quincy Adams. Monroe vetoed a bill in 1822 that would have authorized the collection of tolls on the National Road. Monroe then received an advisory opinion from the Supreme Court that the federal government had the authority to build internal improvements without the need for a constitutional amendment. But many in the South continued to oppose federal power over infrastructure spending, fearing that it would be a springboard for the federal government to interfere with slavery.

President Andrew Jackson vetoed a bill that would have extended the Maysville Road that ran solely through Kentucky, claiming it violated his principle that projects be of national scope. He also expressed constitutional concerns and requested that an amendment be processed to clarify federal authority in this area. Like Jefferson, Jackson was always concerned about debt and that major infrastructure projects would prevent "the repayment of the national debt," Watson writes. He also no doubt saw the Maysville Road project as a major victory for his main rival, Henry Clay, which added to his desire to veto the project.[18]

Banking and Inequality

The expansion of the market economy led to a rapid growth in per capita income in the country in the years after the War of 1812. But just as Jefferson feared, that growth led to ever greater inequality in the United States. The economists Peter H. Lindert and Jeffrey G. Williamson have found that inequality increased between 1774 and

1860 "for the United States as a whole, for every region, among free households alone, and among slave and free combined." Manufacturing had replaced "artisans with unskilled [labor] and this hollowed out the middle class," they find. The increasing rate of urbanization in the United States also contributed to inequality, with cities growing from 6 percent of the population in 1800 to almost 20 percent in 1860. While wealth creation was much faster in urban areas, so too was the growth of income inequality. But inequality also increased in the South, driven by the wealth that was accumulated by large-scale enslavers.[19]

Different political leaders and their respective parties responded to the growth of the market economy and concerns over income inequality in different ways. Andrew Jackson's response can be seen in his veto of the charter renewal of the Second Bank of the United States in July of 1832. Jackson vetoed the bill, seeing it as increasing the structural causes of inequality. While Jackson believed that inequality was sown into the nature of man and that "distinctions in society will always exist," he also opposed laws that "add to these natural and just advantages" any type of "artificial distinctions . . . [that] make the rich richer and the potent more powerful," as he wrote in his veto message. Both Jefferson and Jackson understood that people have differing skills and abilities, and both wanted to avoid an aristocracy tied to either birth or social connections. The monarchies of Europe controlled both the government and the economy, and blocked the average person, regardless of ability, from reaching their full potential. Jackson saw the bank as an institution that was granted a privileged position in society because of its corporate charter, a government benefit that at the time was available only to a limited few. For both Jefferson and Jackson, a smaller government with less power would avoid such situations by eliminating benefits to the already wealthy and powerful.[20]

There was also a certain sense in the minds of Democrats that some professions were simply illegitimate, particularly those that did not include manual labor of one form or another. Banking and speculators in markets were particularly egregious. Democrats saw "wealth passing continually out of the hands of those whose labor produced it . . . into the hands of those who neither work nor save," one person wrote at the time. Many Democrats "were certain that the central agency of corruption had been government," historian Lawrence Frederick Kohl argues. They believed that the Whig use of active "government was designed to advance the interests" of the already rich. Much as Jefferson thought that Federalist economic policies would lead to a monarchy, so too the Jacksonians feared a new aristocracy was being formed under the Whig approach.[21]

The Sale of Public Land

The Democrats wanted the price of public land in the South and West to be affordable to small farmers. At the price that was then being charged, "only wealthy planters and speculators could afford to buy," Watson writes. Clay and the Whigs were opposed to this and preferred that the price be kept high, and that the proceeds be used to fund internal improvements. Clay would eventually propose that the land sales proceeds be returned to the states as a compromise measure, which was incorporated into legislation. That bill would eventually be approved by Congress, but Andrew Jackson vetoed it.[22]

☙☙☙

As we have seen, the Democrats were concerned with artificial inequality, which arose because government favored the wealthy over the average person. Some saw the world in terms of class conflict, with the working class and farmers battling against wealthy bankers and businessmen. For the Whigs, class conflict was chimerical. "Not only were the interests of the classes identical, but there were . . . no classes in America," Arthur M. Schlesinger Jr. has written of Whig philosophy. Inequality of wealth was simply the natural outcome of differing skills and abilities. As the evolutionary anthropologist Avi Tuschman has written, liberals tend to see inequality as occurring because of "outer, structural injustice" while conservatives view inequality as coming from "individual capabilities." This was reflected in the Democratic and Whig worldviews toward inequality.[23]

As one historian has written, the Whigs believed that the government should "promote the general welfare, raise the level of opportunity for all men and aid individuals to their full potentialities." Yet as Daniel Walker Howe has pointed out, the Whigs shared less in common with modern liberals than this statement would imply. Most importantly, "Whig policies did not have the object of redistributing wealth or diminishing the influence of the privileged" unlike modern liberals. Whigs considered themselves conservatives who valued order and wanted all "Americans to exercise self-control," Kohl writes.[24]

The Whig answer to the problem of inequality was a reliance on upward mobility. Today's wage worker could become tomorrow's business owner. "No man in America is doomed by the necessity of his circumstances to die in the same condition, in which he was born," one Whig newspaper proclaimed. Whigs believed that their system of government sponsored economic development that would assist all people who were willing to work hard. "The unquestionable operation of all these things had been not only to increase property, but to equalize it, to diffuse it, to scatter its advantages among the many," the Whig Daniel Webster said at the time. Upward mobility was still a reality in the years prior to the Civil War, when "all men aspire to economic independence," according to Foner. But that world was rapidly changing as industrialization continued to expand. It has been estimated that by 1860 almost 60 percent of the labor force was not economically independent.[25]

Liberalism/Republicanism and the Parties

The core of liberalism is a concern about the individual and the protection of rights, while republicanism is concerned with an overarching public good. Adherents of liberalism "considered the state as the primary threat" to individual liberty, as George Will has written. Both philosophies were present during the founding era and were also present during the age of Jackson. Tocqueville talked about the importance of individualism in America but also about how self-interest needed to be properly understood. "I must say that I have seen Americans making great and sincere sacrifices for the common good and a hundred times I have noticed that when needs be, they almost always gave each other faithful support."[26] To Tocqueville, self-interest properly understood had collective spirit about it.

In some ways it is easy to see the Democrats of Jackson as the inheritors of the liberal tradition, with their focus on the importance of the individual, while the Whigs carried on the republican tradition with their support of the use of government action to advance the overall interest of the society. But Whigs were more comfortable in the market economy that was developing and in an individual ethos that was directed by self-interest. Yet neither party was totally at home in the new market economy that was being created, nor in a purely individualistic notion of society.[27]

The Democrats were certainly the party of the common man, and they had great concern for individual dignity and for the equality of all white men. "Jacksonian America demanded, and the values of the age extolled, personal independence," Kohl writes. The party had a focus on the importance of natural rights, which were perceived as a gift from God. "The rights of man belong to him as man. . . . They belong to man as an individual," one Democratic newspaper wrote. Yet the Democrats had a sense of insecurity in an impersonal world where individual self-interest was the sole motivation. Since Democrats represented the common people of the period, they feared domination by the rich and powerful who were so successful in the emerging market economy. Banks, credit, and governmental sponsorship of corporations were all seen as ways to keep the average person in his place. "No man who owes more than he can immediately pay feels that his soul is free," one Democratic newspaper wrote. They often felt looked down upon by the rich who were more successful in the new economy produced by the Market Revolution. Democrats tended to look at "the banker's world" as an impersonal one staffed with people who were "arrogant" and "cold" and lacked compassion. Whereas Democrats viewed themselves as united by "universal love" in their support for the common people.[28]

Democrats would have been more comfortable in an earlier era of small farmers, as Jefferson was. Historian Kohl succinctly summarizes the views of the followers of Jackson as follows: "Jacksonians pictured an America in which urbanization would be limited, government and institutions small, wealth widely and relatively evenly distributed, and men's relations simple and natural." It was not the world that was emerging around them.[29]

Members of the Whig Party were more successful in the world that the Market Revolution was creating. They tended to be the merchants, bankers, and new industrialists. So too were "wage earners and others who felt they had a stake in the growth of manufacturing," Howe writes, although many laborers who were paid low wages found themselves attracted to the Democrats. The market economy that was developing in antebellum America was more paternalistic than that which would occur in the years after the Civil War. Most business were small to medium size and were largely family owned. "Truly big corporate business, impersonal and bureaucratic, did not arise until the middle of the nineteen century," Howe argues, and so "economic innovation and social stability could still seem compatible."[30]

If Henry Clay was the political apostle of the Whig philosophy, Henry Carey was its intellectual apostle. Carey supported political activism to industrialize American society and create well-paid jobs and "varied career opportunities" that would benefit all men. For Carey, those who had fulfilling jobs would then be able to enjoy life more fully and develop a greater "desire for knowledge" and a "love for literature and art." Government-directed capitalistic economic development was the means to achieve this end. As with other Whigs, Carey believed in upward mobility as the answer to inequality. He too feared the development of large-scale urban areas where wage earners would be exploited by distant capitalists. "The society [Whigs] envisioned would be designed to encourage talent and virtue," Howe writes.[31]

But Whigs were also not completely satisfied with the market economy since it was not "compatible with social order as they knew it," as Howe explains. Whig economic philosophy only partly fit modern conceptions of laissez-faire capitalism. Their approach to society was grounded in tradition. "Whigs had an intense desire for order, both in themselves and in society at large," Kohl writes. Whigs tended to carry on the conservative tradition of top-down leadership and deference they inherited from the Federalists, although they placed their faith in Congress and not the presidency. They also wanted to ensure that the actions they undertook in the economic sphere would benefit "the community, that in some larger sense their individual actions served their fellow man," according to Kohl. Henry Clay once remarked that "every portion of the republic is indirectly . . . interested in the welfare of the whole." Whigs were very supportive of private associations in American life, such as the home, churches, and schools. One can see in their orientation the significant influence of republicanism.[32]

Free Labor and Slave Labor

The Democratic Party may have been concerned with equality, but this was limited to equality for white men. The Democrats were the party of white supremacy during the antebellum period. As previously stated, they were concerned about inequality related to economic class but not inequality based on race or gender. The members of the party from the North tended to be made up of those who felt they were losers in the new market economy, who were in a tenuous alignment with Southern enslavers.[33]

Whigs, on the other hand, tended to practice a more traditional politics of deference, a carryover from the colonial and Federalist traditions. Yet they were more open to appeals against slavery, given their more hierarchical view of society, since "they could help [B]lacks without having to acknowledge their equality," Howe argues. Henry Clay, an enslaver himself, always thought that slavery was evil. His views harkened back to those of many of the founders, who thought slavery was inconsistent with America's revolution. Clay had been the president of the American Colonization Society, which supported the gradual emancipation and colonization of enslaved people. Some believed that the kinds of industrialization that Clay supported would eventually endanger slavery, which did not bother Clay in the least. In 1849, he proposed that all enslaved individuals born after a certain date in Kentucky be set free at the age of twenty-five and then be sent to Africa. Clay did not believe that Black people and whites could live together as equals. He freed his own enslaved people in his will.[34]

One thing that both Jackson and Clay agreed on was that the issue of slavery should be kept off the national agenda. It was simply too explosive an issue, one that could tear the nation apart. Yet the politics of slavery began to emerge in the 1830s with the rise of the abolitionist movement. Led by men like William Lloyd Garrison and Frederick Douglass, who had escaped slavery, they challenged the idea of gradual emancipation accompanied by colonization. Abolitionists wanted the immediate end to slavery in the United States without any form of compensation to enslavers. Garrison, among others, believed in the equality of all people, a position well outside of mainstream opinion at the time.

Garrison eschewed politics, preferring to operate as an outside agitator. Others were not so hesitant to become involved in the political process. Garrison and his American Anti-Slavery Society (AASS) caused a political uproar when they flooded Southerners with 175,000 antislavery tracts. With the support of Andrew Jackson, Southern postmasters refused to deliver the incendiary materials. The abolitionists also bombarded Congress with petitions to eliminate slavery. The former president John Quincy Adams, now a member of Congress, was no abolitionist. Yet when Southerners attempted to ignore the petitions, Adams stepped in, arguing that the right to petition Congress was provided for in the Constitution. Southerners then adopted a gag rule. Threats of violence from Southern politicians silenced many Northern congressmen, but not Adams. He was finally able to overturn the gag rule in 1844.

Abolitionism was gradually changing the terms of the political debate in the North. In the South, politicians continued to dig in their heels. The South had become increasingly dependent on the growing of cotton with slave labor, and as this occurred, their rhetoric on slavery had begun to change. Whereas Southern leaders during the founding era saw slavery as an evil system that was inconsistent with the American Revolution's call for liberty and equality, a new generation of Southern leaders had begun to argue that slavery was a benevolent institution. John C. Calhoun, who had led the nullification effort in South Carolina, said slavery "is, instead of an evil, a good, a positive good." Calhoun tried to appeal to the newly emerging capitalist class in the North, where labor strife over wages and working conditions was occurring. "Calhoun had an ingenious solution for the section problem: in return for the South's services as a balance wheel against labor agitation, the solid elements in the North should join her in a common front against all agitation of the slavery issue," historian Richard Hofstadter writes.[35]

It was a grand bargain that the North ultimately refused to join. For one thing, wage labor had become increasingly important in the North as the Market Revolution continued apace. For Whigs, the wage worker was of central importance. Those who worked freely for wages had the opportunity to rise in the ranks and ultimately own their own business, which enslaved people could never do. Democrats originally were less enamored of the idea of the wage laborer, dating back to Jefferson, believing those who were dependent on their employer "could never be truly free, nor could a dependent class constitute the basis of a republican government," historian James McPherson writes. But the way in which the market economy had expanded by the mid-1840s had caused many Northern Democrats to become supporters of "free labor," even if that labor was now largely made up of wage workers.[36]

The free labor movement grew in part out of the continuing expansion of the boundaries of the United States in the 1840s from the annexation of Texas and territory gained in the Mexican-American War. Free labor became linked with the free soil movement. David Wilmot of Pennsylvania introduced a proviso to an appropriation bill for the Mexican-American War that would ban slavery from any new territory acquired as part of the war. It was designed to promote the interests of working-class whites, "to preserve to free white labor a fair country," in Wilmot's own words, where "the sons of toil, of my own race and own color," could have the ability to be successful. The free soil and free labor movement reflected "an affirmation of the superiority of the social system of the North—a dynamic, expanding capitalist society, whose achievements and destiny were almost wholly the result of the dignity and opportunities which it offered the average laboring man," Eric Foner writes. It also offered to Northern Democrats and Whigs, who were dissatisfied with their own party's position on slavery, a new home that would emerge in the 1850s as the Republican Party.[37]

Free labor was wed to free soil for many Northern Democrats through westward expansion, which provided a safety valve for those who seemed stuck in low-wage jobs in the Northeast. It was in the small towns and farm communities of the Old Northwest Territories that people could obtain property to farm or to open a new business, thereby opening opportunity for upward mobility. The Democrats had long supported low prices for western land "to afford every American citizen of enterprise the opportunity of securing an independent freehold," as Andrew Jackson framed it. The Whigs, for their part, had not been particularly interested in further territorial expansion of the United States. But they too favored upward mobility, "which assured that today's laborer would be tomorrow's capitalist," according to Foner. Support for upward mobility and a greater level of equality wed together disaffected Northern Democrats and Whigs.[38]

The North would increasingly decry the "Slave Power" in the South, where a small number of plantation owners controlled much of the wealth and political power. They feared that the continued expansion of slavery "threatened the rights of free people and corrupted the republic," historian Adam Rothman has written. Divisions among Northern capitalists further contributed to the growing divide between North and South. Whereas the older merchant class in the North was tied economically to the cotton economy, the new industrialists felt no such attachment. They "had a virulent distaste for slavery and slave-holders, who they feared would undermine the free labor republic on which their vision of a rapidly industrializing nation rested," Edward Baptist argues.[39]

The Union Collapses

The split between North and South became further exacerbated during the 1850s over the expansion of slavery. The decade opened on a note of optimism with the Compromise of 1850, which had been cobbled together by the ailing Henry Clay and pushed over the finish line by Senator Stephen A. Douglas of Illinois. The compromise allowed California to enter the Union as a free state, with future admissions determined based on popular sovereignty. The fugitive slave law was strengthened, which caused great controversy in the North.

But the compromise would not hold. Douglas, who wanted a transcontinental railroad to run through Chicago, needed Southern votes to do this. In the process of negotiating the Kansas-Nebraska Act, Douglas agreed to repeal the Missouri Compromise, further inflaming tensions. Kansas, where popular sovereignty was to be used to decide on the fate of slavery, soon became the site of a mini civil war between pro- and antislavery forces.

Each of these issues allowed a little-known politician from Illinois an opening to establish a national reputation. Abraham Lincoln, from a most humble background, had become a successful lawyer in the state. He was not so lucky in his political career, having served short terms in the Illinois state house and one term in Congress. Yet the Kansas-Nebraska Act had stirred him "as he had never been before." Douglas believed that the will of the majority was always right, and so he placed his faith in the doctrine of popular sovereignty as the answer to how to deal with the expansion of slavery. Lincoln thought that popular sovereignty was no solution at all to the problem of the spread of slavery. "The doctrine of self government is right—absolutely and eternally right—but it has no just application" to the issue of slavery, Lincoln said. The reason is that the "[N]egro is a man" and "there can be no moral right in the enslaving of one man by another."[40]

Lincoln and Douglas faced off in their famous debates for the 1858 senate seat in Illinois. While Douglas retained his seat, Lincoln's political career was kicked into high gear. Lincoln had always been a Whig and a strong supporter of an activist government along the lines of Clay's American System. In 1854 he wrote that "the legitimate object of government is to do for a community of people, whatever they need to have done, but can not do, *at all*, or can not, *so well do*, for themselves—in their separate, and individual capacities." Lincoln rejected the top-down approach the Whigs generally embraced and preferred a more Jeffersonian approach. "The principles of Jefferson are the definition and axioms of free society," he said in 1859. Richard Hofstadter writes that Lincoln spoke "with sincerity for Jeffersonian principles while supporting Hamiltonian means," such as active government.[41]

As the Whig Party collapsed in the 1850s, Lincoln moved to the emerging Republican Party. Lincoln was a great supporter of free labor and the idea of upward mobility. "The man who labored for another last year this year labors for himself, and next year he will hire others to labor for him," Lincoln said. Lincoln's support for free labor and the advancement of the common person was "at the core of his criticism of slavery," Hofstadter writes. He would emerge as the dark-horse candidate for the Republican presidential nomination in 1860. His strong support for limiting the further spread of slavery would lead him to victory in the election that year, and to the secession of the South from the Union.[42]

During the Civil War, Lincoln and the Republican Party would fully embrace the use of an active government to win the war but also to promote the needs of average Americans in the North, as we shall see in the next chapter.

Endnotes

1   Sean Wilentz, *The Rise of American Democracy: Jefferson to Lincoln* (New York: W.W. Norton, 2005), p. xvii; Jill Lepore, *These Truths: A History of the United States* (New York: W.W. Norton, 2018), p. 182–183.

2   Jon Meacham, *American Lion: Andrew Jackson in the White House* (New York: Random House, 2008), p. 303; Henry L. Watson, *Andrew Jackson vs. Henry Clay: Democracy and Development in Antebellum America* (Boston: Bedford / St. Martin's, 1998), p. 16.

3   Fraser, *Growth*, p. 293–294; Eric Foner, *The Story of American Freedom* (New York: W.W. Norton, 1998), p. 54–55.

4   Wilentz, p. 302–303.

5   Jon Meacham, *Thomas Jefferson: The Art of Power* (New York: Random House, 2012), p. 484–485.

6   Hamilton, quoted in *The Federalist Papers* (New York: New American Library, 1961).

7   Nancy Isenberg and Andrew Burstein, *The Problem of Democracy: The Presidents Adams Confront the Cult of Personality* (New York: Viking, 2019), p. xiv; on political science research on the issue, see Christopher H. Achen and Larry M. Bartels, *Democracy for Realists: Why Elections Do Not Produce Responsive Government* (Princeton: Princeton University Press, 2016). The authors write about the misguided "folk theory" that sees the public as well informed about government policy and likely to "leaders who will do these things." Alas, the authors present evidence that this is not the case. The evidence

shows that people pay scant attention to politics and vote based on "how they feel about the nature of things" and on "political loyalties typically acquired in childhood." See chapter 1.

8   Fraser, *Growth*, p. 312.

9   Michael Lind, *Land of Promise: An Economic History of the United States* (New York: Broadside Books, 2012), p. 84; Daniel Walker Howe, *What Hath God Wrought: The Transformation of America, 1815–1848* (New York: Oxford University Press, 2007), p. 1; Watson, p. 8.

10 The statistics for the percentage of farmers was downloaded on August 13, 2020, from https://www.digitalhistory.uh.edu/disp_textbook.cfm?smtID=11&psid=3837; see Douglass C. North, *The Economic Growth of the United States 1790–1860* (New York: Norton, 1966), for a discussion of the growth of exports of cotton (p. 75) and how most of the South remained outside of the market system (p. 130). See also Fraser, p. 180, for how the expansion of cotton affected the North.

11 Louis Hartz, *The Liberal Tradition in America* (San Diego: Harcourt Brace & Co., 1955), p. ix.

12 William K. Bolt, *Tariff Wars and the Politics of Jacksonian American* (Nashville: Vanderbilt University Press, 2017), p. 1; Watson, p. 21.

13 Wilentz, p. 247.

14 Fraser, *Growth*, p. 359–364.

15 Fraser, *Growth*, p. 370–376.

16 Brian Balogh, *A Government Out of Sight: The Mystery of National Authority in Nineteenth Century America,* (Cambridge: Cambridge University Press, 2009), p. 123–125.

17 Daniel Walker Howe, p. 87 and p. 118.

18 Watson, p. 77–78.

19 Peter H. Lindert and Jeffrey G. Williamson, *Unequal Gains: American Growth and Inequality since 1700* (Princeton: Princeton University Press, 2016), chapter 5.

20 Fraser, *Growth*, p. 331 and p. 341.

21 Lawrence Frederick Kohl, *The Politics of Individualism: Parties and the American Character in the Jacksonian Era* (New York: Oxford University Press, 1989), p. 191–206.

22 Watson, p. 85.

23 Arthur M. Schlesinger Jr., *The Age of Jackson* (New York: Book-of-the-Month, Inc., 1945), p. 270; Avi Tuschman, *Our Political Nature: The Evolutionary Origins of What Divides Us* (Amherst: Prometheus Books, 2013), p. 250–251.

24 Daniel Walker Howe, *The Political Culture of the American Whigs* (Chicago: University of Chicago Press, 1979), p. 20; Kohl, p. 63.

25 Kohl, p. 66 and p. 220–221; Eric Foner, *Free Soil, Free Labor, Free Men: The Ideology of the Republican Party before the Civil War* (London: Oxford University Press, 1970), p. 31–32.

26 Will, p. xxiv; Tocqueville, p. 594–595.

27 I am indebted to both Kohl's book on individualism during the Jackson era and also Howe's book on the Whigs for an understanding of how both parties continued to carry forward elements of both liberalism and republicanism.

28 Kohl, p. 28–44.

29 Kohl, p. 52.

30 Howe, *The Political Culture*, p. 13 and p. 104–105.

31 Howe, *The Political Culture*, p. 108–122.

32 Kohl, p. 64 and p. 79.

33 Watson, p. 16.

34 Howe, *The Political Culture*, p. 38 and p. 132–133; Robert. V. Remini, *Henry Clay: Statesman for the Union* (New York: W.W. Norton, 1991), p. 26–27 and p. 693.

35 Richard Hofstadter, *The American Political Tradition* (New York: Knopf, 1948), p. 81–84.

36 James McPherson, *Battle Cry of Freedom: The Civil War Era* (New York: Oxford University Press, 1988), p. 23.

37 Foner, *Free Soil*, p. 11.

38 Foner, *Free Soil*, p. 20.

39 Adam Rothman, "The Slave Power in the United States, 1783–1865," in Steve Fraser and Gary Gerstle, eds., *Ruling America: A History of Wealth and Power in a Democracy* (Cambridge: Harvard University Press, 2005), p. 64; Sven Beckert, "Merchants and Manufactures in the Antebellum North," in Fraser and Gerstle, chapter 3 and p. 109.

40 Eric Foner, *The Fiery Trial: Abraham Lincoln and American Slavery* (New York: W.W. Norton & Company, 2010), p. 67–68.

41 Abraham Lincoln, *Selected Speeches and Writings* (New York: Penguin, 1992), p. 91; Hofstadter, p. 100–102.

42 Foner, *Free Soil*, p. 30; Hofstadter, p. 105.

Chapter 4

Activist Government during the Civil War

[The government's] legislative power clearly extends to the passage of laws affecting trade, commerce, and labor of the country.
　　—Representative Israel Washburn Jr.

. . . that this nation, under God, shall have a new birth of freedom . . .
　　—Abraham Lincoln, The Gettysburg Address

The United States now entered a great civil war between Northern society, which was dedicated to free labor, and Southern society, which wanted to protect slavery. The war also represented an experiment in whether the ideology of Hamilton or Jefferson would prove successful.

In some ways a line could be drawn from Hamilton's Federalists to the Whigs of Henry Clay, and now to Lincoln and his Republican Party. As we have seen, the conservative party during this period of history believed in an active government to promote a mixed economy and free labor. On the other side stood Jefferson's original Republican Party, which became the Democrats under Andrew Jackson. Both Jefferson and Jackson believed in limited government, but they were also strongly supportive of the American Union. The South stood for small government, states' rights, a rural economy, and slavery, yet the newly seceded states lacked many of the nuances of Jefferson's own position on slavery and the role of the common man, and had now formed a new and separate government dedicated to the perpetuation of slavery and white supremacy.

The North would go on to win the war. But it would take far longer, and at much greater cost, than anyone could have imagined at the beginning. There is no single reason that the North won the war. Partly it was because it had a greater industrial base than the South and a greater number of men it could tap into. But it also had a willingness to use active government in a more effective manner than the South. The differences in areas like financing the war, taxation, infrastructure, and direct aid to people had an impact on the outcome of the war. And as Lincoln proclaimed at Gettysburg, the United States would undergo a new birth of freedom as the war proceeded. Yet the South, with its adherence to small government, would be forced to also adopt the use of a more assertive government if it hoped to win independence.[1]

Financing the War in the Union

President Lincoln selected Salmon P. Chase to run the Treasury Department. Chase had been one of his rivals for the presidency in 1860, and Lincoln was determined to create unity in his cabinet among the Republican Party, given he was facing the secession of so many of the Southern states. Chase was in some ways an odd appointment, since he had no experience in financial matters but had built his reputation as an antislavery advocate in Ohio. Yet that very reputation, and his run for the presidency in 1860, meant Lincoln could only entice him into the cabinet with one of the senior positions. Since secretary of state had gone to another major rival, William Seward, only the treasury secretary remained.

When Chase took over the Treasury Department, the Union was out of money. Just as the extraordinary expenses of the war hit for soldiers and equipment, the Union faced a deficit of $65 million. Chase initially sought the support of eastern bankers to raise money, offering $8 million in bonds at an interest rate of 6 percent. But he was disappointed that many of the bids were priced at a steep discount, some as low as 90 percent of the par value of the bonds. He rejected any bid that was less than 94 percent of par and was only able to yield $3 million in funding. Chase, who had flirted with both the Whig and Democratic Party and had even changed his views on "the banking system to align himself with the Democrats," had a somewhat skeptical view of bankers, as did many in the West. This was no doubt a remnant of Andrew Jackson and his hatred of banks. When Chase issued another $5 million in treasury notes, New York banks refused to bid on them. "Unfortunately, the Secretary so irritated bankers by rejecting private bids for the notes that they refused to bid for the Treasury notes at all," historian Heather Cox Richardson writes.[2]

Chase needed to innovate, and he found the assistance he needed in a young Philadelphia banker named Jay Cooke. Chase already knew other members of the Cooke family, so young Jay was not a stranger to him. What initially solidified their relationship was when Cooke arranged for the $5 million in treasury notes to be placed with other Philadelphia bankers. Then in the summer of 1861, Chase proposed a popular loan, one sold directly to the public, to "reduce the nation's dependence on uncooperative bankers" as Richardson frames it. In late 1862, Chase named Jay Cooke the general subscription agent for the entire country. Cooke broke the bonds down into ever smaller amounts, with some as low as fifty dollars, in order to sell them to the general public. "Cooke's campaign was a roaring success; northern men, women, and even former slaves bought" a substantial portion of the debt, Richardson writes. In total, sixty percent of the $2.3 billion of war costs was funded through debt financing.[3]

Even though Chase had changed his stance on banking for a brief time to appeal to the Democrats, he still believed in many of the old-line Federalist and Whig ideas: that the federal government should control the money supply and have some form of national banking system. He and Congress acted out of desperation since bond sales in 1861 were simply insufficient to raise the money needed to finance the war. As a second financing mechanism, they began to issue paper money. A fear that paper money would lead to rampant inflation dated back to the American Revolution, when the Confederation Congress had largely financed that war with paper money in the form of continental notes. That money quickly depreciated, giving rise to the saying "not worth a continental." Many also thought it was unconstitutional to issue paper money, since the Constitution only mentioned the coining of money.

It may come as a surprise to the modern reader, but the federal government did not issue paper money prior to the Legal Tender Act of 1862. Instead, state banks issued their own notes that circulated as money. It was a confusing system, subject to counterfeiting, and one in which the face value of bank notes often varied from their actual value. The notes of small and obscure banks often traded at a steep discount since people did not know how solvent the bank was.

The greenbacks that the Union issued, so known because they were printed on green paper, were not backed by gold or silver. "They were based instead on the good faith of the government," Richardson writes. The inflationary impacts of the greenbacks were rather mild compared to what had happened during the Revolutionary War, because they represented approximately 15 percent of the cost of the war.[4]

The Union controlled the money supply without inflation in part through banking reform. Since Jackson had destroyed the Second Bank, the United States had not had a national bank, just state banks. There was no oversight over state banks, which continued to issue their own bank notes at the same time that the greenbacks had begun to circulate. "Lincoln urged that Congress, instead of repeatedly issuing greenbacks, pass a national bank bill and tax state bank notes to contract the currency," Richardson writes. Both Lincoln and Chase feared the return of inflation if state banks were not reined in.[5]

In February 1863 the National Banking Act was passed by Congress and signed by the president. It was pushed forward in the Senate by John Sherman, the younger brother of Union general William Sherman. Senator Sherman told his colleagues that "all private interests, all local interests, all banking interests, the interests of individuals, everything, should be subordinate now to the interest of the Government." The law did not provide for one central bank but instead allowed for national banks to be chartered by the federal government. It was hoped that many of the state banks would be converted to federal banks, but the enticements and penalties in the 1863 law were not strong enough to achieve this goal. The law was amended several times, the last one in 1865, which increased the tax on state bank notes to 10 percent. Conversions to federal banks thereafter began to increase rapidly.[6]

Taxation

Taxation at the federal level had come primarily in the form of tariffs. No one disputed the need for tariffs to raise revenue, but Southerners had always opposed a tariff that protected domestic industry. During 1857, tariffs were reduced substantially, and when the Panic of 1857 occurred, the nation began to run a deficit. Prior to the election of 1860, Justin Smith Morrill proposed a new and innovative tariff bill in the House. Whereas the Whigs had supported a protective tariff to protect manufacturing, the Republicans now supported higher tariffs to protect other parts of the domestic economy. "I would treat agriculture, manufacturing, mining, and commerce . . . as members of one family," Morrill explained. While the Morrill tariff failed in Congress before the secession of the South, it quickly passed Congress on March 2, 1861, after the Southern states had seceded. "Over the course of the war, Congress would continue to raise tariff rates and cut the free-trade list in an effort to generate even more revenue," historian Sharon Ann Murphy writes.[7]

There were a whole series of other revenue-raising measures that Congress implemented to finance the war. One was a 3 percent tax on all manufacturers. The second was the introduction of a progressive income tax. To collect the taxes, Congress created the Internal Revenue Bureau. The income tax began at a low rate, but it gradually increased to 5 percent on incomes from $600 to $5,000, 7.5 percent up to $10,000, and 10 percent for incomes over $10,000. Congressman Morrill, who had been the author of the new approach to tariffs, said that "the weight [of taxation] must be distributed equally not upon each man in an equal amount, but a tax proportionate to his ability to pay."[8]

Taxation at these levels ended after the war as Republican support for an active government began to wane. In 1868 Congress eliminated the manufacturing tax, and the income tax ended in 1872. Overall, taxation contributed about 20 percent of the cost of the war, with bonds totaling over 60 percent. The Union only needed to rely on printing greenbacks for a small percentage of its war expenses. The South would not be so fortunate.[9]

Other Union Governmental Policies

The Union implemented a whole series of policies and laws that placed the federal government in the role of advancing economic development. These included the Homestead Act, land grants for colleges, and financing of the transcontinental railroad.

The distribution of land at low prices had advocates going all the way back to the original ordinances that had organized both the Northwest and Southwest Territories. Whigs had opposed the distribution of free land, preferring that it be sold to finance internal improvements. The issue of public land sales had been what initially sparked the famous Webster-Hayne debate that occurred in early 1830, which soon morphed into a debate over the nature of the federal union. The idea of free land was taken up by the Free Soil Party in the late 1840s, and now Republicans supported the idea.[10]

Prior to the Civil War, Southern Democrats blocked Homestead legislation, since they feared it would lead to an expansion of free labor (versus slave labor) in the West. But with the outbreak of the Civil War, Republicans introduced the Homestead Act in late 1861. It allowed a citizen to acquire up to 160 acres of land for free once they had lived on it for five years. Republicans saw it as a way to "harness individual labor into the agricultural sector of the economy, thus increasing the North's economic base," according to Richardson. Republicans during this period saw government playing a central role in promoting the economy. "With us the Government is simply an agency through which the people act for their own benefit," Republican congressman Owen Lovejoy said. In May of 1862 Lincoln signed the Homestead Act, opening opportunity for many people who acquired land through its provisions.[11]

Representative Morrill initially introduced a bill under which the federal government would donate land to the states to be used for establishing agricultural colleges. Each state could receive up to thirty thousand acres of land in the West per member of Congress. They could then sell the land and use the proceeds to subsidize the cost of constructing new colleges, which were to focus on practical education that advanced agriculture and engineering. Some of the most important state colleges in the country were built with support from the law that was passed in 1862, including Ohio State, Penn State, and Michigan State Universities.[12]

Building a transcontinental railroad had played an indirect role in leading to the Civil War. In 1854, Senator Stephen A. Douglas of Illinois wanted the transcontinental railroad to begin in Chicago and take a northern route to San Francisco. Southerners wanted a route through the South. As part of the Kansas-Nebraska Act, Douglas obtained his northern route, but he paid a steep price, agreeing to undo the Missouri Compromise so that Kansas could choose whether to allow slavery or not. Violence in Kansas contributed to the rise of the Republican Party and the election of Lincoln. Douglas's railroad would have to wait for the Civil War years to come to be financed and constructed, and by then he was dead.

During the war, the North feared that the West Coast would break off from the Union because it was so isolated. Building the transcontinental railroad was seen as a way to link the West with the rest of the Union. In 1862 a bill was introduced that would allow the federal government to create a new railroad company, the Union Pacific, which would build the part of the railroad that would run from Kansas to present-day Utah. It was the first incorporation by the federal government since the Second Bank of the United States. The Central Pacific, which had already been incorporated in California, would run east from Sacramento, and meet up with the Union Pacific. The Republicans in Congress were willing to use the national government in an expansive way to achieve its economic and war aims.[13]

The Union Pacific was led by a man named Grenville Dodge. In 1859, Dodge had seen Lincoln give a speech in Council Bluffs, Iowa. Lincoln was told that "the young engineer knew more about railroads than any two men in the country," Stephen Ambrose writes. Lincoln, who had represented railroads as a lawyer, ultimately grilled Dodge about a transcontinental railroad. "What is the best route for a Pacific railroad in the West?" Lincoln asked. Dodge replied that the town they were in would be the best starting point. Ultimately, the Central Pacific began construction in Omaha, Nebraska, just across the state line from Council Bluffs.[14]

The Central Pacific had come together under the leadership of a young engineer named Theodore Judah. He had a vision to build the transcontinental railroad and had gone to California to organize a corporation to do that. "Backing Judah was a collection of Sacramento store-keepers who called themselves the Associates," historian Richard White writes. The group included Collis P. Huntington, Leland Stanford, Mark Hopkins, and Charles and Edwin Crocker. There was not an experienced railroad financer among them, since none thought the railroad was feasible. "None of us knew anything about railroad building," Crocker would later admit. But Judah did, and he was the one who found the route through Donner Pass that would ultimately be used for the railroad line that would run east from Sacramento.[15]

In 1862 Congress passed the first law to help fund the transcontinental railroad, but it was inadequate for the massive task. Dodge warned Lincoln about the inadequacies of the law and recommended that the government build the railroad. Lincoln indicated that was impossible in the middle of a war, but he would try to strengthen the law. Congress too saw the problems. "I do not believe that there is one man in five hundred who will invest his money, and engage in the building of this road, as the law stands," one congressman said.

The Pacific Railway Act of 1864 extended the financial incentives to build the railroad. It loaned the Union Pacific and Central Pacific $50 million in government bonds and allowed the two companies to issue their own bonds in the same amount that would be senior to the government bonds. The government would pay the interest on the $50 million in bonds until they matured in thirty years. Ultimately, the companies would only be asked to pay back the bonds with simple interest, which was a significant subsidy that Richard White has estimated was valued at an additional $43 million. The railroad companies received both the right of way where the track was laid and also a significant amount of land (over 131 million acres), along with the rights to any minerals found on the land. The transcontinental railroad was ultimately completed in May of 1869, when the golden spike was driven into the ground at Promontory, Utah. It was not without controversy or substantial corruption.[16]

Financing the War in the Confederacy

Before the South could contemplate how to finance the war, they had to establish a system of government. The Constitution of the Confederate States, adopted March 11, 1861, was essentially a duplicate of the American Constitution with some key exceptions. Whereas the Framers of 1787 refused to use the word *slavery* in the document, the Confederate Constitution was explicit in its protections for slavery, stating that no "law denying or impairing the right of property in negro slaves shall be passed." The Confederate Constitution also made it clear, in its preamble, that "each State was acting in its sovereign and independent character," thereby incorporating the theory that the Confederacy was a compact among sovereign states and not a new nation. It also reflected the small-government philosophy that the South adhered to. "The provisions of the Confederate Constitution were carefully crafted to forestall the possibility that the new government would ever attempt anything like the programs of Alexander Hamilton and Henry Clay for national economic development," the economic historian Michael Lind has written. The new central government would not be allowed to fund internal improvements, and the Confederate Constitution placed strict limits on tariffs. Yet ultimately the Confederacy would have to implement some rather draconian policies to acquire and produce weapons and feed and pay its soldiers.[17]

The Confederate Constitution placed a significant limit on raising revenue from tariffs by excluding any type of protective tariff. "In February 1861, the Confederacy adopted its first tariff, which was almost identical to the Tariff of 1857," Murphy writes. The rate on imported goods was set at 5 percent, which resulted in a reduction for European imports, but an increase for any goods coming in from the North. When the North implemented a blockade of Southern ports, the tariff produced very little in revenue. The South mainly relied on a property tax to raise revenue, which produced about 5 percent of total revenues. Out of desperation for funding, the Confederacy finally implemented an income tax in 1863. The top rate ultimately reached 25 percent for wealthy individuals, but the combination of all tax sources only provided about 9 percent of all war expenses.[18]

Borrowing too proved problematic for the Confederacy. Foreign loans were a limited means since other countries lacked confidence that the South could win the war and "were unwilling to demonstrate such open support for slavery," as Murphy writes. Since Southerners had always distrusted banks, there were not nearly as many banking institutions as there were in the North, although Virginia, the Carolinas, and Tennessee did have some established public banks. The Confederate treasury secretary had some success marketing bonds directly to the public, especially to rich Southerners. About 33 percent of the cost of the war was borne through borrowing.[19]

Printing money was the major means by which the Confederacy financed the war. However, they did not make their currency, known as graybacks, legal tender, and so people could decline to take them in payment. Overall, the Confederacy issued over $1 billion in graybacks, which amounted to over 50 percent of the cost of the war. As expected, inflation was rampant in the South. "By the end of the war, prices were ninety-two times higher than they were at the start," Murphy writes. The South's smaller and rural-based economy, along with its antigovernment sentiment, contributed at least in part to its defeat in the Civil War.[20]

❧ ❧ ❧

While the Confederacy entered the war committed to states' rights and small government, in one of the great ironies of history, survival required the opposite. Because the South's economy relied largely on the export of agricultural products like cotton, its war mobilization was far more dependent on governmental controls than the North.

The first challenge the South faced was for soldiers and materials. During the first year of the war, volunteers were sufficient, but then the "bloom faded from Southern enthusiasm for the war," historian James McPherson writes. In 1862 the South implemented a draft, a full year earlier than the North. It would eventually include all able-bodied white men between the ages of eighteen and fifty-five. The draft worsened class conflict, since plantation owners received one exemption for every twenty enslaved people they held and rich men could also buy substitutes, giving way to the slogan "A rich man's war but a poor man's fight." The draft proved to be the most unpopular governmental policy, clearly seen as a contradiction of the small-government philosophy of the South.[21]

In terms of munitions, the South was in a tough position because of its lack of industry. "No foundry in the South except the Tredegar Iron Works had the capability to manufacture heavy ordinance," McPherson writes. During the first year of the war, the South acquired weaponry from Europe. But thereafter it implemented what Michael Lind has described as "Confederate Socialism." It began to build factories to produce gunpowder, arms, and artillery.[22]

While the North was subsidizing the transcontinental railroad, the South subsidized local rail lines. The Confederacy did this despite a prohibition in the Confederate Constitution to aid with internal improvements. In February of 1862 the Confederate Congress approved a bill that allowed the government to aid in the construction of a rail line from Danville, Virginia, to Greensboro, North Carolina. The South also took a much more direct role "over operations, schedules, and the impressment of railroad property" than the North, according to historian Richard Franklin Bensel. While the North also passed a law giving the military similar controls, it largely relied on contracts with railroad companies to shuttle troops and materials as needed.[23]

The Confederacy faced an enormous challenge in feeding both its soldiers and its citizens. Cotton fields were converted to corn to help with this. The main meal for many soldiers was a mix of cornmeal and salted pork, making salt production important. Before the war, the South had purchased salt from the North. "The war forced the rapid development of southern salt mines, but transportation priorities for war materials . . . kept supplies scarce and prices high." The South also turned to a form of price controls to feed the army. It established prices below market value, which it paid to farmers, plantation owners, factories, and others for the goods needed to sustain the military. Since the public was often paid in depreciated graybacks, they received little in return.[24]

Both the draft and the impressment of goods contributed to the problem of feeding the general public. With men away fighting the war, there was no one to plant the crops. "A rise in desertions from the army in 1862 resulted from the distress of men's families," according to McPherson. One of the worst incidents that resulted from hunger in the Confederacy were the bread riots that occurred in many cities and towns in 1863. In Richmond, a group of women marched to the governor's office to seek an end to hunger. "Bread, Bread!" and "Our children are starving while the rich roll in wealth," they cried. At one point the mob grew to over one thousand people who began to break into shops to steal food. They were finally met by President Jefferson Davis, who condescendingly greeted the group largely made up of mothers, tossing a few coins at them. He then told the crowd to disperse or the soldiers that had been mobilized would fire on them. The crowd finally disbanded, and in response the "Richmond city council expanded its welfare food aid," according to McPherson. But food shortages were far from over and would sap the strength of the Confederacy."[25]

Violations of civil liberties occurred on both sides. In the North, Lincoln suspended habeas corpus in certain areas where Southern sympathies were strongest and, at times, throughout the nation. Large numbers of people "who were believed to be secessionist sympathizers were soon being arrested . . . and held in prison without being charged without any violation of law and without recourse to trial," historian David M. Potter writes. Lincoln's action was controversial at the time, since it was unclear under the Constitution where the power to suspend habeas corpus existed, and at one point the Supreme Court ruled that Lincoln's actions were unconstitutional, which Lincoln ignored. Lincoln was not overly concerned with respecting "constitutional niceties protecting individual rights," as historian David Donald writes, while the fate of the nation hung in the balance. In addition to the survival of the Union, Lincoln was also concerned about the future of democratic government, as he told Congress in July of 1861: "It presents to the whole family of man, the question whether a constitutional republic, or a democracy—a government of the people, by the same people—can or cannot, maintain its territorial integrity, against its own domestic foes."[26]

Jefferson Davis too found it necessary to suspend habeas corpus and to declare martial law at various times. But he did it based on the actions of the Confederate Congress, which only issued the authority for short periods of time. These occasions caused criticism in the South, even from Davis's own vice president, Alexander Stephens. Stephens thought the suspension of habeas corpus was unconstitutional. Another critic complained that "the road to liberty does not lie through slavery." Davis's more limited use of the suspension of habeas corpus probably reflected the fact that his government did not face the types of internal threats as the Union did.[27]

A New Birth of Freedom

Lincoln entered the war with one overriding goal: the preservation of the Union. Lincoln's theory was that secession reflected an illegal rebellion, an insurrection by certain Southerners. Lincoln maintained that the Union "was much older than the Constitution," dating all the way back to "the Articles of Association in 1774" and strengthened by the Declaration of Independence, as he argued in his first inaugural address in 1861. Given this, "no State . . . can lawfully get out of the Union . . . acts of violence . . . against the authority of the United States, are insurrectionary." To do otherwise would require him "to acknowledge that the Union was not a perpetual one and that secession was constitutional," Donald writes.[28]

Given the superior population and industrial capacity of the North, the South adopted a defensive strategy modeled after Washington's during the Revolutionary War. So long as they didn't lose, the Confederacy would win. Yet Jefferson Davis and the other Southern leaders had difficulty maintaining the strategy. There were "demands by governors, congressmen, and the public for troops to defend every portion of the Confederacy," McPherson writes. Southerners also wanted to fight, believing it was dishonorable not to and that they were superior soldiers. "The idea of waiting for blows, instead of inflicting them, is altogether unsuited to the genius of our people," the *Richmond Examiner* wrote. The Army of Northern Virginia, led by general Robert E. Lee, proved to be a formidable opponent in the early years of the war, besting the Union in many battles.[29]

Confederate victories at Bull Run (twice) and Fredericksburg, and the stalemate at the terrible battle of Antietam, put Lincoln in an awkward position. He kept having to fire Union generals for incompetency, or in the case of George McClellan, for lack of a willingness to attack Lee's army. Lincoln once sent a telegram to McClellan stating: "If General McClellan does not want to use the Army, I would like to borrow it . . ." The Union reached the depths of despair at Chancellorsville in May of 1863, when Lee's army defeated Joseph Hooker's troops. When he learned of the news, Lincoln said, "My God! My God! What will the country say?" Yet the victory came at a high price for the Confederacy, with thirteen thousand casualties and the loss of Stonewall Jackson. Despite heavy Union losses, Hooker's army escaped.[30]

The Southern defensive strategy cracked wide open in the aftermath of Chancellorsville. Lee convinced Davis to press the attack, and he soon invaded the southern part of Pennsylvania near Gettysburg. The Union held the high ground and ultimately won a massive victory over a three-day period in July 1863. The Union saw twenty-three thousand men killed or wounded while the South, strained for soldiers, lost twenty-eight thousand, more than a third of Lee's army. "No matter how many battles he had won, Lee had never succeeded in capturing or destroying an army . . . and its great offensive power was forever broken" after Gettysburg, historian David M. Potter writes.[31]

It wasn't just the inability of Lee to break the Union army, but also victories that the North was extracting in the western theater of the war. The rivers of the western area, especially the Mississippi, "pointed like pistols in the heart of the Confederacy." General Ulysses S. Grant had arisen as a very formidable foe on the western front. A graduate of West Point, Grant had fought in the Mexican-American War, but problems with alcoholism had forced him to resign from the army in 1854. When the Civil War broke out, Grant became a colonel for the Twenty-First Illinois regiment. He would soon become a general, wreaking havoc on the Confederacy.[32]

On the same day that the Union won the battle at Gettysburg, the Confederate fortress at Vicksburg, Mississippi, with thirty thousand men, surrendered to Grant. The Union now controlled the Mississippi River. "Though the war was destined to continue for almost two more bloody years, Gettysburg and Vicksburg proved to have been its crucial turning point," McPherson writes.[33]

As the war proceeded, Lincoln began to change his mind about the purpose of the war. Part of this was forced on him by military necessity. By July of 1862, Lincoln began to see the many advantages of issuing a proclamation freeing the enslaved people in those states that were part of the Confederacy. The enslaved population was used by the South to do work that otherwise would have been done by soldiers, and by freeing them as the Union army occupied territory, former enslaved people could instead do that work (and eventually fight) for the North. Framing the issue as a military necessity provided Lincoln with the constitutional basis he needed to act. On September 22, 1862, Lincoln announced that the Emancipation Proclamation would free "all persons held as slaves" in any state that was in rebellion against the Union, thereby freeing 3.1 million people from bondage effective January 1, 1863.[34]

Lincoln was gradually redefining the purpose of the Civil War, from one that was being fought solely to preserve the Union to one to end slavery, advance freedom and equality, and preserve self-government. He took his most famous step in this direction in Gettysburg at the dedication of its cemetery on November 19, 1863. In closing, Lincoln made clear that the cause for which soldiers were dying was a "new birth of freedom" and the preservation of "government of the people, by the people, for the people." Yet Lincoln was still ambivalent about the role of Black people in American society, and as late as 1862 continued to support colonization for freed Black people. He was also ambivalent about a constitutional amendment to bar slavery, but finally came around as a way to consolidate the Republican Party as he approached reelection in 1864. Once he got behind amending the Constitution to ban slavery, he threw the full weight of his office behind it. By the end of 1865, the Thirteenth Amendment had been ratified, long after Lincoln was assassinated at Ford's Theatre on April 14, 1865.[35]

With Lincoln dead, his successor and the Congress ended up in a major dispute over Reconstruction. Originally born in North Carolina in 1808, Andrew Johnson, and his family, were part of the lowest rung of white society, people whose status was tied to "white supremacy [which] gave people in the Johnsons' social position a sense of identity that softened the reality of their downtrodden existence," according to historian Annette Gordon-Reed. Johnson wanted to allow the Southern states to reenter the Union in essentially the same position they had been in before they left, with the exception that slavery would now be banned. Black codes were soon introduced in the South that placed the newly freed African Americans into a situation nearly as bad as slavery. In 1866 the Ku Klux Klan (KKK) was formed and violence erupted against the newly freed peoples as a way to reinstitute white supremacy.[36]

It was at this point that the Radical Republicans wrested Reconstruction policy away from President Johnson. Even before the outbreak of the Civil War, there had been more radical elements of the Republican Party that "favored more drastic action against slavery than merely preventing its westward expansion," Eric Foner writes. During Reconstruction, the Radical Republicans had a completely different view of what the future of the nation should be compared to Johnson's view.[37]

Andrew Johnson would eventually be impeached, in large part because of his racist views and Reconstruction policies, although the actual charges against him had nothing to do with Reconstruction but rather dealt with his firing of the secretary of war. Congress had passed the Tenure of Office Act to better control Johnson, which stripped him of the power to fire executive-branch officials until a Senate-confirmed appointment had been made. Johnson escaped conviction in the Senate by one vote.[38]

The Republicans would ultimately implement two amendments to the Constitution. The Fourteenth Amendment provided for birthright citizenship and equal protection under the law, while the Fifteenth Amendment provided for Black male suffrage. The amendments were an attempt to eliminate what the Radical Republican Thaddeus Stevens called the "'political blasphemy' that the United States was and should remain "a white man's government'" as Eric Foner writes. The Fourteenth Amendment was able to pass in large part because the Republicans had mandated that Black people be allowed to vote in the South, even prior to the Fifteenth Amendment, which meant that for a short period of time Southern state legislatures were controlled by Black people. "Without [B]lack suffrage in the South, there would be no Fourteenth Amendment," Foner writes.[39]

The Radical Republicans unequivocally believed that the federal government was supreme and set about to completely change not only the governments that had been established in the South, but also Southern society. Having won a substantial victory in the midterm elections in 1866, the Radical Republicans in Congress now had the voting strength to pursue their agenda. Congressman George W. Julian proposed that what was needed in the South was "government, the strong arm of power, outstretched from the central authority here in Washington" to rule in the former Confederate states. The Reconstruction Act of 1867, passed over Johnson's veto, established five military districts governed by a military general. In order to be readmitted to the Union, each state would have to ratify the Fourteenth Amendment, bar former Confederates from voting, and approve new constitutions that included voting for Black people.[40]

In 1868 General Ulysses S. Grant, the hero of the Civil War in the North, was elected president. He was able to win because of the overwhelming support of Black men. Already there was a degree of ambivalence about Reconstruction in the North, which had always harbored its own racism. Yet the actions of the KKK, and other white supremacist groups in the South, so shocked the nation that Congress passed the Enforcement Acts and Ku Klux Klan Act in the early 1870s. "President Grant used the powers granted him by the Enforcement Acts to crush the Ku Klux Klan," Foner writes. The attorney general of the United States used the Klan Act to try many Southerners. The two actions protected Black people and restored a semblance of order in the South, but it would not last.[41]

A rapidly expanding economy in the aftermath of the Civil War soon crashed with the Panic of 1873. Northern support of Reconstruction waned even further, as support for remaking the South based on the free labor ideology of the North eroded, replaced by tensions between labor and capital and overt racism. The Panic of 1873 led to major Democratic gains in the 1874 midterm election for the House. As the North retreated from Reconstruction, Southerners continued their counterrevolution to retake state governments, eliminate the ability for Black people to vote, and reestablish the rule of white people. In the disputed presidential election of 1876, Rutherford B. Hayes emerged as the winner when he agreed to remove federal troops from the South. Reconstruction was over.[42]

But it was not only Reconstruction that ended, so too did the Republican Party's support for activist government, as we shall see in the next chapter. It would not be revived again until the Progressive Era near the turn of the new century.

Endnotes

1 For a useful summary of the advantages the Union had, see David Potter, *Division and the Stresses of Reunion: 1845–1876* (Glenview: Scott Foresman, 1973), p. 114–116.

2 Richardson, p. 30–36; for Chase's background and his flirtation with different political parties, see Doris Kearns Goodwin, *Team of Rivals: The Political Genius of Abraham Lincoln* (New York: Simon & Schuster, 2005), p. 112; Sharon Ann Murphy, *Other People's Money: How Banking Worked in the Early Republic* (Baltimore: Johns Hopkins University Press, 2017), p. 149.

3 Murphy, p. 155–157; Richardson, p. 38–63.

4 Richardson, p. 71–76; Murphy, p. 155.

5 Richardson, p. 85.

6 Richardson, p. 87; Murphy, p. 158–161.

7 William K. Bolt, *Tariff Wars and the Politics of Jacksonian America* (Nashville: Vanderbilt University Press, 2017), p. 196; Richardson, p. 105; Murphy, p. 147.

8 Richardson, p. 133 and p. 117.

9 Murphy, p. 146.

10 Fraser, *Growth*, p. 356–359; Richardson, p. 145.

11 Richardson, p. 143–149.

12 Richardson, p. 155.

13 Richardson, p. 176–177.

14 Stephen E. Ambrose, *Nothing Like It in the World: The Men Who Built the Transcontinental Railroad 1863–1869* (New York: Simon & Schuster, 2000), p. 23–24, p. 89.

15 Richard White, *Railroaded: The Transcontinental Railroads and the Making of Modern America* (New York: W.W. Norton, 2011), p. 18; Ambrose, p. 72.

16 Ambrose, p. 87 and p. 94; White, p. 22–24.

17 Michael Lind, *Land of Promise: An Economic History of the United States* (New York: Broadside Books, 2012), p. 131.

18 Murphy, p. 139–140.

19 Murphy, p. 141–142.

20 Murphy, p. 142–143.

21 Richard Franklin Bensel, *Yankee Leviathan: The Origins of Central State Authority in America, 1859–1877* (Cambridge: Cambridge University Press, 1990), p. 135–136; McPherson, p. 429–433.

22 Lind, p. 134; McPherson, p. 320.

23 Bensel, p. 148–150.

24 McPherson, p. 440; Bensel, p. 159.

25 McPherson, p. 618.

26 Potter, p. 111; David Herbert Donald, *Lincoln* (New York: Simon and Schuster, 1995), p. 303–304.

27 McPherson, p. 434–435; Bensel, p. 140.

28 Abraham Lincoln, *Selected Speeches and Writings* (New York: Vintage Books, 1992), p. 286–287; Donald, p. 302.

29 McPherson, p. 336–337.

30 McPherson, p. 645; Potter, p. 137–138.

31 McPherson, p. 664; Potter, p. 139.

32 Potter, p. 130, Ron Chernow, *Grant* (New York: Penguin, 2017), p. 84 and p. 136.

33 Potter, p. 140–141; McPherson, p. 665.

34 Fraser, *Growth*, p. 590.

35 Fraser, *Growth*, p. 594.

36 Perhaps the best book on reconstruction is Eric Foner's, *Reconstruction: America's Unfinished Revolution, 1863–1877* (New York: Harper Perennial, 2014); this section is largely taken from Fraser, *Growth*, p. 597–602.

37 Eric Foner, *The Fiery Trial: Abraham Lincoln and American Slavery* (New York: W.W. Norton & Company, 2010), p. 84.

38 Fraser, *Growth*, p. 604.

39 Eric Foner, *The Second Founding: How the Civil War and Reconstruction Remade the Constitution* (New York: W.W. Norton, 2019), p. 57.

40 Fraser, *Growth*, p. 603–604.

41 Fraser, *Growth*, p. 605–608; Foner, *Second Founding*, p. 121.

42 Fraser, *Growth*, p. 609–613.

CHAPTER 5

The Gilded Age and the Retreat of Government

. . . millionaires . . . may fairly be regarded as the naturally selected agents of society . . .
—WILLIAM GRAHAM SUMNER IN SUPPORT OF SOCIAL DARWINISM

. . . abolish poverty, give remunerative employment to whoever wishes it . . .
—HENRY GEORGE, PROGRESS AND POVERTY

The Republicans had, to a large degree, been pursuing the Federalist and Whig policies of using government to promote industry in the United States. Still, the type of direct government aid implemented during the Civil War, which assisted average Americans, was unique, a product of several factors. One was the views of Lincoln and some parts of the Republican coalition who believed government needed to assist the average person when necessary. Present in the Republican Party was also the Democratic inheritance of support for the common man reflected in the Free Soil Party and the free labor movement.

In the aftermath of the war, industry was now largely self-sustaining. Large industrial conglomerates began to form in railroads, steel, and oil. The owners of such businesses, and many politicians, preferred a hands-off, laissez-faire approach to the economy. The Gilded Age, so named by Mark Twain, ran from around 1865 to 1900. The name was appropriate, equated to a "gilded piece of jewelry" by the historian Edward T. O'Donnell, in which "one only need scratch the surface of the thin gold layer to find" the problems beneath. It was during this period that parts of the Republican Party abandoned their support for active government, which Democrats had never supported. The result was the triumph of laissez-faire capitalism, the growth of income inequality, and labor strife. Still in the future lay the idea of a mixed economy where government would regulate capitalism and provide direct aid through the social welfare state. Still, by the end of the Gilded Age, government would be forced to respond to the problems that arose from unregulated capitalism.[1]

One of the major questions that arose during the period was whether democracy and the growth of capitalism could coexist. The founders had worried about the excessive concentration of power in government, but now many individual capitalists had significant economic power that could threaten the very nature of the American republic. And the balance between individualism and the common good had tipped ever more toward the individual, leaving large portions of the population on their own.

The Growth of Industry and Inequality

The United States had been moving toward an industrial future since at least the War of 1812. "By 1860 the nascent outline of the modern American economy of mass consumption, mass production, and capital-intensive agriculture was visible," McPherson writes. The Civil War had pushed the economy ever further along the path to industrialization. Industries such as coal, pig iron, and rails needed for railroad construction expanded. So too did the beginnings of large-scale companies that used mechanization and new technologies for the purposes of mass production. Also of importance was the greater centralization of finance that occurred due to the implementation of banking and monetary reform that we saw in the last chapter. As McPherson writes, "the consequences of these acts were to increase the domination of the country's credit, transportation, and marketing structure by eastern bankers, merchants, and investors."[2]

If the Civil War helped to set the stage for the continued economic growth of the United States, the years between 1876 and 1900 saw massive growth in industrial capitalism. It was a time of great progress and optimism. The economic historian J. Bradford DeLong marks 1870 as the beginning of the "long twentieth century," when economic growth really took off, not just in the United States but around the world. Led by globalization, the industrial laboratory, and the modern corporation, humanity began to escape dire poverty. By the turn of the new century, the United States was the largest industrial power on earth, and by the outbreak of World War I, the country had overtaken Great Britain as the leader in per capita income. The gross domestic product grew by almost 4 percent per year and was outpaced by industrial production, which grew at over 5 percent per year.[3]

The Unites States had numerous advantages that allowed it to achieve such tremendous economic growth. The North American continent had both rich farmland and natural resources like coal, iron ore, lead, zinc, and copper. Other emerging industrial powers like Japan and France had to import some or all of these minerals. Oil was discovered in western Pennsylvania in 1859, which initially provided for the production of kerosene for lighting homes and then later for running the internal combustion engine with gasoline.[4]

American industry was also fostered by new inventions and innovations and improvements to existing technology. Steam engines became more efficient and increasingly replaced animal labor. World trade flourished with improvements in ship building, which opened markets for American goods and agriculture. It was during this era that typewriters and telephones were invented, improving communications. Thomas Edison invented the electric light bulb in 1879, which spawned a whole new electrical industry. "Edison and his associates also had to invent machinery for generating electricity and new devices and techniques for transmitting and applying the new source of power," historian Carl N. Degler has written.[5]

Mechanization of the workplace, already underway before the Civil War, began to accelerate. Compared to Europe, wages were higher in the United States. To compete, businesses had to cut costs, and they did so by using machines. This increased the need for a greater level of education among the workforce. "To employ these devices to the best advantage requires the intelligence of the American workmen . . . witless men behind witty machines would be of no use," a commissioner of patents wrote in 1900. Expenditures on education increased significantly during this period to provide a more skilled workforce.[6]

Perhaps the most important contribution to economic growth was the expansion and improvement of the American railroad system. In 1860 there were 30,000 plus miles of track, which grew to over 190,000 miles by 1900. Before 1860, shipping was largely done by river steamboats and canal boats. The expansion of the railroad system in the postwar years, including the completion of the transcontinental railroad in 1869, meant trains had become the major means for transporting goods and people. "By the turn of the century the railroads tightly knitted together an economy that was now fully national in scope, and nearly every town of any size was served by a railroad," economics writer John Steele Gordon concluded. The railroads even led to the introduction of standard time with eastern, midwestern, mountain, and western time zones.[7]

Railroads were the first large-scale employer in the country, with over one million workers by 1900. It was also a complex operation to manage and "the first industry to evolve a cadre of professional managers who specialized in railroad administration," historian H. W. Brands writes. Some parts of the railroad system—the major branches—operated as a natural monopoly. The owners controlled rates and charged larger and long-haul shippers a lower rate, causing friction with small farmers and manufacturers. Trunk lines, spurs that connected smaller towns, tended to be more competitive, with multiple lines serving an area. Excessive competition along the trunk lines caused some railroads to go bankrupt. Ultimately, the monopolistic nature of the major railroads would create pressure for government to recognize that they were a natural monopoly that required regulation.[8]

Capitalism as an economic system can create great wealth and defeat scarcity in human societies. As the historian Joyce Appleby has written, "capitalism is a cultural system rooted in economic practices that rotate around the imperative of private investors to turn a profit" usually by creating greater efficiencies and innovations in the production of goods and services. But unregulated capitalism of the kind found during the Gilded Age also led to great inequities of wealth in society and substantial levels of poverty, to the point where critics wondered whether democracy could survive.

Income inequality grew as industry expanded, much as Jefferson had feared during the 1790s. While income inequality had been steadily increasing since 1800, "income gaps continued their long march upward in the North," at a faster rate than before in the years after the Civil War, Lindert and Williamson report. By 1870, the top 10 percent of American households held 30 percent of income, and the top 20 percent held over 55 percent. The bottom 40 percent had only 11 percent of income. During the period from 1870 to 1900, urbanization and industrialization led to ever greater growth levels but also to expanding income inequality, especially among the top 1 percent. "The top 1 percent share rose from 9.8 percent to 17.8 percent" from 1870 to 1910, according to Lindert and Williamson. Disparities in overall wealth were even more pronounced, with the top 1 percent owning 51 percent of all wealth in 1890, and the bottom 44 percent owning 1.2 percent.[9]

The growth of income inequality during the Gilded Age can be illustrated by reviewing the life stories of several successful businessmen, who are sometimes referred to as the *robber barons*. Capitalism requires access to money, and one of the major money men of the era was J. P. Morgan. He was born in 1837, a year that saw a major panic in the American economy. He was a blue blood, his father having also been a banker who built a fortune from money he inherited from his father. John Pierpont Morgan attended the best schools in Boston and Europe, and then in 1857 he entered Wall Street as an investment banker. "He made a promising start in commodities, displaying a shrewd grasp of what people would pay for various things and an intuitive understanding of the larger currents affecting the Atlantic economy," H. W. Brands writes.[10]

Morgan did not fight in the Civil War, hiring a substitute to take his place. In 1861 he opened his own investment firm. He made plenty of money during the war by speculating in securities and commodities.

By 1865 he reported an income of $50,000 at a time when the average day laborer made a dollar a day. But Morgan's real impact was in rationalizing the railroad industry to eliminate excessive competition and reduce overbuilding. Morgan understood that the Panic of 1873 had in part been caused by bond defaults of the railroads. When the owner of the New York Central, William Vanderbilt, decided to sell a substantial number of shares, Morgan not only assisted in the sale that netted his firm $3 million, but he also insisted on a seat on the board. He then negotiated what was known as the "corsair compact," which reduced unneeded competition between the New York Central and the Pennsylvania Railroad. Thereafter "the industry's leading association looked to [Morgan] whenever competition became oppressive," and he would host a summit at his lavish New York home, directing the participants to reduce competition if they wanted his firm's assistance with future financings.[11]

By the time of his death in 1913, Morgan was worth somewhere over $1 billion in today's dollars. Yet his wealth paled in comparison to that of John D. Rockefeller. While Morgan was from old money, Rockefeller was largely a self-made man. Rockefeller's father, William, was a con artist, a snake oil salesman, and a philanderer. His mother, Eliza, was a Baptist and the disciplinarian in the family. John was born in 1839 and inherited the business acumen of his father and the discipline of his mother, qualities that made him a fabulously successful businessman, one that was "money mad" in the words of one of his contemporaries.[12]

Oil was discovered near Titusville, Pennsylvania, in 1859. It would soon replace whale and coal oil as a source for lighting homes and factories. "The man who provided cheap light would not merely let farmers read their almanacs after supper but allow the factory-working sons and daughters of farmers to tend looms and lathes before breakfast," Brands writes. Rockefeller became that man, not by drilling for oil but by refining it into kerosene and lubricants for machines. He would later refine oil into gasoline to run the internal combustion engine. Just like other moguls of the age, Rockefeller paid for a substitute to fight in the Civil War for him. "He began as a clerk, studied bookkeeping, and became a wholesaler, trading in and speculating in commodities," Richard White writes. Rockefeller then formed a partnership and began the process of oil refining.[13]

Rockefeller, like many capitalists, hated competition. He believed too much competition was detrimental, and so he began a process of eliminating his competitors. He was a clever businessman who understood how to control costs. He was also ruthless in how he dealt with those who stood in his way. In 1870, he formed the Standard Oil Company, the first of the major large and monopolistic trusts (large-scale monopolistic corporations) of the era. Yet overproduction remained a problem, so he formed a cartel with several other large refiners that engaged in a conspiracy to "apportion the market in a way that preserved their profits—and, not incidentally, crowded out their competitors," according to Brands.[14]

When the cartel collapsed, Rockefeller decided to buy out his competition. He would typically make a fair purchase offer, but if they did not sell, he would then use whatever means were needed to run others out of business. Given Standard Oil's size, Rockefeller could afford to cut his own prices and even operate at a loss for a period of time until the competition conceded. It was through these means that he came to largely control the refining business in Cleveland. With the Panic of 1873, Rockefeller saw an opportunity to expand his control over the business in Pittsburgh, Philadelphia, and New York. "By 1875 he controlled all the major refining centers," Richard

White writes. He then turned his attention to the production side. Rockefeller also "pioneered vertical integration, manufacturing railroad cars, investing in pipelines, and buying up oil land," according to Michael Lind. Standard would later become not only the largest refiner but also the largest producer of oil.[15]

Control of the oil business made Rockefeller a very wealthy man. "I believe the power to make money is a gift from God," he told one reporter. And make money he did. By some estimates, he was worth over $400 billion in today's dollars, more than Bill Gates or Jeff Bezos ever made. He also believed that his money should be used for "the good of my fellow man according to the dictates of my conscience." In this, he combined the rugged American individualist with great concern for the common good. He was a very generous philanthropist, but he also pioneered the creation of a corporate monopoly to eliminate competition.[16]

Andrew Carnegie was to steel what John D. Rockefeller was to oil. Carnegie's story is remarkable, one of those rags-to-riches tales that seem to only happen in America, and even then, very infrequently. Born in Scotland in 1835, he was from a family of "fiery Scottish Chartists who for years had been agitating for political liberty, human rights and religious toleration," for the working class, James MacGregor Burns writes. Andrew's father was one of those put out of work by the Industrial Revolution that was underway in the British Isles. Ever resourceful, his mother moved the family to the United States, and they settled near Pittsburgh.[17]

Carnegie was twelve years old when he went to work, initially in a textile mill. He quickly moved on, working as a bobbin boy, and then as a messenger for the telegraph company. Once he taught himself Morse code, he was able to assume the job of telegrapher. He ultimately landed a job with the Pennsylvania Railroad. Young Carnegie has been described as "observant, quick, steady, resourceful, everlastingly competent," and by 1859 he became a superintendent of a railroad. With the money he made, he shrewdly invested in sleeping cars and oil. He too hired a replacement, so he did not need to serve in the Civil War, and by 1863 he reported an income of $48,000, most of which he earned through his investments.[18]

But Andrew Carnegie ultimately made his mark in the steel business. By 1872 he went full-time into the making of steel using the newly developed Bessemer technology. He believed that vertical integration was the best means to dominate the steel industry. "Carnegie by the end of the century came to control raw materials, transportation, manufacturing, distribution and finance," according to Burns. As with Rockefeller, he focused on cost cutting, which allowed him to dominate his competition. His cost-cutting measures extended to labor, and both the blue-collar workers he employed and his own managers received low salaries, although he made millions. By some estimates Carnegie was worth over $300 billion in today's dollars.[19]

Carnegie never completely lost his Chartists roots. In 1886 he wrote, "my experience has been that trade-unions upon the whole are beneficial both to labor and capital." Yet this was largely lip service since Carnegie did everything he could to keep unions out of his mills. In 1889 the Amalgamated Association of Iron and Steel Workers had successfully been able to negotiate a contract that set work rules and wages at Carnegie's main plant. When the contract expired in 1892, Carnegie attempted to eliminate the union once again. Violence erupted during the labor dispute, and the workers were finally forced to back down and accept pay cuts of up to 60 percent.[20]

While on the one hand he amassed great wealth and beat back the demands of his workers for higher wages, Carnegie was also a philanthropist. In 1889 he published his "Gospel of Wealth." He believed that movements like socialism and communism were doomed to failure for rewarding laziness. "Upon the sacredness of property civilization itself depends," he wrote, since the best interests of society "are promoted" by giving "wealth to the few." Yet Carnegie also believed that society would be best served if the wealthy would administer their wealth for the common good by donating to worthy causes.

Justifications for Great Wealth

Andrew Carnegie provided one justification for the great wealth that was accumulated by the few during the Gilded Age. But there were other rationalizations as well. The Gilded Age could be called the age of laissez-faire capitalism. At its core, this was the philosophy that government should "leave us alone" and stay out of economic affairs.

There has always been a streak of libertarianism in America, dating all the way back to the pre-Revolutionary era. The *Cato Letters*, written by two Englishmen named John Trenchard and Thomas Gordon, were widely read in the colonies in the years leading up to the break with Great Britain. Liberty was placed at the forefront of values for the libertarians. Yet the *Cato Letters* also expressed a concern that inequality could destroy a republic. Jefferson and his followers in the 1790s combined these two threads together, preferring a weak central government with largely independent and equal landowners as citizens. Part of the Jeffersonians' battle with Hamilton and the Federalists was over their banking and industrial policies. Jefferson feared such policies would create great inequalities of wealth and the creation of a new monarchy in the United States, thereby destroying the republic. Jefferson's Republican Party was attempting to bridge the conflict between liberalism and republicanism, as we saw in chapters 1 and 2.[21]

During the Gilded Age, the pendulum had swung toward the extreme libertarian side, with a focus on individualism and economic liberty. The equilibrium between liberty and equality, between individualism and the common good, had become unbalanced. Both Arthur M. Schlesinger Sr. and Arthur M. Schlesinger Jr. have argued that there are cycles in American history. In 1986 Schlesinger Jr. defined "the cycle as a continuing shift in national involvement between public purpose and private interest." Public purpose can sometimes be equated with democratic values like "equality, freedom, social responsibility, and the general welfare," whereas private interest can be aligned with capitalism, including "the sanctity of private property, the maximization of profit, the cult of the free market, and survival of the fittest," as Schlesinger Jr. argued. For many people, the environment we find ourselves in today looks increasingly like a new Gilded Age, with extremes of wealth and a focus on individualism.[22]

"Survival of the fittest" was used to justify extremes of wealth that had emerged during the Gilded Age. It was originally coined by the British scholar Herbert Spencer from the work of Charles Darwin, who published his *On the Origin of Species* in 1859. "I am simply carrying out the view of Mr. Darwin in their application to the human race," Spencer wrote in 1891. In Spencer's view, the rich had obtained their wealth because they were the most fit, and any attempt to "help the poor, either by private or public aid . . . interfered disastrously with the improvement" of humanity, as the economist John Kenneth Galbraith has written. Spencer's work found a ready audience in the United States and was promoted by the Yale professor William Graham Sumner, who wrote that "the millionaires are a product of natural selection . . . they get high wages and live in luxury, but the bargain is a good one for society," since out of this the society became wealthier.[23]

Within the Republican Party a new faction emerged known as the Liberal Republicans. They were supporters of a laissez-faire approach to the economy and harkened back to a Jeffersonian approach to small government. Yet they lacked Jefferson's support for democracy and equality among the common man. They rooted their ideology in science and believed that there were natural laws that were as powerful as the laws of physics. To Liberal Republicans, markets were part of natural law since "they had already decided that nature operated like the market," according to the writer Louis Menand. Government should be left to experts, who would ground their policies in social science and "would identify the range of human behavior and mark the boundaries beyond which it was useless for governments to go," White explains. Given their support for expertise, Liberal Republicans supported civil service reform and opposed the spoils system.[24]

The Liberal Republicans supported Grant's election in 1868 and hoped he would implement many of their preferred policies. These included a return to the gold standard, support for free trade, and an end to the political corruption that marked the era. They would be sadly disappointed, and soon became a part of the Republican coalition known as the Half-Breeds—those opposed to the Grant administration.[25]

There was also an elitist and antidemocratic strain within the Liberal Republican movement. They were largely anti-immigrant, since immigrants were supported by the political party machines, especially the Democrats in major cities like New York. They also wanted to see an end to Reconstruction in the South, since they equated Black people with the urban poor, as part of a dangerous class of people. As White writes, the liberals were sympathetic to the Southern elites. "The best men, North and South, believed that expanding the franchise was a mistake. It inevitably yielded corruption."[26]

Voices of Dissent

Voices of dissent to the prevailing doctrine of laissez-faire capitalism ranged from the radical approach of the Marxists to the more moderate voice of Henry George.

In 1848 the journalist Karl Marx, along with his co-author Frederick Engels, had released the *Communist Manifesto*. They were not the first to call for a socialist revolution against the established power of capitalism, but they were perhaps the most famous. "The history of all hitherto existing society is the history of class struggles," Marx and Engels wrote. The class struggle of the current age was between those who owned capital and those who worked for the owners. In one rousing section, the authors proclaimed: "Let the ruling classes tremble at a communistic revolution. The proletarians have nothing to lose but their chains." While Marxism would gain some adherents in the United States, communism would resonate more in Europe and finally lead to a revolution in Russia in the twentieth century, a country with a very limited capitalist economy at the time.

A homegrown and more moderate response was put forward by Henry George. He was born in 1839 in Philadelphia "almost within the shadow of Independence Hall," as his biographer Edward T. O'Donnell writes. Young Henry had two major influences that affected his life. One was his Christian faith, which taught him to be concerned about the fate of his fellow man. The other was the free labor ideology of the 1850s, in which workers were seen as moving from a dependent status as wage earners to independent business owners. Yet his own experiences with the booms and busts of the capitalist system soon made him realize how hollow this dream was becoming. In 1865 he reached a low point when he was forced to beg for money to feed his family. Had the man he approached not been willing to help, "I think I was desperate enough to have killed him," George later recalled. It was in the aftermath of this incident that George became concerned about the monopoly power of the rich and the poverty of the poor. "To say that the people of a country shall consist of the very rich and the very poor, is to say that republicanism is impossible," he wrote in 1871. Many of the founding generation would have agreed.[27]

By early 1870 it appeared that George had fulfilled his own version of the Republican labor ideal, becoming part owner of several California newspapers. But then the Panic of 1873 hit, and by the end of 1875 his newspapers had failed. Still, George would look back at his failure and see "good fortune in the guise of evil" when he wrote *Progress and Poverty*, released in 1879.[28]

George looked at the nation and "instead of a golden age, America was trapped in [a] state where the beguiling glitter of progress was offset" by poverty, as O'Donnell writes. It was a world in which "amid the greatest accumulations of wealth, men die of starvation." The problem was not, as the Marxists argued, that the capitalists had taken all of the profit. Those who invested in a business had a right to a return on their investment and were producers just as workers were. The problem was with landowners, whose property increased in value due to general economic growth, not due to anything they did. George gave an example from the gold rush's impact on land values in San Francisco. "In 1848 property there had been essentially worthless. . . . Five years later the same lot sold for tens of thousands of dollars," according to H. W. Brands. Essentially, George was pointing out the problem of unearned income. "The great cause of inequality in the distribution of wealth is inequality in the ownership of land," George wrote.[29]

His solution was a single land value tax that would replace all other taxes. Only land value (and not buildings) would be subject to the tax, as would minerals on the land, including coal and oil. In essence, the tax would apply to the appreciation of land values and would be a substitute for the confiscation of private property as proposed by socialists. "It is not necessary to confiscate land, it is only necessary to confiscate rent," George wrote, with rent being the profit of escalating land values. The proceeds of the tax would be used for a variety of public benefit projects and would be another way to achieve "the dream of socialism" without the need to implement socialism, which George knew was unpopular in many quarters.[30]

While George's ideas were popular among the working class, they have never been tried, perhaps in part because most political leaders know that such an onerous tax burden on land would be extremely unpopular in practice. In addition, George's proposals were clearly a threat to the concept of private property. Still, his ideas continue to be raised, even today, in part because they were an attempt to balance individualism with the common good.[31]

Wage Labor, Urbanization, and Poverty

Booms and busts were a part of the capitalist landscape. In 1873, another major panic began when Jay Cooke & Company went bankrupt. This was followed by railroad failures and business bankruptcies, with unemployment perhaps reaching as high as 30 percent. The panic brought into stark relief the underlying problem of the Gilded Age. Labor, farmers, and the poor all struggled while a few people became very wealthy.[32]

Wage Labor

By the time of the Gilded Age, wage labor was becoming the norm. "Excluding farmers, wage workers by 1870 outnumbered the self-employed," according to Richard White. To replace the Jeffersonian ideal of the independent farmer or worker, a new theory began to emerge called contract freedom, that a wage worker was free to work for whom he chose. Yet even a supporter of laissez-faire capitalism like E. L. Godkin, a journalist and editor of the *Nation*, saw that this was a lie. "What I agree to do in order to escape from starvation . . . I agree to do under compulsion." Workers increasingly turned to labor unions for protection of their interests, and business owners resisted the formation of unions, with the power of the state behind them. Violence would soon ensue.[33]

The closest thing to a general strike occurred in the United States in the summer of 1877. It was triggered by the sustained reduction in wages for those who worked for the Pennsylvania Railroad. Over a three-year period starting with the Panic of 1873, the railroad had reduced pay by over 20 percent and increased work hours. Still, it was not enough for the railroad to sustain its operations, and further wage cuts were implemented in 1877. This was soon followed by wage cuts on the Baltimore and Ohio, whose workers walked off the job. The strike soon spread throughout much of the country in a "chain reaction" with "news of a strike in one place spark[ing] eruptions in other towns, cities and regions," White finds. And strikes weren't restricted to just railroad workers but soon spread to workers in other fields. The striking workers were popular among the general public and in many working-class parts of the country. Business owners called on the power of federal, state, and local governments to put down the strikes, and violence ensued in Baltimore, Pittsburgh, Philadelphia, and other cities. By August, the strike was over, with the power of the government siding with the business class.[34]

The ruling class in America seemed to be trembling in response to the Great Railroad Strike of 1877, imagining "communist revolutionaries in league with workers and the dangerous classes in an assault on free labor and property," White writes. While the ruling class may have feared a communist revolution, the appeal of Marxism in America was quite small at this point, restricted to a small group known as the Workingmen's Party that had begun in 1876. But later adherents of socialism would have a greater impact, pushed by the continued intransigence of both American business and government to provide unions with the ability to protect workers.[35]

It wasn't that all workers did poorly. The highly skilled, who were largely native-born whites, did much better. They were focused on fields like carpentry, locomotive engineering, and machine building. For the unskilled, poverty "remained a chronic, often inescapable feature of working-class life," as the historian Eric Arnesen frames it. A middle class, attached to large businesses as clerks and middle managers, also began to emerge during the latter part of the Gilded Age.[36]

The Knights of Labor, open to "to skilled and unskilled, men and women, immigrants and [B]lacks," initially had great success in attracting members. From 1877 to 1886, their membership grew from 30,000 to over 750,000. The organization was committed to policies designed to advance the working class, from better wages to an eight-hour day. They also opposed large monopolies and the power they held over government. "Shall these great corporations control the government, or shall they be controlled by the government?" one labor leader asked. At the height of their success, the Knights began to collapse, in part due to the continued hostility of both business owners and government officials, who combined to break many of the strikes the Knights were involved in. This happened even though the Knights were a moderate force that was "opposed to labor violence, class conflict, and socialism," James MacGregor Burns writes. The Haymarket Square bombing that occurred in 1886 in Chicago also had an impact. While the Knights were not involved, they were tainted by the anarchists that had organized the event, and their membership declined rapidly.[37]

A different approach to labor organizing was reflected in the efforts of the American Federation of Labor (AFL), which began in 1886. Under its leader, Samuel Gompers, it focused on organizing the skilled crafts. The AFL attempted to have a role for its members within the industrial system, but even this was "resisted by modern corporate managers, who viewed unions as unnecessary interference in their rights to set wages, determine conditions, and rule the workplace as they saw fit," according to Arnesen. During the 1890s the AFL would lose several strikes, including one in the steel industry against Andrew Carnegie at Homestead, Pennsylvania. In 1894, the American Railroad Union, under its leader Eugene V. Debs, lost another major strike against the Pullman Palace Car Company. Once again, the federal government, under President Grover Cleveland, supported the company and sent in army troops "to protect railroad property and to disperse strikers," as Arnesen writes. So long as the power of government was on the side of the industrialists, working-class Americans would continue to struggle.[38]

Urbanization and Poverty

"The United States was born in the country and has moved to the city," Richard Hofstadter wrote in 1955. During the Gilded Age, urbanization expanded rapidly. In 1860, at the outbreak of the Civil War, 80 percent of the population lived in rural areas and 20 percent in urban areas. By 1900, that had changed to a 60/40 split. By 2019, urban areas contained over 80 percent of the population. The raw numbers are even more startling. While only 6.2 million people lived in urban areas in 1860, by 1900 that number had reached over 30 million. Urbanization was most pronounced in the Northeast, where over two-thirds of the population lived in urban areas.[39]

Where did all these people come from? About half left farms, since mechanization meant that fewer farmers were needed to produce food, which still suffered from overproduction and falling prices. Farms were also failing in the aftermath of "the depressions of the mid-1870s and mid-1890s," historian Robert G. Barrows writes. Black Americans too had begun a slow migration from their existence as sharecroppers in the South. They not only moved to urban areas in the North but also began to populate cities in the South. The other half came from immigration. In the 1880s over five million people immigrated to the United States, more than double the largest number that had come during any decade. Many of these new immigrants were from Italy, Poland, Russia, and the Austro-Hungarian Empire. They tended to settle in cities.[40]

With the increase in urban population came numerous problems of poverty, along with health and safety problems. Life spans declined, infant mortality increased, and people grew shorter during the Gilded Age. At least some of these problems were caused by the spread of disease, including malaria, yellow fever, cholera, and dysentery. People were not yet aware that many of these diseases were carried in contaminated water and air, spurred on by people living in crowded areas where human waste contaminated the water supply. Once public officials discovered that germs were carried largely in drinking water, cities began to hire civil engineers to design upgrades and improvements to the water and wastewater systems. "By early 1880 a basic modern water infrastructure was in place in most cities," according to White. Only government, this time at the local level, could provide such improvements to life in cities. But often these improvements only benefited the wealthy and the middle class.[41]

Contaminated milk was another contributor to the problem of infant mortality. Caused by sick cows or bacteria carried in tainted water, milk made many children sick. By the 1890s, improvements in the milk supply began to be mandated, although the major improvements would finally occur in the twentieth century with the introduction of pasteurization. "Infant mortality plummeted," the political scientists Jacob Hacker and Paul Pierson write.[42]

"It was the best of times, it was the worst of times," Charles Dickens wrote in *A Tale of Two Cities*. He could have easily been writing about life in America's cities during the Gilded Age, where wealth and poverty stood side by side. In New York alone, there were over one thousand millionaires, most of them recently wealthy. Many "sought to mark concretely their arrival in the city's highest circles of wealth and prestige by building themselves magnificent mansions on Fifth Avenue," O'Donnell writes. Not only did they live in mansions, but they threw wild parties that rivaled the court of Versailles before the French Revolution. None was quite as lavish as the ball thrown in 1883 to celebrate the completion of the Vanderbilt Mansion. Not only were the guests requested to dress as European aristocrats, but Mrs. Alva Vanderbilt's sister-in-law came "dressed as The Electric Light in an evening gown fitted with gas jets that periodically spouted flames." All this opulence, what the social critic Thorstein Veblen dubbed *conspicuous consumption*, took place in an environment where many New Yorkers lived in abject poverty.[43]

Many of the urban poor lived in tenements in a design that looked like a dumbbell. White writes that "in New York the dumbbells numbered five or six stories, four apartments on a floor with a narrow airshaft in the center for air and light." Ventilation was horrible, very few had access to bathrooms, and in a fire "they were deathtraps." No wonder the word *tenement* came to symbolize poverty. The poor who lived in them worked long hours and could barely afford both rent and food. And many of the environmental benefits that improved the water and sewer systems in cities never reached the poor.[44]

An Inadequate Political Response

Why did the political system not respond to the problems that so many encountered during the Gilded Age? There is no one answer to the question, since it revolved around ideology, political gridlock, the corruption of the era, and a lack of strong presidential leadership. During the Gilded Age, a number of grassroots movements also emerged that pushed for reforms. As we shall see in the next chapter, none was more important than the Populists, whose ideas presaged the Progressive Era and the New Deal. At the end of the Gilded Age, the Democratic Party would, for the first time, nominate a candidate for president who proposed using the powers of government to help the average person.

Ideologically, many Gilded Age politicians in both major parties subscribed to a laissez-faire view of economic affairs. There were also Republicans who still believed in an activist government, following the long tradition that ran from Hamilton and the Federalists through Henry Clay and the Whigs, who supported policies designed to foster industry, including the protective tariff. The historian Heather Cox Richardson, in her book about the history of the Republican Party, argues that the party has swung between expanding equality and opportunity for all and protecting the interests of money and property. "Property was the heart of individualism, Republicans argued, and any effort to regulate business or to levy taxes was a direct attack on the American system," Richardson writes. The Republican Party reflected an underlying tension in American history between classical republicanism with its concern for the public good and classical liberalism, with its focus on the individual. During the Gilded Age, the Republican Party increasingly began to move away from its commitment to equality, which had flourished during the Civil War and the early years of Reconstruction, to become a party that represented the wealthy and business owners. Attempts to assist the working class or small farmers were portrayed as efforts to inflict "communism" or "socialism" on the nation.[45]

This internal shift caused the Republican Party to split apart during Grant's reelection bid in 1872. The Liberal Republicans, who were also referred to as Half-Breeds because they no longer supported Grant, pushed for a series of reforms that White summarizes as including "abolition of the tariff, civil service reform, return to the gold standard, [and] curbing of democracy." They were opposed to widespread voting for Black people, poor people, and women. It was an odd mix of progressive ideas (like long overdue civil service reform) and reactionary politics (the limits on voting). Limitations on voting placed the Liberal Republicans in league with Southern Democrats. Both wanted to "destroy the political power of African-Americans and organized workers" to ensure that no laws would pass to "redistribute wealth" as Richardson writes.[46]

The Liberal Republicans nominated the newspaper editor Horace Greeley to run against Grant. Due to their role in the Civil War, the still-disgraced Democrats also nominated Greeley. But Grant swept to victory with the support of the regular Republicans (sometimes called the Stalwarts), along with the business and finance community. In response to the Panic of 1873, Congress adopted legislation authorizing the reissuance of greenbacks to inflate the economy. Farmers and debtors were particularly hard hit by deflation. Grant vetoed the bill, to placate liberals, who were supporters of hard money and the gold standard. The Democrats then swept to victory in the 1874 midterm election, attacking the Republicans as being in the pocket of the rich. "In the House they went from a 70 percent majority to a 37 percent minority," White observes.[47]

A period of electoral gridlock ensued in the aftermath of the Panic of 1873 and the midterm election of 1874. "Between 1875 and 1897 each major party held the presidency and a clear majority in both houses of Congress for only a single two-year period," the historian Charles W. Calhoun writes. Gridlock was the result, making it difficult to pass sweeping legislation or address many of the problems of the era. The balance between the two parties was reflected in the electorate as well. While Republicans tended to win the presidency during this period, this was only because of the Electoral College. Both Hayes in 1876 and Harrison in 1888 lost the popular vote but won the presidency.[48]

Politics during the Gilded Age was marked by corruption, which contributed to the lack of progress on festering social problems. The monopoly power that was held by men like Rockefeller and Carnegie bled into politics, where they "used their tremendous wealth to stop or avoid regulations and subvert the democratic process," as the legal scholar Zephyr Teachout frames it. Former president Hayes would write in 1886 that the government was no longer of the people but a "government by the corporations, of the corporations and for the corporations," in a play on Lincoln's words at Gettysburg.[49]

Part of the corruption was linked to the growth of the railroads, including the building of the transcontinental railroad. In 1864 the Union Pacific took ownership of a company named Crédit Mobilier, a sham construction and finance company. The company overcharged the government for construction of its portion of the transcontinental railroad by perhaps twice the actual costs, lining the pockets of the owners of the Union Pacific. Stock in the company was sold to politicians for below market prices to ward off regulation of the railroads. The scandal broke during the Grant administration's second term, implicating both of his vice presidents and other high-ranking officials, including future president James A. Garfield. "The second Grant administration became synonymous with . . . scandal," according to White, including other ominous-sounding transgressions like the Whiskey and Indian Rings.[50]

It was also the age of the political machine. The most infamous of these was the Democratic Party's Tammany Hall in New York, but all major cities had some form of a political machine, some of which were under Republican control. They were successful because they provided services to those in need, especially to recent immigrants. "Perhaps the party bosses' greatest achievement was to meet people's basic needs of food and shelter without robbing them of their self-esteem," James MacGregor Burns writes. Yet they also mixed such useful services to the poor, during an era when government refused to do this, with kickback schemes and other favors to businesses to advance their political power. William "Boss" Tweed of Tammany was known to have stolen over $200 million from New York City before being taken down by Governor Tilden. Yet Tweed may not have been all that different from other robber barons in "his corruption, greed and ability to knit together government and private capital," according to White.[51]

The strength of the two main political parties was rooted in the spoils system. Dating back to Andrew Jackson, the winner of an election at all levels of government used patronage to fill government jobs with loyal supporters. The recipients were then required to use part of their salaries to pay dues to the political parties. Instead of government jobs being awarded based on merit, they instead went to dedicated party men, robbing government of the expertise required to run many functions. One of the plum assignments was the collector of the New York Custom House, which in the 1870s was filled by future president Chester A. Arthur. As one of his biographers writes, his salary "was twelve thousand dollar a year, but his actual income exceeded fifty thousand dollars" because he received a percentage of fines levied for catching smugglers. Perhaps this is one among many reasons why political engagement was so high during the Gilded Age, since the parties doled out patronage in the form of government jobs.[52]

Voter fraud was also rampant because there was no secret ballot. Instead, political parties printed their own ballots on different colored paper and had "ticket peddlers" pay people to accept them. Voter intimidation by employers also occurred. Selling votes was not unheard of and could garner a man anywhere from $250 to $500. "Probably no election in the whole nineteen century was so infamous for the buying of votes and stuffing of ballot boxes as that of 1888," one historian writes. Reform of the system would finally begin in that year, when Louisville, Kentucky, adopted the Australian secret ballot, which soon spread throughout the country. It went a long way toward reforming the electoral system of the nation.[53]

Weak presidential leadership during the Gilded Age also contributed to the lack of progress on major issues during the era. A 2021 survey of historians by C-SPAN ranked the presidents who followed Grant and came before William McKinley in the following order.

C-SPAN Ranking of Gilded Age Presidents[54]

Name	Term	Rank
Grover Cleveland (D)	1885–1889 / 1893–1897	25
James A. Garfield (R)	1881	27
Chester A. Arthur (R)	1881–1885	30
Benjamin Harrison (R)	1889–1893	32
Rutherford B. Hayes (R)	1877–1881	33

Lincoln, Washington, and the two Roosevelts (Franklin and Theodore) were listed as the top four of the forty-six men that have held the office. As Arthur M. Schlesinger Jr. has observed, the president is the central player in the American political system. "Great presidents possess, or are possessed by, a vision of an ideal America," Schlesinger once wrote. Alas, none of the men who held the office from 1877 until 1897 possessed substantial vision to steer the ship of state in a reformist direction. Part of this was no doubt the fault of the voters themselves, who elected them.

James Bryce, the Scottish historian, provided one explanation for why the presidents of the Gilded Age were such a mediocre lot. In his three-volume work called The American Commonwealth, published in 1888, he argued that men during the era looked to business rather than government to make their mark. Due to the political divisions of the period, "a safe man [was] preferred" to a brilliant man, since they "would not anger partisans in their own parties or . . . could help carry a key swing state," as Richard White succinctly frames it.[55]

James A. Garfield is a good example of a decent man who rose to the top, even though no one thought of him as one of America's leading men. Born in a log cabin in 1831 to a poor family, he originally went to work on the canals as a young man. He eventually attended Williams College in Massachusetts, where he became interested in politics and developed his skills as a public speaker. By 1859, he was in the Ohio legislature as an antislavery Republican who campaigned for Abraham Lincoln, although he would later believe Lincoln was too weak on the South in the aftermath of the Civil War and would become a part of the Radical Republicans.[56]

Many of his positions on issues were like those of the Liberal Republicans, but Garfield attempted to steer a path between the various factions in the Republican Party. Still, he was more clearly identified with the positions of the Half-Breeds, who supported a modest version of civil service reform. At the 1880 Republican Convention, Garfield supported John Sherman for the presidential nomination. In return, Sherman promised to throw his support to Garfield should he fall short of the nomination. Sherman was one of the three front-runners, along with former president Grant and Speaker of the House James G. Blaine, another of the Half-Breeds. When none of them could secure the nomination, Garfield emerged on the thirty-fifth ballot as the dark-horse compromise candidate.

He then selected Chester A. Arthur as his vice president. As we have seen, Arthur was a spoilsman from New York; he was also friends with Senator Roscoe Conkling, one of the leaders of the Stalwart faction of the party. It was Garfield's attempt to consolidate the party's faction, and he went on to defeat the Democratic candidate, General Winfield Hancock, in a very close and nasty election.[57]

Garfield was shot by Charles Guiteau in July of 1881 and died a few months later. Guiteau was a Stalwart and a disgruntled office seeker. Garfield's death was the impetus for Congress to finally pass the Pendleton Act in the aftermath of the 1882 midterm elections. Arthur, the old spoilsman, signed the bill. It began the process of civil service reform that would, over the next twenty years, replace the spoils system with a professional cadre of government workers.

The Pendleton Act was not the only reform measure to be passed during the Gilded Age. Concerns over the monopoly power of large businesses also led to the adoption of the Interstate Commerce Act in 1887, which established the Interstate Commerce Commission (ICC) to monitor the railroads. The law was weak, and the ICC found itself with little support. "The result was feeble enforcement of the law, considerable evasion of it, and a series of Supreme Court decisions that weakened federal regulation to the point of emasculation," Burns writes. The other major law to pass was the Sherman Antitrust Act in 1890, to further reduce the power of monopoly capitalism. It was another vague piece of legislation that ultimately had limited impact because courts interpreted its provision narrowly. Still, each of these bills established important precedents for further government action to regulate the economy.[58]

Additional reform efforts would continue to roil politics in the 1890s, forced in part on the political system and its leader by grassroots agitation from third parties. None was more important in this regard than the People's Party, or the Populists. They began to push the government to take a more active role to solve the problems that average people were experiencing, and new leadership would soon emerge to lead this effort in both political parties.

Endnotes

1   Edward T. O'Donnell, *Henry George and the Crisis of Inequality: Progress and Poverty in the Gilded Age* (New York: Columbia University Press, 2015) p. xix.

2   McPherson, p. 14–15, p. 453, p. 816–817; Potter, p. 206–207.

3   Lindert and Williamson, p. 171; J. Bradford DeLong, *Slouching Towards Utopia: An Economic History of the Twentieth Century* (New York: Basic Books, 2022), p. 1–3.

4   Carl N. Degler, *The Age of the Economic Revolution: 1976–1900* (Glenview: Scott Foresman, 1977), p. 28.

5   Degler, p. 32–33.

6   Degler, p. 31.

7   Degler, p. 18–22; John Steele Gordon, *An Empire of Wealth: The Epic History of American Economic Power* (New York: Harper Perennial, 2004), p. 235.

8   Gordon, p. 236; H. W. Brands, *American Colossus: The Triumph of Capitalism 1865–1900* (New York: Random House, 2010), p. 22.

9   Lindert and Williamson, chapters 6 and 7; O'Donnell, p. xxv.

10 Brands, p. 67.

11 Brands, p. 81–82; see also H. W. Brands, *The Money Men: Capitalism, Democracy, and the Hundred Years' War over the American Dollar* (New York: Norton, 2006), p. 164–165.

12 Brands, *American Colossus*, p. 71–72.

13 Brands, *American Colossus*, p. 72–73; Richard White, *The Republic for Which It Stands: The United States during Reconstruction and the Gilded Age 1865–1896* (New York: Oxford University Press, 2017), p. 342.

14 Brands, *American Colossus*, p. 86–87; White, *The Republic*, p. 343.

15 Brands, *American Colossus*, p. 88; White, *The Republic*, p. 344; Lind, p. 161.

16 Brands, *American Colossus*, p. 88.

17 Brands, *American Colossus*, p. 77; James MacGregor Burns, *The Workshop of Democracy: From Emancipation to the Era of the New Deal* (New York: Vintage Books, 1986), p. 102.

18 Brands, *American Colossus*, p. 77; Burns, p. 103.

19 Burns, p. 104.

20 Philip Dray, *The Is Power in a Union: The Epic Story of Labor in America* (New York: Doubleday, 2010), p. 169; Christopher Klein, "Andrew Carnegie Claimed to Support

Unions, But then Destroyed Them in His Steel Empire," retrieved April 6, 2021, from https://www.history.com/news/andrew-carnegie-unions-homestead-strike.

21 I develop these themes in *Emergence*, p. 42–44 and *Growth*, chapter 1.

22 Arthur M. Schlesinger Jr., *The Cycles of American History* (Boston: Houghton Mifflin, 1986), p. 26–27; for a recent work that compares our era to that of the Gilded Age, see Robert D. Putnam with Shaylyn Romney Garrett, *The Upswing: How America Came Together a Century Ago and How We Can Do It Again* (New York: Simon & Schuster, 2020). They argue that "Tocqueville saw in our nation's democracy . . . an attempt to achieve a balance between the twin ideals of freedom and equality," p. 2.

23 John Kenneth Galbraith, *The Age of Uncertainty: A History of Economic Ideas and Their Consequences* (Boston: Houghton Mifflin, 1977), p. 44–46.

24 White, *The Republic*, p. 176–179.

25 White, *The Republic*, p. 181–188.

26 White, *The Republic*, p. 193–202.

27 O'Donnell, p. 1–27.

28 O'Donnell, p. 34 and p. 41.

29 O'Donnell, p. 43–50; Brands, p. 375.

30 O'Donnell, p. 51–55; White, *The Republic*, p. 452–456.

31 For modern attempts to revive Henry George, see Annika Neklason (April 15, 2019), "The 140-Year-Old Dream of 'Government with Taxation,'" *The Atlantic*. Retrieved June 9, 2021, from https://www.theatlantic.com/national/archive/2019/04/henry-georges-single-tax-could-combat-inequality/587197/.

32 O'Donnell, p. 34; White, *The Republic*, p. 266.

33 White, *The Republic*, p. 237–238.

34 White, *The Republic*, p. 345–354.

35 Galbraith, p. 91; White, *The Republic*, p. 351.

36 Eric Arnesen, "American Workers and the Labor Movement in the Late Nineteenth Century," in Charles W. Calhoun, ed., *The Gilded Age: Perspectives on the Origins of Modern America* (Lanham: Rowman & Littlefield, 2007), p. 57.

37 Burns, p. 176.

38 Arnesen, p. 64–69.

39 Robert G. Barrows, "Urbanizing America," in Calhoun, p. 101–103.

40 Barrows, p. 105–107.

41 White, *The Republic*, p. 502; Jacob S. Hacker and Paul Pierson, *American Amnesia: How the War on Government Led Us to Forget What Made America Prosper* (New York: Simon & Schuster, 2016), p. 50.

42 White, *The Republic*, p. 477–483.

43 O'Donnell, p. 73–74; Jack Beatty, *Age of Betrayal: The Triumph of Money in America, 1895–1900* (New York: Alfred A. Knopf, 2007), p. 174–175.

44 White, *The Republic*, p. 512–513.

45 Heather Cox Richardson, *To Make Men Free: A History of the Republican Party* (New York: Basic Books, 2014), p. xv.

46 Richardson, *To Make*, p. 96.

47 White, *The Republic*, p. 274.

48 Charles W. Calhoun, "The Political Culture: Public Life and the Conduct of Politics," in Calhoun, ed., p. 242.

49 Zephyr Teachout, "Monopoly versus Democracy: How to End a Gilded Age," *Foreign Affairs*, January–February 2021, retrieved July 9, 2021, https://www.foreignaffairs.com/articles/united-states/2020-12-08/monopoly-versus-democracy; Christopher Klein, "How the Gilded Age's Top 1 Percent Thrived in Corruption," retrieved July 9, 2021, from https://christopherklein.com/2020/01/30/how-the-gilded-ages-top-1-percent-thrived-on-corruption/.

50 White, *The Republic*, p. 255–256 and p. 273.

51 Burns, p. 264–265; Degler, p. 298; White, *The Republic*, p. 197.

52 Zachary Karabell, *Chester Alan Arthur* (New York: Times Books, 2004), p. 25.

53 Zephyr Teachout, *Corruption in America: From Benjamin Franklin's Snuff Box to Citizens United* (Cambridge: Harvard University Press, 2014), p. 178–179; Degler, p. 92.

54 The C-SPAN survey of presidential rankings can be found at https://www.c-span.org/presidentsurvey2021/?page=overall.

55 Brands, *American Colossus*, p. 349–350; White, *The Republic*, p. 752.

56 This biographical sketch is drawn from Ira Rutkow, *James A. Garfield* (New York: Times Books, 2006).

57 Rutkow, p. 48–63.

58 Burns, p. 214–217; Degler, p. 40–41.

CHAPTER 6

Grassroots Democracy—The Populists

We believe that the power of government—in other words of the people—should be expanded.
—THE PEOPLE'S PARTY PLATFORM

The 1890s prove to be the hinge years, a time when support for pure laissez-faire capitalism would come under major assault. This was led by the Populist movement, with its roots in rural America and its call for the use of activist government to counter the growing power of the capitalist class in America. The two major parties would both see a reform leader arise in their ranks to contest the 1896 election.

The Populist Movement

"Power grows out of the barrel of gun," according to Mao Zedong. But the use of force to achieve political ends in a democracy means the system has failed. Lincoln certainly thought this, declaring at Gettysburg that the Civil War was being fought to ensure that "government of the people, by the people, for the people, shall not perish from the earth." The attempt by the South to leave the Union through force because they lost an election was the death knell of democracy. In our times, former president Donald Trump tried on January 6,

2021, to use violence to overturn a free and fair election that he lost. As I write these words, the verdict of history is still out on whether his efforts will fatally undermine democracy.

Power in a democracy comes not from violence but from the ability to persuade people of the rightness of your cause. In this regard, organizing people, whether from the top down or the bottom up, is one approach to achieving power. Another is the influence that money can bring in a democracy to advance various policy positions or causes, most of which benefit the wealthy. Populism, which had deep roots in the American experience dating back to the American Revolution and continuing through the age of Jackson, reappeared once again during the latter part of the Gilded Age. It was the ultimate bottom-up movement. James MacGregor Burns described the movement this way:

> *Somewhere in central Texas, sometime in the late eighties. In the twilight splendor of the Plains, men and women march along dusty trails toward the glow of a campfire in the distance. . . . These people walk with hope and pride. [They] see stretching for miles ahead and behind thousands of people marching with them. . . . These people will be part of an arresting venture in popular grass-roots democracy.*[1]

Populism emerged from the problems that farmers experienced during a period of rapid industrialization and urbanization. In the 1870s farmers began to organize through the Grange movement, a cooperative approach "to reduce the costs of farm machinery, insurance premiums, [and] interest on loans," according to Degler. One of the biggest problems farmers faced was dropping crop prices for wheat, corn, and cotton—caused by overproduction. Deflation exacerbated the problem. Since the Grange movement was nonpolitical, farmers soon joined the Farmers' Alliance and became active in politics, initially through the Greenback-Labor Party.[2]

The lack of money in circulation was particularly acute for farmers in the South, Midwest, and West. In the South, the crop-lien system, or sharecropping, had developed as a replacement for slavery. Both Black and white farmers were stuck in the system. "To secure essential supplies for farming and household sustenance, cash-poor farmers were forced to go to a merchant (sometimes their actual landlord), who advanced supplies in return for a share of the crop," historian Elizabeth Sanders writes. Interest rates on the money borrowed was exorbitant, sometimes reaching up to 100 percent. Sharecroppers simply could not get ahead. Farmers in the Midwest and West also found themselves in debt due to the costs of purchasing land and supplies. They typically sold a single cash crop like wheat or corn. Their struggles with debt and lack of cash also led them to support a more expansionary money supply.[3]

Farmers joined with labor to support the short-lived Greenback Party in 1880. The Greenback movement wanted the government to take control of the nation's money supply. "Corporate control of the volume of money has been the means of dividing society into hostile classes," according to the Party's platform in 1880. But their candidate for president, James B. Weaver, polled only 3 percent. Third parties in America have a difficult time due to the winner-take-all nature of the electoral system. Party loyalty during this period was very strong, especially in the South, where whites remained loyal to the Democrats and Black people to the Republicans.[4]

The Farmer's Alliance was the next step in organizing farmers. Its goal was to unite farmers in the North and the South and bury the animosities of the Civil War. But to do this, they had to accept the segregation of Black from white farmers. Black farmers were not welcome in the Southern Farmers' Alliance and formed their own Colored Farmers' Alliance. "The growing acceptance of the universality of white supremacy tied the knot of this newly found national harmony" between the farmers from the North and the South, as historian Charles Postel writes. It would also foreshadow the racism that would infuse the entire Populist movement.[5]

Populism had some success in the 1890 midterm elections at the state level, especially in the Midwest. "In Kansas the People's Party won control of the legislature and elected five of seven congressmen," according to White. In Nebraska two of three congressional seats were won by Populists. At the national level, the People's Party was first launched in May of 1891. Delegates were overwhelmingly from the Midwest and West. A year later, the People's Party met in Omaha to adopt a platform of reform measures designed to advance the cause of working people, whether laborers or farmers. They met in the aftermath of labor violence that had occurred in Homestead, Pennsylvania, at Carnegie's steel mill, in which Pinkerton's and ultimately the state militia had intervened on the side of industry. There had also been a violent uprising between strikers and strikebreakers at the silver mines in Coeur d'Alene, Idaho. The People's Party was attempting to merge both workers and farmers into one organization.[6]

In important ways, the People's Party was very forward-looking, especially in using government to advance the interests of working-class people. "We believe that the power of government—in other words of the people—should be expanded . . . to the end that oppression, injustice, and poverty shall eventually cease in the land" its party platform proclaimed. That platform reflected many of the reforms that would later be implemented by the Progressives and during the New Deal. The platform included the following:

> a more expansive money supply, including the issuance
> of greenbacks and the unlimited use of silver;

> a subtreasury plan that the Farmers' Alliance had been
> pursuing to expand credit for farmers;

> a graduated income tax and an eight-hour workday "to
> combat the maldistribution of wealth"; and

> nationalization of the railroads, telephone, and
> telegraph systems to fight monopoly power.[7]

"After the Populists, government responsibility for the prosperity of the economy would be a more acceptable tenet of democratic social thought," Degler writes, at least among parts of the American public. This forward-looking view was matched in part by the role that women played in the movement. During the Gilded Age the ideal of womanhood was still centered on the home. Yet the Populist movement had a number of women who assumed leadership roles. One of the most famous was Mary Lease, who moved from Pennsylvania to Kansas after the Civil War, where she became one of the first female lawyers in the state. She was also known as a fine speaker with "a deep, rich contralto, a singing voice that had hypnotic qualities" one observer recalled. She once told the farmers of Kansas they needed to "raise less corn and more Hell."[8]

Yet Populism faced its own problems, particularly over the issue of race. "When in 1891 the Colored Alliance sponsored a cotton pickers' strike, the white Farmers' Alliance suppressed it," according to White. The Southerner Alliance also decided to stick with the Democrats rather than endorse the People's Party in 1892. Since the Populists had little to no support among farmers in the Northeast, nor among the emerging middle class, the party fared poorly in the 1892 presidential election. Their opposition to immigration also doomed them among recently arrived city dwellers. Their base of support in the West, South, and Midwest made them a regional party and gave them only 38 percent of the electorate to poll from. With the South sticking with the Democrats, they really had no chance of victory. Weaver, once again the candidate for the reform effort, made the case that government had given over too much power to the large industrial trusts. "The great object . . . is to restore to Congress its Constitutional and exclusive control over the great limbs of commerce, money, transportation and telegraphy," Weaver argued. He did garner 8.5 percent of the total vote and twenty-two electors from Kansas, Colorado, Nevada, and Idaho. The Populists also won at least 30 percent of the vote in nine western states.[9]

The Democrat Grover Cleveland swept to victory in a rematch with the incumbent Republican president Benjamin Harrison and brought in a Democratic Senate and House. Southern Populists, who stuck with the Democrats, had helped to bring the party total victory in the election. It would be a short-run win, with another recession lurking just around the corner, as Cleveland took the presidency for a second time.[10]

The Failure of the Cleveland Administration

Grover Cleveland had lost the election of 1888 to Benjamin Harrison, the grandson of President William Henry Harrison. While Cleveland proposed reductions to tariffs, Harrison campaigned on the protective tariff to "preserve the American market for American producers, and to maintain the American scale of wages." This was his attempt to lock in the support of both capital and labor. Harrison barely squeaked out an Electoral College victory in 1888 and lost the popular vote to the incumbent Cleveland by 100,000 votes.[11]

His presidency occurred during a period when the lure of Populist reforms was gaining ground. Harrison was an activist president, but much of his policy agenda was designed to protect business, which had supported him with their money and votes in 1888. He was "beyond question the best business administration the country had ever seen," according to one businessmen's club. Harrison did achieve some early reform measures, including the Sherman Antitrust Act and the Silver Purchase Act. But high tariffs were proving unpopular with the electorate, especially with Populists in the Midwest and West who paid more for products because of high tariffs but were at the mercy of the market themselves. Right before the midterm elections, the Republicans passed the McKinley Tariff Act, which "lowered rates on a few items but raised them on everyday items, sometimes dramatically," Richardson writes. The Democrats were able to portray "the Republicans as servants of trusts and warned of sky-rocketing prices," according to one of Harrison's biographers. The Republican Party lost the House in the 1890 midterm elections by a two-to-one margin, as many western and midwestern Republicans moved away from them, although they retained a small majority in the Senate.[12]

Such was the situation in the run-up to the 1892 election, when Cleveland defeated Harrison and reentered the White House. During his time out of office, "Cleveland had become much more sympathetic to the needs and concerns of the businessmen and eastern bankers," according to historian Henry F. Graff. It was an odd place for a member of the Democratic Party to find themselves. Cleveland himself had known hardship, growing up the son of a preacher in upstate New York. A wealthy neighbor had loaned him the money to go to college in Ohio, and he ultimately earned a law degree. Returning to New York, he had been elected mayor of New York City, governor of the state, and a one-term president. But the conservative Cleveland had a very limited view of the role of government, saying in his inaugural address that "the lessons of paternalism ought to be learned . . . that while the people should patriotically and cheerfully support their government its functions do not include the support of the people."[13]

It was a chilling philosophy at the very moment that the economy was about to crash once again into another depression. Until the 1929 crash, the depression of 1893 was known as the Great Depression. The excessive competition of railroads, which were deeply indebted to European banks, was part of the cause. So too was a strict adherence to the gold standard, which had caused the deflation of the era. "In 1892–93 the combination of Europeans liquidating investments and a poor cotton harvest caused gold reserves to fall dramatically, credit to become more expensive and investment to decline," White writes.[14]

The conservative Cleveland, who was an adherent of hard money, then pushed for the repeal of the Silver Purchase Act that Harrison and the Republicans had enacted. Cleveland and other supporters of the gold standard believed it had led European banks to move their capital from the United States. The repeal measure split the Democratic Party, many of whom supported the use of silver to add liquidity into the system, and so Cleveland had to depend on Republican votes to pass the bill. His actions were the exact opposite of what should have occurred, which is to pump more liquidity into the economic system during a depression. In his defense, this was prior to modern notions of how to manage a financial crisis, which were pioneered by the Englishman John Maynard Keynes during the Great Depression of the 1930s. It was also before the Federal Reserve System was established in 1913. As the historian Carl N. Degler has written, "the amount of money in circulation, instead of being responsive to the needs of the economy as it should have been," was limited by the artificial supply of gold.[15]

The depression worsened and gold continued to leave the country. At one point 25 percent of the railroads were in bankruptcy and over fifteen thousand businesses had failed, along with many banks. Unemployment exploded across the nation, with sustained rates of over 10 percent for five to six years. Many people who previously considered themselves part of the middle class now had to stand in bread lines or go to a soup kitchen. "In scores of American cities . . . municipal governments, churches, and other private charities tried to stem the tide of starvation," historian Jackson Lears writes.[16]

Cleveland soon found himself confronted by an army of unemployed men in the spring of 1894, led by Jacob Coxey. Coxey, an Ohio Populist and successful businessman, wanted the government to hire men to build public works as a way to put people back to work. It was a radical idea for its time, to be funded through the sale of $500 million in bonds. When they arrived in Washington, DC, Coxey and his supporters were confronted by federal troops that Cleveland had called out. Coxey was arrested for "walking on the grass" and his army was dispersed. But Cleveland's actions made him "a target of national ridicule," as White writes.[17]

This was soon followed by the Pullman Strike in which Cleveland used federal troops to end the strike. In the midterm election of 1894, the Republicans retook the House and added seats in the Senate. It was the beginning of the ascendancy of the Republican Party "with the American voter outside the South that would endure for a generation," historian Lewis L. Gould writes. The Populist Party also was defeated, but their movement would soon gravitate to the Democratic Party in 1896, as a young leader emerged.[18]

William Jennings Bryan and the Democratic Party

He was born in the tumultuous year of 1860 in the small Illinois town of Salem. His father was a self-made man, a lawyer and politician, whose political hero was Andrew Jackson. Like Jackson, Silas Bryan believed in the equality of all white men and in limited government. He also shared Jackson's racism.[19]

Young Will was raised in a religious household and he ultimately became a Presbyterian, brimming "with hope for the salvation of all Americans," according to Michael Kazin, Bryan's biographer. Bryan attended Illinois College, where he developed the oratorical skills that would serve his political career well. As orators, his role models were Henry Clay and Daniel Webster. When he married Mary Baird, he not only found the love of his life but also a woman who aided his rise in politics. "She managed his correspondence, helped prepare his speeches, edited his articles, and on occasion even negotiated with his fellow politicians," Kazin writes.[20]

Bryan attended law school in Chicago, but he felt lost in the big city. It was also in Chicago where Bryan began to show concern about the plight of the working class and a Democratic Party that took advantage of those they were supposed to serve. After law school, he and Mary moved to Lincoln, Nebraska, where Bryan began a successful law practice with an old friend from law school.[21]

During Bryan's formative years, the Democratic Party had begun to split between the conservatives and a new group of reformers. The conservatives maintained the old Jeffersonian support for small government and states' rights, but they had lost Jefferson's commitment to egalitarianism. The reformers were under pressure from their own constituents, many of whom were farmers or laborers, who were attracted to the Populist cause. They began to "revise the party's gospel of hostility to federal intervention" on behalf of average citizens. Bryan would soon join their side.[22]

In 1889 the corn harvest was so large that it caused a sharp drop in prices. This was followed a year later by drought, placing the farmers of Nebraska in further distress. It also opened opportunity for the Populist movement in the state to gain traction in the midterm elections of 1890. Bryan ran as a reform Democrat and called for control over large trusts and for the minting of silver as a way to relieve the debts of farmers. William Jennings Bryan was able to ride the Populist wave, and to utilize his skills as an orator, to win election to the House of Representatives. He was the first Democrat to win in a Republican state. Along the way, he had begun to earn a national reputation. The *Omaha World-Herald* wrote that Bryan "had the physical and mental qualities to make him a remarkable man in the history of the nation."[23]

In his first major speech in the House, Bryan attacked high tariffs with a moral fervor, insisting that they were "a massive subsidy to some of the wealthiest" people in the country, as Kazin frames it. Bryan didn't oppose a tariff for raising revenue, he only opposed the protective tariff, harkening back to debates between Whigs and Democrats during the days of Henry Clay and Andrew Jackson. He also supported "a graduated income tax upon the wealth of the country" which would "fall most heavily upon the rich" to raise revenue that would be lost by lowering tariffs.[24]

As Bryan's district continued to change, he was brought ever further into the Populist orbit. He barely won reelection to the House in 1892 and then began to stake his career on the issue that would later define him, the use of silver as an alternative form of currency for the United States. From a modern perspective, it seems unlikely that bimetallism (the use of both gold and silver, albeit at a sixteen-to-one ratio) would have resolved the many problems facing farmers and working people. Silver "was no more responsive in amount to the needs of" the economy, as Degler writes.[25]

Yet there was something both symbolic and egalitarian in the issue of silver that resonated during the era. The perception was that money and credit were focused on the Northeast, leaving little for farmers in the Midwest and South. Interest rates on loans were also higher outside of the Northeast. To the extent that silver was added to the money supply, it would help to inflate the economy and benefit average people.[26]

By 1894 Bryan's ambition drove him to run for the Senate. But as a Democrat, even with the support of the Populists, he was tied to the now-unpopular Cleveland and lost his bid when the Republicans swept to power in both Washington, DC, and Nebraska. Though out of office, Bryan pledged "to fight the battles of the people for what I think is right and just." And so, he set off on a quixotic quest for the presidency, even though, at thirty-four, he was not yet old enough to fill the office.[27]

Bryan brought to his pursuit of the presidency some important gifts, especially his oratory. He was a magnetic speaker, part actor, part Old Testament prophet. As his biographer Michael Kazin writes, his voice was described as "sonorous and melodious," "deep and powerfully musical," "soothing but bold" and "clear as a cathedral bell." His speeches often bordered on the demagogic, convincing even those who disagreed with him. Yet he was also an astute politician, able to convince Populist leaders to eventually support his candidacy. He ran for the nomination on a broad call for social and economic reform, proposing to use the power of the federal government to side with the people rather than the wealthy.[28]

The Democratic Convention was held in Chicago from July 7 to July 11, 1896. Bryan arrived as a clear underdog. The convention was split between the conservative Democrats and the Populist forces that supported free silver and other reforms. But the Populists had a clear majority at the convention, and they carried the day. Bryan cleverly arranged to give the final speech for the Populist side after a day of debate. In perhaps his finest moment in his young life, he made a "Jeffersonian plea for moral equity," according to Kazin. He placed the common man as the equal of the rich and powerful. "The man who is employed is as much a businessman as his employer," he argued, and he placed farmers and miners on the same footing as "the few financial magnates who, in a back room, corner the money of the world." He then closed with the words that echoed in the vast meeting hall. "You shall not press down upon the brow of labor this crown of thorns, you shall not crucify mankind upon a cross of gold," he said while he extended his arms straight out in a Christlike pose. Bryan emerged on the fifth ballot with the nomination.[29]

It was a major turning point for the Democratic Party. The party of Jefferson, which had always been committed to equality for the common white man, had also supported small government to achieve this goal. But time and circumstances, and the nation itself, had changed. The industrial age now made farmers and wage earners dependent on the power of monopoly capitalism. The only force that could counter this was democracy, the use of the power of the government as a countervailing force. The party was now "on a course from their laissez-faire past and toward the liberalism of the New Freedom, the New Deal, and the Great Society" to support the "[redistribution] of wealth and power in America," as Kazin nicely summarizes the party's transformation.[30]

Unfortunately for Bryan and the Democratic Party, their appeal did not yet have a wide enough base of support. Another politician would face Bryan with a more appealing level of support for progressive ideals while also maintaining ties to the business community.

William McKinley and the Republican Party

At first blush William McKinley appears to be a typical Republican politician of the era, on the side of the business community and a major advocate for the protective tariff. He took substantial sums of money from the business community in his run for the presidency in 1896. But McKinley was a more complex figure than this, a transitional figure between the Populists and the newly emerging Progressives.

McKinley was born in Ohio in 1843, seventeen years before Bryan. The state was a microcosm of the United States, with a balanced economy that included both industry and agriculture. Given this, McKinley would become a strong supporter of the protective tariff, which had been a staple of conservative politics from Hamilton through Henry Clay. Ohio was also a major battleground state, the home of numerous late nineteenth-century presidents, including Grant, Hayes, Garfield, and Harrison.[31]

The McKinleys were from the burgeoning middle class that had begun to emerge in the nation during the Gilded Age. It encompassed people in the professional classes, including "medicine, law, economics, administration, social work" and "specialists in business," who were needed in response to the new industrial age, as historian Robert H. Wiebe writes. A new world of white-collar work was on the rise. By the end of the Gilded Age, as the twentieth century dawned, about 20 percent of the population was middle class.[32]

Both McKinley's grandfather and father, William senior, were iron makers, and his father owned a small foundry. Much like Bryan, religion helped to form young William's worldview, instilled in him by his mother. He referred "to himself as a soldier for Jesus" during his time serving in the military during the Civil War. The contacts he made during the war, especially his service under future president Rutherford B. Hayes, would help him launch his own political career in the postwar years.[33]

When McKinley was twenty-eight, he married Ida Saxton, "the very pretty but high-strung daughter of one of Canton's most prominent families," biographer Kevin Phillips writes. The couple knew tragedy when both of their daughters died at a very young age. Ida then developed epilepsy, with William taking care of her. His political popularity may have in part been a product of "the time and attention he devoted to his wife," which caused many to admire his love and devotion to her.[34]

McKinley straddled the political factions that made up the Republican Party. He was a shrewd politician, a man who knew how to "survive the tough school of Ohio politics in the last quarter of the nineteenth century" as the historian Walter LaFeber writes. He was also sympathetic to labor, representing coal miners as a lawyer and supporting arbitration to resolve labor disputes, both in his time in the House of Representatives and as Ohio's governor. The Progressive Robert La Follette once wrote that "McKinley was generally on the side of the public against private interests." Yet he often hid his views, a useful trait for a politician, but one that obscures from the historian the true nature of the individual.[35]

Perhaps it was support for the protective tariff that led some historians to conclude that McKinley was on the side of large-scale industrialists and plutocrats. Yet his interest in the tariff seemed to spring from his support for keeping wages higher. In 1890 he became the author of the McKinley Tariff Act, which was full of excesses, a product of the legislative process of the time. While president he told a member of his cabinet that he knew the bill was flawed at the time it was crafted, "but I thought then, and think now [1897], that it is for our best interests to return gradually to a much less drastic system of tariff." McKinley also had a hard time seeing the connection between tariff protection, the growth of monopolies, and the creation of vast fortunes during the Gilded Age. Perhaps this was because "it was not that way in [his hometown of] Canton which hummed with protected industries while the owners lived unostentatiously," Phillips writes.[36]

The tariff bill may have partly cost McKinley his house seat in 1890. But that loss also allowed him to return to Ohio and be twice elected governor of the state. It kept him out of Washington during the great depression of 1893 and allowed him to criticize Cleveland and the Democrats for the economic calamity the nation faced. With the help of his chief advisor, the wealthy businessman Mark Hanna, McKinley was able to secure the Republican nomination for president on the first ballot. His relationship with Hanna, a longtime operative in the Republican Party, was used against him in the campaign, in which McKinley was made to look like "a puppet of the plutocratic 'boss' Mark Hanna," according to Phillips.[37]

The Election of 1896

With the benefit of hindsight, it is easy to see that Bryan's campaign was in trouble from the beginning. The headwinds that Cleveland's unpopularity produced made it a difficult year to run as a Democrat. The party was also split, and the conservatives nominated their own presidential candidate, Illinois senator John Palmer, who was committed to maintaining the gold standard. Many of the country's major newspapers were opposed to Bryan, seeing him as too radical. Bryan was able to garner the Populist nomination, an action that Richard Hofstadter referred to as the "suicide" of that movement. "When a third party's demands become popular enough, they are appropriated by one or both of the major parties and the third party disappears," Hofstadter wrote of the Populists.[38]

Bryan's biggest deficiency was his inability to knit together the working-class interests in the nation, especially hourly wage earners and farmers in the Northeast. "Labor had nothing concrete to gain from free silver and would only suffer if a change in the currency drove up prices for food and other necessities," Kazin writes. Farmers in the Northeast, who were not dependent on one-crop staple farming "realized that the Populist proposals were not designed to help them," according to Hofstadter. Major industries further threatened labor with major layoffs should Bryan win and his policies be implemented. Eugene V. Debs, who would later run for president as a socialist, was the only major labor leader to support Bryan. In his whirlwind tour of the country, Bryan downplayed the silver issue in many places, instead focusing on a common enemy, the wealthy.[39] This theme was foreshadowed at the Democratic Convention when Bryan had said:

> *There are two ideas of government. There are those who believe that if you must legislate to make the well-to-do prosperous, their prosperity will leak through on those below. The Democratic idea has been that if you legislate to make the masses prosperous, their prosperity will find the way up through every class that rests upon it.*[40]

McKinley could not match Bryan's speaking ability, nor did he try. He instead waged a front-porch campaign, with supporters coming to his home in Canton. Hanna ran a shrewd and modern campaign, sending out speakers to shore up support in battleground states, and flooding the mail with campaign flyers. McKinley's campaign was fueled by contributions from the business community, who were fearful of the radical Bryan. John D. Rockefeller alone contributed $250,000, and combined business donations totaled over $3.5 million, a massive sum for the times. Of the campaign, Theodore Roosevelt said, "Hanna advertised McKinley as if he were a patent medicine."[41]

McKinley charged Bryan with playing the politics of class warfare, a charge that would resurface against any Democrat that attempted to meld the working class into a political movement in the future. Yet McKinley also had a wide appeal among those people who now lived in urbanized areas or who were dependent on industrialism, which was the direction the nation had been moving toward during the Gilded Age. For many of these people, tariffs protected their businesses and jobs. McKinley also straddled the silver issue. He had historically supported both gold and silver as sources of money, but his support of silver was predicated on "an international conference, with British concurrence in drawing up binding guidelines" that all would follow.[42]

At first glance the election was not close. McKinley ushered in a major party realignment for the Republicans that would last until Franklin D. Roosevelt's election in 1932. He garnered 51 percent of the popular vote and 271 electoral votes to Bryan's 176, carrying the entire Northeast, most of the Midwest, and Oregon and California. Yet had Bryan garnered approximately 38,000 additional votes in six key states (California, Delaware, Indiana, Kentucky, Oregon, and West Virginia), he would have been elected president.[43]

Bryan also won the solid South, in part because Black people were being barred from voting. As the historian Carl N. Degler has noted, "the rivalry between Populists and Democrats in the 1890s suddenly revived the southern whites' old Reconstruction-born fear" of Black domination in the electoral sphere, since they could potentially hold the balance of power between the two parties. The systematic disenfranchisement of African Americans began in the 1890s through literacy tests, poll taxes, and other means. Bryan, the great advocate of the common man, said little to nothing about the adoption of Jim Crow laws in the South, and the Populist movement carried the taint of racism.[44]

Still, the election of 1896 was a turning point. As Kevin Phillips has written, "McKinley and Bryan were both in their ways remarkable men—tribunes of the people, not the interests . . . when the dust settled, America's urban and industrial future was narrowly victorious, but many of the reforms Bryan had held out eventually became law." This would occur during the Progressive Era that bubbled up from below—and sparked remarkable leaders in both major parties who would dominate the political landscape of the early twentieth century. The Progressives would move the nation from its extreme focus on individualism to a more balanced approach that also included a revival of republicanism.[45]

Endnotes

1   Burns, p. 180.

2   Degler, p. 71.

3   Elizabeth Sanders, *Roots of Reform: Farmers, Workers, and the American State: 1877–1917* (Chicago: University of Chicago Press, 1999), p. 111–112.

4   Sanders, p. 108–117.

5   Charles Postel, *The Populist Vision* (New York: Oxford University Pres, 2007), p. 173–184; Sanders, p. 118.

6   White, *The Republic*, p. 652; Sanders, p. 128; Degler, p. 116–117.

7   White, *The Republic*, p. 749.

8   Degler, p. 118; Stacy A. Cordery, "Women in Industrializing America," in Calhoun, ed., p. 120; Burns, p. 185–186; Postel, p. 69.

9   White, *The Republic*, p. 747; Alan Ware, *The Democratic Party Heads North, 1877–1962* (Cambridge: Cambridge University Press, 2006), p. 74; Joseph Fishkin and William E.

Forbath, *The Anti-Oligarchy Constitution: Reconstructing the Economic Foundations of the American Democracy* (Cambridge: Harvard University Press, 2022), p. 166.

10 White, *The Republic*, p. 755.

11 Charles W. Calhoun, *Benjamin Harrison* (New York: Times Books, 2005), p. 54–58.

12 Richardson, *To Make*, p. 123 and p. 130; Calhoun, p. 107–109.

13 Henry F. Graff, *Grover Cleveland* (New York: Times Books, 2002), p. 3–10 and p. 117; Brands, *American Colossus*, p. 433.

14 Burns, p. 226; White, *The Republic*, p. 771.

15 White, *The Republic*, p. 772; Degler, p. 131–132.

16 Jackson Lears, *Rebirth of a Nation: The Making of Modern America, 1877–1920* (New York: Harper, 2007), p. 169–172; the unemployment rate is reported as being as high as 20 to 25 percent on some internet websites, but I have used the figures found at the Economic History Association, retrieved July 29, 2021, from https://eh.net/encyclopedia/the-depression-of-1893/.

17 Burns, p, 226; White, *The Republic*, p. 804–807.

18 Lewis L. Gould, "Party Conflict: Republicans versus Democrats, 1877–1901," in Calhoun, ed., p. 276.

19 Michael Kazin, *A Godly Hero: The Life of William Jennings Bryan* (New York: Anchor Books, 2006), p. 4–5.

20 Kazin, p. 8–14.

21 Kazin, p. 15–16.

22 Kazin, p. 21.

23 Kazin, p. 26–28.

24 Kazin, p. 33; the quotes from Bryan are from the Congressional Record from March 16, 1892, retrieved August 12, 2021, from https://www.govinfo.gov/app/collection/crecb/_crecb/Volume%20023%20(1892).

25 Kazin, p. 33–39; Degler, p. 132.

26 Fishkin and Forbath, p. 170.

27 Kazin, p. 34.

28 Kazin, p. 48.

29 Kazin, p. 60–62.

30 Kazin, p. 56.

31 Kevin Phillips, *William McKinley* (New York: Times Books, 2003), p. 9–15.

32 Robert. H. Wiebe, *The Search for Order: 1877–1920* (New York: Hill and Wang, 1967), p. 112; Michael McGerr, *A Fierce Discontent: The Rise and Fall of the Progressive Movement in America* (New York: Free Press, 2003), p. 43.

33 Phillips, p. 13–16 and p. 24.

34 Phillips, p. 25–27.

35 Walter LaFeber, *The New Empire: An Interpretation of American Expansionism 1860–1898* (New York: Cornell University Press, 1963), p. 327; Phillips, p. 29–34.

36 Phillips, p. 43–45.

37 LaFeber, p. 328; Phillips, p. 66–73 and p. 4.

38 Kazin, p. 63–64; Richard Hofstadter, *The Age of Reform* (New York: Vintage Books, 1955), p. 97 and p. 107.

39 Kazin, p. 69; Hofstadter, p. 99.

40 White, *The Republic*, p. 845–846.

41 White, *The Republic*, p. 845.

42 White, *The Republic*, p. 846; Phillips, p. 52.

43 White, *The Republic*, p. 849. It should be noted that White indicates that a change of twenty thousand votes in the six states mentioned would have given Bryan the victory. But this is not accurate based on the state-by-state results that are shown on Wikipedia at https://en.wikipedia.org/wiki/1896_United_States_presidential_election#Results_by_state.

44 Degler, p. 138–139; Kazin, p. 91–92.

45 White, *The Republic*, p. 849; Phillips, p. 84.

CHAPTER 7

The Progressives

*This new movement is a movement of truth, sincerity and
wisdom, a movement which proposes to put at the service of
all of our people the collective power of the people through their
Government agencies.*
　—Theodore Roosevelt

The Progressive Era was a time when American society undertook a massive series of reforms designed to rebalance the rampant individualism of the Gilded Age with concerns for the larger public good. It had components that were instituted from the bottom up, largely from the newly emerging middle class. Yet the movement was also led by remarkable new leaders, including Theodore Roosevelt in the Republican Party and Woodrow Wilson in the Democratic Party. While different historians have dated the era in various ways, we will generally cover the period from the mid-1890s to 1920.

Overview of the Progressive Era

There have always been competing visions of what America is about. As we explored in earlier chapters, classical liberalism, with its focus on the importance of each individual and the protection of basic rights, has always been a part of the American ideal. But so too has classical republicanism, with its concern for the public interest and the protection of the community. During the Gilded Age, the balance between these two visions had shifted radically toward a focus on individualism. "Progressives differed among themselves in many ways, but they shared a critique of hyper-individualism," according to political scientist Robert D. Putnam and writer Shaylyn Romney Garrett.[1]

The philosophy of individualism and a laissez-faire approach to the economy had allowed for the rise of very powerful individuals as we saw in the last chapter, including men like Carnegie, Rockefeller, and Morgan. While they advanced the American economy through innovation (and at times cut-throat business practices), they also caused a sea change in American society. Individuals were now powerless against the forces of industrialism and the rise of trusts. Reforms during the Progressive Era were meant to rein in such forces through the power of government. "Many middle-class Americans who enjoyed the benefits of industrial capitalism feared that individuals had less control over their lives," the historian Steven J. Diner writes. The middle class formed the backbone of the Progressive movement.[2]

Where did this middle class come from? As Diner writes, it was an offshoot of the Industrial Revolution, which had created such growth in the years after the Civil War. The historian Robert H. Wiebe breaks the middle class into two broad categories. One was the newly emerging group of professionals in "medicine, law, economics, administration, social work, and architecture. The second comprised specialists in business, labor and in agriculture." One of the hallmarks of the Progressive Era was the movement toward professionalization in many of these fields, including in the management of government itself. In colleges and universities, science began to be applied to fields that studied human beings, like political science and sociology, leading to an attitude that all problems could be solved through rational analysis.[3]

Part of the Progressive reform efforts were a response to the underlying changes that were occurring in American society. Urbanization and industrialization had occurred in tandem, fueled by the movement of people from farms to cities and the introduction of new immigrants from Southern Europe. Many of these newcomers crowded into rapidly growing cities, yet the housing and environmental conditions were often subpar at best. "The stench rising from open privies, garbage-strewn alleys, and stagnant water produced a stink enough to knock you down," Burns writes. Worse than just the stink were the unhealthy living conditions that led to shortened lives, as we saw in the previous chapter.[4]

The sense of dislocation and loss of community was acute for many people. While there was a great deal of hope that American society was making progress, there was also a concern that the small-town sense of community that had existed in the countryside (whether in the United States or in Europe) had been lost. People responded both before and during the Progressive Era by beginning to join a whole host of civic groups. Between 1870 and 1920, "half of all of the largest mass membership organizations in American history" were founded. This included groups like the Red Cross, the Knights of Columbus, the Rotary Club, the PTA, and the Sierra Club. "Virtually all of these organizations, regardless of race or gender, tended to encompass both middle-class and working-class members," Putnam and Garrett write, and were a "reaction against the individualism and anomie of this era of rapid social change."[5]

Progressivism was, in some important ways, a conservative movement. Rather than attempting wholesale changes in the nation's economy, which socialism offered, it was a movement designed to reform and not replace capitalism. While some went the socialist route, many rejected the "narrow and rigid economic determinism of Marx," as one activist wrote. Overall, Progressives rejected both "socialism and individualism alike," looking for "the golden mean" as economist Richard T. Ely framed it. Progressives hoped to remove the impetus for socialism by removing "each individual case of injustice," as Louis Brandeis said in 1906.[6]

Jane Addams and Social Justice

Many of the major themes of Progressivism can be seen in the life of Jane Addams. Born in 1860 as the Civil War was about to erupt, she was the daughter of a very successful self-made man. John Addams "owned mills, invested in lands and railroads, and presided over a local bank," historian Michael McGerr writes. Yet he never forgot his humble beginnings, and always gave back to his community. Addams knew Lincoln, whom he referred to as "the greatest man in the world," and Lincoln referred to him as "my dear Double-D'ed Addams."[7]

After the death of her father in 1881, Jane was a lost soul. She finally found her purpose after traveling to Europe in 1887 and seeing the great works of charity that had been undertaken in London. Returning to Chicago, she set out "to rent a house in a part of the city where many primitive and actual needs are found." It was in Chicago that she opened Hull-House, which would ultimately include "a nursery, a kindergarten, a variety of clubs and classes for women and children, and a boardinghouse for working women," according to McGerr. Addams also rejected the idea of individualism, seeing in the Pullman Strike of 1894 the evils of rampant industrialism. "A large body of people feel keenly that the present industrial system is in a state of profound disorder, and that there is no guarantee that the pursuit of individual ethics will ever right it."[8]

Addams was not alone in her views. She was joined by many Christian ministers who promoted the Social Gospel, an attempt to live the gospel message of Jesus to help the poor and downtrodden. As Jon Meacham has written, they "saw good works as a critical element of Christianity." The theologian and Baptist minister Walter Rauschenbusch was one of the prime proponents of the Social Gospel. His Second German Baptist Church in New York bordered Hell's Kitchen, so he saw firsthand the problems of urban poverty. Rauschenbusch saw Jesus as a man of action, less concerned with personal piety "and more concerned with the ethics of human relations and public morality." Rauschenbusch thought the way to alleviate the problems of poverty and crime was to move away from "competitive life . . . into an organic cooperative life."[9]

Addams and the adherents of the Social Gospel soon became advocates for greater governmental activism to ameliorate the problems of the period, including poverty, crime, and health and safety issues. There was also an element of the Progressive movement that focused on improving the behavior of people. This was grounded in the belief that by improving the environment that people lived in, individual behavior would also improve. Part of this was an attempt "by old stock Americans to impose a uniform culture based on their values," as historian John Whiteclay Chambers II writes. This impulse had a nativist taint to it, as an attempt to change the culture of newly arriving immigrants.[10]

Perhaps the most famous (or infamous) example of this type of social engineering was Prohibition. Temperance movements had deep roots in American society. Abolitionism grew out of the Christian temperance movement. Carrie Nation, who later renamed herself

Carry A. Nation, began disrupting the operations of saloon keepers in Kansas, a supposedly dry state, in the 1890s. The movement gained a substantial amount of support in the South, where "two-thirds of the counties in former Confederate states had become dry by 1907," Chambers writes.[11]

Just as with other elements of the Progressive agenda, there was an anti-immigrant element of the movement for Prohibition. Some saw the influence of foreigners, like Italian Catholics, in the drinking of wine. "The fact that the American beer industry was dominated by companies with German names would contribute substantially to the successful climax of the movement during the era of the First World War," historian Richard M. Abrams writes. The Anti-Saloon League was able to push what became the Eighteenth Amendment through Congress in 1917 as the United States entered World War I against Germany. It was ratified the following year.[12]

Women's Suffrage

During the long sweep of American history, there has always been a push for greater equality for women, followed by a reactionary response. With the expansion of voting rights for men during and after the American Revolution, many men worried that women too would push for the right to vote. Some men even admitted that women should be treated as equals. Richard Henry Lee, who had introduced the resolution approving independence in the Continental Congress in 1776, told his widowed sister that he "would at any time give my consent to establish their right" to vote. In New Jersey, women who owned at least fifty pounds were allowed to vote in the years between 1776 and 1807, but this was not widely accepted in other states and would eventually be overturned. The abolitionist movement had a solid core of women who played leadership roles, and the pursuit of equal rights in antebellum America culminated in the Seneca Falls Convention in 1848. The movement was led by women like Elizabeth Cady Stanton and Susan B. Anthony. In a play on Jefferson's words, the Declaration of Sentiments stated "that all men and women are created equal."[13]

The Progressive Era saw a continuation of the struggle for equal rights for women. The movement was characterized by two sometimes conflicting goals. One was "to protect women from exploitation" as one historian frames it. In this regard, laws were adopted in the workplace to protect women from dangerous conditions and provide a minimum wage. The other was to continue to promote equal rights, of which gaining the vote was the most important.[14]

The movement for voting rights was given impetus in the post–Civil War world when western states, looking to attract women, allowed for female suffrage. Wyoming was the first, in 1869, followed by Colorado, Idaho, and Utah in the 1890s. Middle- and upper-class women organized with their working-class counterparts, lobbying at both the state and national level for the vote. They eventually gained the support of President Woodrow Wilson in the buildup to American participation in World War I. The Nineteenth Amendment was finally ratified in 1920, although full equal rights for women remains an elusive goal even today.[15]

The Rise of Professionalism

In the late 1880s and continuing throughout the Progressive Era, certain fields became more professional, including medicine, law, engineering, social work, and governmental service. During the Jacksonian age, the licensing of physicians was abolished, since it was viewed as "undemocratic and monopolistic," Diner writes. This was part of an ever-expanding movement to denigrate expertise in all fields in pursuant of democracy. Support for this approach began to erode as scientific knowledge spread ever further during the late nineteenth century. By 1901, spearheaded by the American Medical Association, many states began to require a college degree and passage of an examination to practice medicine.[16]

Lawyers, through the American Bar Association, also attempted to tighten requirements to enter the legal profession by requiring college degrees and passing exams. But they met with major resistance from state legislators, many of whom had followed the traditional route of studying law with an already-established lawyer. Some of the restrictions that the ABA sought had an element of racism to them, as they were designed "to restrict the number of immigrants, Jews, African-Americans, and others of working-class origins in [entering] the profession," Diner writes. Even a distinguished legal scholar like Louis Brandeis was opposed by many elites for a seat on the Supreme Court in 1916 because he was Jewish and had taken on powerful corporations.[17]

Government was not immune from the movement toward professionalization. As we have seen, initial efforts were made during the Gilded Age to reform public employment in order to eliminate the spoils system and the influence of party machines and replace them with an expert cadre of government workers. It was during the Progressive Era that the professional management of cities began. In 1913, the city of Dayton, Ohio, adopted the council-manager form of government in which an elected city council hired a nonpolitical city manager to run the city. The city manager was responsible for the city budget and finances and hired other professionals to manage the affairs of the city, including police, fire, public works, and recreational services. Most small and medium-size cities in the United States use the council-manager system today.[18]

State governments also underwent reform, much of it targeted at expanding democracy and breaking the power of corporations and the wealthy to control the government. "What the majority of the Progressives hoped to do in the political field was to restore popular government" through "direct primaries, popular election of Senators, initiative, referendum, recall, the short ballot," and other such reforms, Richard Hofstadter has written.[19]

Yet, in one of those ironies of history, the movement to create good government may have had the opposite effect on democracy. Participation rates in voting fell dramatically during the Progressive Era, from 83 percent in the presidential election of 1876 to 49 percent by 1920. Historians and political scientists have long debated the reasons for this, and a full examination is outside of the scope of this work. But a few observations are in order.[20]

One obvious reason for the drop in voting was the beginning of Jim Crow segregation in the American South, which overlaps with the Progressive Era. With the end of Reconstruction in 1876, the South had begun the process of creating an apartheid system in which separate but unequal facilities were provided to Black people, which reached its zenith in the early twentieth century. Strict segregation of Black people extended to hotels, schools, restaurants, transit, and even water fountains. This form of overt discrimination was sanctioned by the Supreme Court's 1896 decision in *Plessy v. Ferguson*. Not only were facilities separated, but Black people were subject to state-sanctioned violence, including lynching, for stepping outside of what white society considered acceptable.[21]

During Reconstruction, the Republican Party had encouraged Black Americans to vote, since they supported the party. But during the 1890s, Southern states began to rewrite their Constitutions to systematically exclude Black people from voting through poll taxes, literacy tests, and other means. Many of these measures also affected poor whites. Putnam and Garrett write that "nearly 620,000 [B]lack registered voters were purged from Southern rolls, leading to a drop in voter registration rates of 84.5 percent." In Mississippi alone, the number of African Americans who were registered to vote dropped from 147,000 to 9,000 during the 1890s.[22]

Participation rates also declined in the North as well. The question was *why*. The historian Jon Grinspan, in his book entitled *The Age of Acrimony*, describes how the Gilded Age was a time of high turnout but also a time of rabid partisanship and political violence. In an interview, he discussed how it was an era in which both good and bad existed side by side, a time of incredible engagement accompanied by a loss of civility. Grinspan argues that Americans made an intentional choice to tone down politics, which had grown partisan while failing to resolve the problems of the day. "After 1890 or so, a new alliance began working toward the secret cause of making politics so dry and quiet that fewer of those 'inferior types' wanted to participate, often explicitly viewing mass turnout as harmful," Grinspan writes. While it is true that there were some, particularly the Liberal Republicans we met in chapter 5, who wanted to discourage democracy, it seems hard to believe that the Progressive leaders, who were pushing for more direct democracy, were attempting to tamp down participation, as Grinspan portrays the situation.[23]

Rather than being the result of a conscious choice by Progressive leaders, the drop in voter turnout was a side effect of the various reforms that were implemented. The Progressives were attempting to reduce the role of political parties, particularly political machines, and bosses. In doing this, the power of the machines to drive turnout in return for something tangible was broken. The benefit may have been a government job awarded through the spoils system or the provisions of social services that were provided to new immigrants and the urban poor. Grinspan recognizes this, writing that "millions turned out to vote for crooks and demonstrate for demagogues, not because they were fools, but because they got something material or psychological from their participation." As government became the province of professionals, the role of parties in awarding patronage jobs or providing social services was ended.

Some of the high turnout during the Gilded Age may also have been the product of corruption, as we saw in chapter 5. "At all levels of government voters were purchasable, and elections purchased," historian Jack Beatty writes. He reports that in one Ohio county "85 percent of the electorate had either sold or bought votes" over a forty-year period ending in 1910. This was not an isolated incident, and ballot box stuffing also occurred. Introduction of the secret ballot made this less possible, as did laws that cracked down on electoral fraud. Beatty writes that fraud "flourished everywhere, inflating those suspiciously high nineteenth-century turnouts."[24]

The Role of Journalism

Journalism played a major role in influencing public policy during the Progressive Era, due to its "business of exposure," as Richard Hofstadter has referred to it. The writers and reporters of the era were able to expose the corruption of large industrial businesses and their ties to government officials. Teddy Roosevelt called these reporters *muckrakers,* and he was able to use the work they produced to advance his own progressive causes as president through the bully pulpit.[25]

One of the most important publications was *McClure's Magazine.* Samuel S. McClure, only thirty-six when he began the publication during the depression of 1893, was known as a genius. An immigrant from Northern Ireland, he knew poverty, as his family struggled to survive after the death of his father. His mother eventually moved him and his three brothers to Indiana, where she remarried. Sam ultimately attended Knox College in Illinois and was named editor in chief of the student newspaper during his senior year. He worked for a variety of publications before he launched his own magazine.[26]

McClure hired a stable of outstanding journalists. His magazine was designed "to deal with important social, economic and political questions" and to become "a power for good." Ida Tarbell became the first hire. She was known as the "mother hen" to a solid group of reporters that included Ray Stannard Baker, Lincoln Steffens, and William Allen White. Tarbell was from the oil region of Pennsylvania. Her father had been a successful independent oil producer until he was put out of business by Standard Oil, which manipulated freight rates to their advantage.[27]

Tarbell's twelve-part series on Standard Oil reflected the core practice of investigative journalism. She wanted to avoid writing a "hit" piece and set out to tell both sides of the story. As such, she showed the brilliance of Rockefeller and Standard's business practices while also writing of "how the ascendancy of the company was aided at every stage by discriminatory railroad rates and illegal tactics—bribery, fraud, criminal underselling and intimidation," Doris Kearns Goodwin observes. Tarbell's work was matched by articles about corruption from the political machines in numerous cities by Steffens and the problems of labor and capital from Baker. "Their disclosures of corrupt linkages between business, labor, and government educated and aroused the public, spearheading the Progressive movement that would define the early twentieth century," Goodwin writes.[28]

The dilemma for liberals had always been that the rich and powerful would manipulate and control government. This had been Jefferson's great fear—that too much power concentrated in the hands of the few would ultimately undermine a republican form of government. Andrew Jackson had worried that governmental assistance to banks and business would contribute to unnatural inequality. Both men had therefore favored limited government. The question was whether government could be used to aid and assist average people. Another journalist, Herbert Croly, would attempt to answer that question.

Croly, who was born in 1869, was one of the seminal writers and thinkers of his age. He provided a new definition of liberalism, one that combined a classical concern for individual rights with the use of an active federal government to advance the good of society. His mother, Jane, was a nationally known writer who supported women's rights, including voting rights, and a more "cooperative control of industry," as the political scientist Edward A. Stettner writes. His father, David, was also a journalist whose worldview derived from Auguste Comte, whose philosophy reflected a positive view of the course of history, grounded in a secular belief that rejected individualism for the good of the greater society.[29]

Croly attended Harvard University, which opened new horizons for him and made him question his parents' Comtean worldview. Leaving before he earned his degree, he began a career in journalism in 1899, just as the Progressive Era was heating up. Six years later, in 1905, he began work on *The Promise of American Life*. George Will, no fan of Progressivism or Croly, has called the book "a manifesto for the progressive movement . . . perhaps the twentieth century's most influential book on American politics."[30]

In *The Promise*, Croly directly took on the laissez-faire economic philosophy of the Gilded Age. "The existing concentration of wealth and financial power in the hands of a few irresponsible men is the inevitable outcome of the chaotic individualism of our political and economic organization, while at the same time it is inimical to democracy, because it tends to erect political abuses and social inequalities into a system." The nation instead needed to repurpose the government and make it "responsible for a morally and socially desirable distribution of wealth."[31]

He built his case in part by reviewing the broad sweep of American history, attempting to reconcile the distinct political philosophies of Hamilton and Jefferson. As Sean Wilentz has written, Croly was attempting to combine "Hamiltonian ends with Jeffersonian means." Since Croly was proposing the use of strong federal government action to control the power of large businesses, he admitted his allegiance to Hamilton. "I shall not disguise the fact that, on the whole, my own preferences are on the side of Hamilton rather than Jefferson." This also gave him a point of agreement with Theodore Roosevelt, who was an ardent Hamiltonian.[32]

Yet Croly recognized Hamilton's Achilles' heel, his opposition to democracy. So, he absorbed that part of the Jeffersonian philosophy, indicating how "Jefferson was filled with a sincere, indiscriminate, and unlimited faith in the American people." Croly wanted to encourage the most skilled and talented to assume leadership roles in society "but only on the express condition that their power is . . . used . . . for the benefit of the people as a whole." He criticized Jefferson for viewing "society to be composed of a collection of individuals, fundamentally alike in their abilities and deserts." This was largely a misreading of Jefferson, who also believed in an aristocracy of talent, as Jefferson wrote to his old friend John Adams in 1813.[33]

Croly was attempting to find the right balance between the individual and the group by rejecting both laissez-faire economics and socialism, and steering a middle course between the two. In the concluding section of the book, he writes: "It is the economic individualism of our existing national system which inflicts the most serious damage on American individuality; and American individual achievement . . . will remain partially impoverished as long as our fellow countrymen neglect or refuse systematically to regulate the distribution of wealth in the national interest." Croly therefore supported the regulation of large businesses and the implementation of an inheritance tax to reduce income inequality.[34]

The Progressive Leaders:
Theodore Roosevelt and Woodrow Wilson

If the Progressive movement was middle class in nature, with many people providing the energy to its policies from the bottom up, part of its success was due to Progressive political leaders from both political parties, men like Robert La Follette, Charles Evans Hughes, and William Jennings Bryan. None were more important than Theodore Roosevelt and Woodrow Wilson.

Theodore Roosevelt

Theodore Roosevelt, or TR, as he was often referred to, was a larger-than-life figure in the American landscape, the first truly great president since Lincoln occupied the office. The political scientist James MacGregor Burns equates him to the founding generation, as a man who embraced "the natural world around him as well as the political flora and fauna" and who "emulated the Founding Fathers in recording his experiences in correspondence, articles and books."TR presided at the wedding of his distant cousin Franklin and his niece Eleanor and stole the show, causing his daughter Alice to comment that "Father always wanted to be the bride at every wedding, the corpse at every funeral, and the baby at every christening."[35]

Roosevelt was born in 1858, two years before the outbreak of the American Civil War. The Roosevelts were a part of the old Dutch aristocracy of New York. His father, also named Theodore, was a great philanthropist who had a special interest in helping poor children. His mother, Mittie, was a child of the South, born in Georgia. She and her family aided the South during the Civil War, which caused a rift in the family and kept Theodore senior from serving in the war.[36]

Teedie, as he was known, was a sickly child who suffered from asthma. Perhaps it was his early health problems, along with his father's philanthropic work, that caused TR to later identify with helping the poor and downtrodden. Teedie adored his father and was able to gain his attention during some of his more sever bouts of asthma. They almost always occurred at night, and sometimes his father "would bundle him up against the cold, servants would be roused to fetch the carriage to door, and father and child would drive off in the dark in the hope that the sudden change of air might bring relief," David McCullough writes.[37]

He spent most of his early life with his family, traveling in Europe, and during his teen years living in Oyster Bay on Long Island. He overcame his physical limitations in his early teens by weightlifting and other forms of physical activity. As Brands writes, he was a "bundle of contradictory traits," loving both the outdoors and reading books. When he was sixteen, his parents decided he should attend Harvard, so he began a period of intense study, and at eighteen he entered the university. Initially lonely being away from his family, he soon made friends that he would keep for a lifetime. He also continued his fitness routine, and although too small to play a major sport, he loved boxing, writing to his parents, "I am training to box among the lightweights in the approaching match for the championship of Harvard."[38]

During his sophomore year tragedy struck the family when his father died. Rutherford B. Hayes had been elected president in the disputed election of 1876. Hayes was a reformer who wanted to clean up the spoils system. As part of that effort, he nominated Theodore Roosevelt senior to replace the future president, Chester A. Arthur, as the collector of customs for the Port of New York, a plum assignment. Roosevelt's nomination was soon engulfed in controversy in the Senate, where the spoilsman Roscoe Conkling stood in his way and defeated his nomination. The strain of the controversy took its toll. "Six days after his rejection by the Senate, Theodore Senior collapsed," Goodwin writes. "Doctors diagnosed an advanced stage of bowel cancer." Perhaps this was the key moment that placed young Roosevelt on a path as a reformer in the political arena and an opponent of machine politics. He would say, "my father . . . was the best man I ever knew."[39]

TR graduated from Harvard nineteenth in his class of 230 members, and then attended law school. Like so many political leaders, he found the law a bit boring, being more "concerned with [the] question of what law is, and not what it ought to be." Roosevelt belonged in politics, where the law is made. At the age of twenty-three, TR was elected to the New York State Assembly. As Doris Kearns Goodwin writes, "he longed to honor his father and family through his own efforts 'to help the cause of better government in New York.'" As with every office he ever held, he made quite a stir, arriving in a burst of energy, determined to take on the power of the political machine in both parties, including Tammany Hall. In his first major battle, he attempted to impeach a corrupt judge who was in the pocket of the financier Jay Gould. Although he lost this one, he gained a reputation with the local press. Teddy was also a bit of a moralist. The historian Geoffrey Ward writes that he looked for a "middle course between change and stability" and was a man who "saw everything in terms of right and wrong." He was also unafraid to stir the pot. When he was threatened by a fellow politician who was part of Tammany Hall, Roosevelt sought him out. "By God, if you try anything . . . I'll kick you, I'll bite you. I'll kick you in the balls."[40]

Tragedy once again struck young Roosevelt's life. On Valentine's Day in 1884, both his mother and his wife, Alice, died within hours of each other. His mother died from typhoid fever, while Alice, who two days before had given birth to a girl, died from Bright's disease. Roosevelt turned his baby daughter, also named Alice, over to his sister, essentially abandoning her during much of her early life. He soon set out for his ranch house in the badlands of Montana. It was "a place to rebuild his broken spirit," Geoffrey Ward writes. He spent his days on horseback, either managing his cattle or hunting a variety of birds and animals. His time in Montana gave him the chance to work with a wide range of men of a different class, and he held his own. When a cowboy dared call him "old four eyes," he pummeled the man. His love of the outdoors and wilderness areas would later lead to one of his enduring contributions to American life: the conservation movement.[41]

The lure of politics soon beckoned again. Roosevelt held a number of positions in government, from a stint in Washington, DC, as a civil service commissioner to a police commissioner in New York City to assistant secretary of the Navy. It was from that position that he clamored for American expansionism in Hawaii and for war with Spain to liberate Cuba. TR, along with his close friend Henry Cabot

Lodge, was part of a group that the writer Evan Thomas has called the "War Lovers" in his 2010 book of the same title. Roosevelt, much like his hero Hamilton, longed for a war so he could make his mark. "It does not seem to me that it would be honorable for a man who has consistently advocated a warlike policy not to be willing himself to bear the brunt of carrying out that policy."[42]

Despite his success, Roosevelt was facing a dilemma in his political career. "Because the bosses distrusted him and the public didn't know him, he was essentially unelectable" to any higher office, Brands writes. The war changed that. His exploits leading the Rough Riders in the Spanish-American War gave him a national reputation. As with so much of his success, he cultivated the reporters who covered the war. His Rough Riders, who were a mix of cowboys, blue-collar men, and elites, made for an irresistible story. After TR successfully led the charge up San Juan Hill, newspapers proclaimed he "had single-handedly crushed the foe." Roosevelt, who had always thought that war was the true "measuring rod," exclaimed after the war: "I've had a bully time and a bully fight. I feel as big and strong as a bull moose."[43]

Theodore Roosevelt then parlayed his success in the war into political success. He returned to New York and ran for governor. To obtain the Republican nomination, he needed to placate New York state senator Thomas Platt, the powerful boss of Republican politics who "detested reformers like Roosevelt," Goodwin writes. Yet Platt also had a problem when a major corruption scandal occurred in the current governor's office, making Roosevelt a potential solution because of his reputation as a reformer. Some supporters wanted Roosevelt to run as an independent, and while Roosevelt too distrusted Platt and his brand of politics, he was a realist who knew he could not win as an independent. And so, TR met with Platt and accepted his endorsement.[44]

This was one of the hallmarks of TR's leadership style. A reformer, he was not willing to burn his bridges to the powerful leaders of his party, knowing this would cost him politically. Roosevelt was always looking for balance, between reform and radical change, between being a maverick yet knowing when to go along.[45]

Roosevelt threw himself into the race for governor, just as he had done with everything in his life, stumping "the state up and down and across and zigzag," Lincoln Steffens wrote. TR won the election by an extremely narrow 18,000 votes.

Just as Platt feared, Roosevelt proved to be a Progressive reformer. During his stint as a police commissioner in New York City, he had come to see the plight of the urban poor, those he had once thought of as people who had "failed in life," but now saw as people who were ill served by the current political and economic system, and a self-serving elite. "I became more set than ever in my distrust of those men . . . who see to make of the Constitution a fetish for the prevention of the work of social reform." During his time in the governor's office, TR was able to get legislation passed "that taxed corporations, limited working hours for women and children, improved sweat shop conditions, and created forest preserves," Ward writes.[46]

Platt soon saw his chance to get rid of Roosevelt when McKinley's vice president died in late 1899. He urged McKinley and his campaign manager, Mark Hanna, to select TR to run as vice president on the Republican ticket in 1900. But Hanna also did not want Roosevelt. "Don't any of you realize that there's only one life between that madman and the Presidency?" Hanna exclaimed. But he was ultimately forced to take him by a Republican Convention that overwhelmingly favored TR.[47]

Then it happened—the scenario that Hanna most feared. While attending the Pan-American Exposition in Buffalo, New York, McKinley was shot by Leon Czolgosz, an anarchist. McKinley died eight days later, on September 14, 1901. Theodore Roosevelt, at forty-two years old, became the youngest man to ever assume the presidency.[48]

Woodrow Wilson

He was born Thomas Woodrow Wilson in December of 1856 in Virginia. His father, Joseph, was a Presbyterian minister originally from Ohio. His mother, Jessie, was a recent immigrant from England. Tommy, as he was known, spent his childhood in the South during the Civil War, largely in Augusta, Georgia. Despite being from the North, his father, like so many Christian ministers from the South, found biblical sanction for slavery and served in the Confederate army for a short period of time.[49]

Tommy's earliest memory was from when he was four years old and heard "that Mr. Lincoln was elected and there was to be war." Wilson, as an academic scholar, published a book called *Division and Reunion* in 1893. He wrote of the South: "they knew that their lives were honorable, their relations with their slaves human, their responsibility for the existence of slavery among them remote." Wilson blamed the North for the Civil War. The racism that was a later hallmark of Woodrow Wilson was born in the South.[50]

If Roosevelt had physical problems as a child, Wilson had his own limitations to overcome. Diagnosed with dyslexia, Wilson "did not learn the alphabet until he was nine, could not read until he was eleven or twelve, and at thirteen still struggled with reading and writing," his biographer Patricia O'Toole writes. It was a strange beginning for a man who would grow into an intellectual. Once he learned to read and write, he found "words that moved a nation" and "guided America onto a new plateau of social responsibility," Brands concludes.[51]

His father was Tommy's first teacher, and as he grew older, Joseph became ever more the taskmaster. "Above all, Dr. Wilson wanted his son not just to absorb but to analyze," Wilson biographer A. Scott Berg observes. Despite his father being occasionally harsh, Tommy loved him, calling him "one of the most inspiring fathers that ever a lad was blessed with." From his mother, Jessie, he learned humility, and remembered "how I clung to her, a laughed at momma's boy."[52]

In 1872, when Wilson was sixteen, the family moved to Columbia, South Carolina, a city that still carried the scars of the Civil War. Young Tommy was now a good student with an abiding interest in history and politics. One of his idols was William Gladstone, the prime minister of Great Britain, whom he called "the greatest statesmen that ever lived. I intend to be a statesman too"—a fateful comment from a man who later made such a major impact on the world of foreign affairs. Fearful that his son intended to become a politician rather than a minister, his father "sent him to Davidson College in North Carolina, a small Presbyterian establishment whose graduates typically went on to divinity school," O'Toole writes. While Davidson helped to deepen his religious faith, it was also the place where he realized politics would be in his future.[53]

In the spring of 1874, Wilson met with Dr. James McCosh, the president of Princeton. Tommy told his father, "I've found I have an intellect and a first-class mind," and decided he wanted to attend the university. Princeton was a fateful place for a future president to go to college, where so much "educational, political, and religious history converged," as Berg writes, including where the father of the American Constitution, James Madison, had attended.[54]

It was at Princeton that Wilson honed his speaking skills as a member of the American Whig Society "until he was recognized as the best debater" in the society. He continued to pursue his love of English politics, discovering Edmund Burke and John Bright. Bright was a man who "refused to separate the spheres of morality and politics," a hallmark of Wilson's own later approach to public affairs. He also began to develop his own theory that America's government should be more like the British system. As a senior he published an article entitled "Cabinet Government in the United States" in which he "urged the United States to adopt the British practice of linking the legislative and executive branches through the cabinet," O'Toole writes.[55]

Given his interest in politics, Wilson attended the University of Virginia law school beginning in 1879, after graduating from Princeton. He quit after eighteen months, finished his legal studies at home, and even opened a law practice. But practicing law was not his true calling. "He shrank from the idea of courting potential clients. He was appalled by the greed and pettiness on display in the courtroom," O'Toole writes. Instead, he launched a career in academia, attending Johns Hopkins University and earning a PhD in government.[56]

In 1885 his dissertation was published as a book called *Congressional Government*, which built on his earlier theme that the American government should operate more like its British counterpart. Wilson bemoaned that Congress spent so much time, through its committee system, in making laws. "Quite as important as legislation is vigilant oversight of administration," Wilson wrote. He also wanted a "broad daylight of discussion" from Congress that went beyond narrow debates over specific legislation. Otherwise, "the country must remain in embarrassing, crippling ignorance of the very affairs which it is most important that it should understand and direct." Wilson wanted to see the British parliamentary system implemented in America, in part as a way to circumvent checks and balances. "As at present constituted, the federal government lacks strength because its powers are divided, lacks promptness because its processes are roundabout, lacks efficiency because its responsibility is indistinct and its action without competent direction."[57]

Wilson eventually landed at his alma mater, Princeton, in 1890. He was married to his first wife, Ellen, and they had three daughters. Now known as Woodrow, he became a celebrity with his writing and speaking engagements. In 1902, Wilson became the president of Princeton as the Progressive Era began to take off. Brands argues that "what connected the sundry elements of this movement was an almost unquestioning faith in education as an instrument of democratic betterment." Wilson, as a public intellectual, was right in the middle of the educational establishment at one of America's elite universities.[58]

Wilson caught the eye of the Democratic leaders and machine bosses, who were looking to break the Republican hold on the presidency. He accepted their nomination to run for governor of New Jersey in 1910, which would serve as a stepping stone to the presidency. Wilson immediately distanced himself from the party regulars, calling for a rebirth of democracy and a focus on "the common interests," easily winning the governorship.[59]

Endnotes

1   Robert D. Putnam with Shaylyn Romney Garrett, *The Upswing: How America Came Together a Century Ago and How We Can do it Again* (New York: Simon & Schuster, 2020), p. 167.

2   Steven J. Diner, *A Very Different Age: Americans of the Progressive Era* (New York: Hill and Wang, 1998), p. 4.

3   Robert H. Wiebe, *The Search for Order: 1877–1920* (New York: Hill and Wang, 1967), p. 112.

4   Burn, p. 245–249; Diner, p. 77, has statistics on the number of immigrants coming into the US during these years.

5   Putnam and Garrett, p, 114.

6   Michael McGerr, *A Fierce Discontent: The Rise and Fall of the Progressive Movement in America* (New York: Free Press, 2003), p. 64–65; Richard M. Abrams, *The Burdens of Progress: 1900–1929*, (Glenview: Scott Foresman, 1978), p. 43–44.

7   McGerr, p. 40–41.

8   McGerr, p. 56–58.

9   Jon Meacham, *American Gospel: God, the Founding Fathers, and the Making of a Nation* (New York: Random House, 2006), p. 144–145; People & Ideas: Walter Rauschenbusch, retrieved November 16, 2021, from https://www.pbs.org/wgbh/pages/frontline/godinamerica/people/walter-rauschenbusch.html; McGerr, p. 66.

10 McGerr, p. 67–68; p. 79–81; John Whiteclay Chambers II, *The Tyranny of Change: America in the Progressive Era 1890–1920* (New York: St. Martin's Press, 1992), p. 142.

11 McGerr, p. 81–83; Chambers, p. 145.

12 Abrams, p. 34; Burns, p. 441.

13 Fraser, *Growth*, p. 218–219.

14 Chambers, p. 97.

15 Chambers, p. 99–101.

16 Diner, p. 176–177.

17 Diner, p. 184–185.

18 Diner, p. 206.

19 Hofstadter, p. 257.

20 Statistics on voting were taken from the United States Elections Project that was retrieved on December 15, 2021, from https://www.electproject.org/national-1789-present.

21 Putnam and Garrett, p. 201–202.

22 Putnam and Garrett, p. 214; Jon Grinspan, *The Age of Acrimony: How Americans Fought to Fix their Democracy, 1865–1915* (New York: Bloomsbury, 2021), p. 214–215.

23 Jon Grinspan interview with WBUR retrieved December 15, 2021, from https://www.wbur.org/onpoint/2021/12/09/in-age-of-acrimony-a-historian-reflects-on-the-last-time-americans-fought-for-democracy; Grinspan, J. (10/29/2021), "What We Did the Last Time We Broke America," *New York Times* retrieved December 15, 2021, from https://www.nytimes.com/2021/10/29/opinion/normal-politics-gilded-age.html.

24 Beatty, p. 215–218.

25 Hofstadter, p. 186.

26 Doris Kearns Goodwin, *The Bully Pulpit: Theodore Roosevelt, William Howard Taft, and the Golden Age of Journalism* (New York: Simon & Schuster, 2013), p. 160–168.

27 Goodwin, *Bully Pulpit*, p. 170–171.

28 Goodwin, *Bully Pulpit*, p. 323–331.

29 Edward A. Stettner, *Shaping Modern Liberalism: Herbert Croly and Progressive Thought* (Lawrence: University Press of Kansas, 1993), p. 1–11.

30 Will, p. 41.

31 I am using the version of the original 1909 book that was republished in 2014 by Princeton University Press. Herbert Croly, *The Promise of American Life* (Princeton, 2014), p. 28–29.

32 Stettner, p. 38.

33 Stettner, p. 40.

34 Croly, p. 503; Stettner, p. 65–69.

35 Burns, p. 325; Geoffrey C. Ward and Ken Burns, *The Roosevelts: An Intimate History* (New York: Alfred A. Knopf, 2014), p. 121.

36 H. W. Brands, *TR: The Last Romantic* (New York: Basic Books, 1997), p. 3–16.

37 David McCullough, *Mornings on Horseback* (New York: Simon and Schuster, 1981), p. 36.

38 Brands, *TR*, p. 19–69.

39 Goodwin, *Bully Pulpit*, p. 45; Brands, TR, p. 79–82.

40 Goodwin, *Bully Pulpit*, p. 67–75; Ward and Burns, p. 27.

41 Brands, *TR*, p. 160–162 and p. 173–175; Ward, p. 35.

42 Evan Thomas, *The War Lovers: Roosevelt, Lodge, Hearst, and the Rush to Empire, 1898* (New York: Little, Brown and Co., 2010); Brands, TR, p. 333.

43 Brands, *TR*, p. 369; Goodwin, *Bully Pulpit*, p. 227–231.

44 Goodwin, *Bully Pulpit*, p. 235–238; Brands, *TR*, p. 365–368.

45 Brands, *TR*, p. 175–177.

46 Goodwin, *Bully Pulpit*, p. 213; Ward and Burns, p. 65.

47 Brands, *TR*, p. 394–398; Ward and Burns, p. 66–67.

48 Brands, *TR*, p. 411–416.

49 H. W. Brands, *Woodrow Wilson* (New York: Times Books, 2003), p. 1–3; Patricia O'Toole, *The Moralist: Woodrow Wilson and the World He Made* (New York: Simon & Schuster, 2018), p. 1–2.

50 A. Scot Berg, *Wilson* (New York, 2013), p. 32.

51 O'Toole, p. 3; Brands, *Wilson*, p. 1.

52 Berg, p. 35–36.

53 O'Toole, p. 4; Berg, p. 45–47.

54 Berg, p. 48–51.

55 Berg, p. 58–63; O'Toole, p. 7.

56 Brands, *Wilson*, p. 9; O'Toole, p. 9,

57 Woodrow Wilson, *Congressional Government* (Boston: Houghton Mifflin, 1885), kindle location 2765 and 2818; John Milton Cooper Jr., *Woodrow Wilson* (New York: Knopf, 2009), p. 48–49.

58 Brands, *Wilson*, p. 8–11; O'Toole, p. 14–15 and p. 18.

59 Brands, *Wilson*, p. 16–18.

CHAPTER 8

National Politics during the Progressive Era

*I feel confident if Jefferson were living in our day he would
see what we see ... without . . . the resolute interference of the
government, there can be no fair play.*
—Woodrow Wilson

*I*t is at this point that the two political parties begin to converge on the
use of government as an active force to control large businesses that
had come to dominate the American economy and the political system.
Theodore Roosevelt was a conservative reformer, a man who feared mob
violence and wanted moderate reforms through governmental action
to better balance the power of large business. He attempted to steer
the Republican Party back to its radical roots that emerged before and
during the Civil War. TR would have a degree of success, but he would
ultimately fail. The political scientist Stephen Skowronek has written
that "a president's political authority turns on his identity vis-à-vis the
established political regime." Roosevelt's presidency occurred when the
existing regime was "relatively resilient" and still had credibility through
its laissez-faire economic philosophy, which meant TR was ultimately
unable to achieve his goal of making the Republicans a pro-government
party. After his term in office, Roosevelt would attempt to regain the
presidency through the Progressive Party.[1]

It was Woodrow Wilson who moved the Democrats forward toward being a pro-government party. Wilson, for his part, was an "opposition leader" facing the same resilient regime as Roosevelt. As such, he too faced strong headwinds. While both TR and Wilson fit into Schlesinger's cycle theory, in that they were presidents during a period when "public action" prevailed, they were unable to fully transform their political parties because the existing philosophy had not been completely repudiated. In Wilson's case, World War I would both strengthen and ultimately lead to the demise of the Progressive movement.

President Theodore Roosevelt

Roosevelt assumed the office of the presidency on September 14, 1901. From the beginning he faced a balancing act. On the one hand, he had not been elected president—McKinley had. He was also warned of a stock market crash if he acted abruptly, so Roosevelt indicated he intended "to continue absolutely unbroken the policy of President McKinley." Yet he also told a small group of friends that following McKinley too closely "would give the lie to all he stood for." He was president and he intended to act like it, he told a group of reporters.[2]

The problem that Roosevelt faced was that he was among those presidents who assumed office affiliated with an existing political regime "that was flush with prosperity, heady with imperial triumphs, and rock solidly Republican," as Skowronek writes. As such, he had a more limited range of options for change than those presidents who come to power when the existing political order has failed to provide answers to the problems of the day, including "Thomas Jefferson, Andrew Jackson, Abraham Lincoln, and Franklin Roosevelt," according to Skowronek. Yet times of great prosperity also offer opportunities to those that seize them. "People enjoying material well-being are more likely to move to higher needs and aspirations—such as the pursuit of liberty, equality, and happiness," as Burns writes.[3]

TR was attempting to move the Republican Party back to its Lincolnesque radical roots, to make "an old party progressive" again. Yet he faced an old guard committed to a belief in laissez-faire individualism and committed to a pro-business point of view. That view was deeply embedded in American conservatism running from Hamilton and the Federalists to Clay's Whigs, although neither of these earlier movements were hostile to active government—nor were they completely committed to laissez-faire. Yet Roosevelt also knew that the times demanded, and his own beliefs dictated, that large businesses be reined in through the actions of the federal government.[4]

As a practical politician, TR knew he faced an old guard in Congress that was beholden to the political bosses and the trusts. He consulted with many of them, including Mark Hanna, who cautioned that he go slow in his annual State of the Union address to Congress in December of 1901. Roosevelt ultimately added wording to the speech that praised "the captains of industry who have driven the railway systems across the continent, who have built up our commerce, who have developed manufactures, [who] have on the whole done a great good to our people." Yet he refused to back down from support for progressive causes like business regulation, unionization, and workplace safety for women and children. He argued that industrial development had caused "serious social problems" and that "the great corporations known as trusts are in certain of their features and tendencies hurtful to the general welfare." Roosevelt did not support prohibition of the trusts, but rather believed they should be "supervised and within reasonable limits controlled" by "proper governmental supervision." He also made clear his support for unionization "when they combine insistence upon their own rights with law-abiding respect for the rights of others."[5]

❦ ❦ ❦

At the turn of the century, corporate mergers had increased rapidly, when "at least 2,274 manufacturing firms merged . . . most of which dominated their industries," legal scholar Tim Wu writes. United States Steel Corporation was one of the largest, created by J. P. Morgan when he merged Carnegie's steel operation with nine other steel companies, which then controlled 25 percent of world steel production. Similarly, the Northern Securities Company, which Morgan created to merge together some of the major rail lines, controlled much of the rail traffic of the country. Roosevelt fired his first major volley on the trusts by supporting the Justice Department's antitrust suit against Northern Securities. When Morgan went to the White House to meet with TR in order to "fix it up" (end the suit), he was informed by the attorney general, Philander Knox, that "we don't want to fix it up, we want to stop it." Roosevelt said that the lawsuit "served notice on everybody that it was going to be the Government . . . who governed these United States." The case would ultimately be decided in a 5–4 decision by the Supreme Court that the government had the right to reject the merger under the Sherman Antitrust Act.[6]

Roosevelt was in the process of establishing a modern activist presidency. He was full of energy and optimism, a magnetic personality that drew people to him, including the press. "He intended from his first day as president to make the national executive the dominant actor in all parts of American life," historian Jeremi Suri writes. He helped to end a coal strike with the surprising aid of Morgan, establishing an arbitration committee that "granted the workers a nine-hour day and a ten percent pay increase," according to Burns, but not union recognition.[7]

In 1903 TR was able to get legislation passed that established the Department of Commerce, investing it with the power to regulate large businesses engaged in interstate commerce. It also included the creation of a Bureau of Corporations with the power to review the internal operations of interstate corporations. This provision led to significant opposition from large businesses, who declared the legislation as socialistic and saw TR as "an extremely dangerous man." Yet Roosevelt was able to place significant pressure on the old guard in the Senate when he revealed that Rockefeller had sent a telegram to half a dozen senators insisting the bill be stopped. No one wanted to appear to be bought and sold, and the bill became law.[8]

The 1904 Election

In order for Roosevelt to implement his Progressive vision, he needed to be elected president in his own right. TR needed to finesse the tariff issue, which had been a part of the conservative creed since the time of Hamilton. Progressives saw the tariff as part and parcel of the problem of large industrial business who were shielded from international market forces, allowing them to grow ever bigger. But Roosevelt feared that "the attempt to revise the tariff [would] split the Republican Party wide open and insure defeat." So he once again settled on a middle course, "mounting a strong defense of protection, [while calling] for a commission of experts that might recommend incremental rate adjustments where necessary," Skowronek writes.[9]

The one man who potentially stood in his way was the hero of the old guard, Mark Hanna. But in February of 1904, Hanna died of typhoid fever, removing him as a potential obstacle. Lacking an alternative leader, the old guard grudgingly supported Roosevelt at the Republican Convention, which nominated him by acclamation. They did saddle him with the conservative Charles Fairbanks as vice president. Roosevelt readily accepted Fairbanks as a concession to the old guard and as a means to consolidate party support behind him.[10]

Meanwhile the Democrats moved rightward, eschewing Bryan and his populism for the conservative Alton B. Parker, known as a Gold Democrat because of his staunch support for the gold standard. "Parker also used his own conservative background and appeals to big business to try to reverse the recent ideological alignment of the two parties," historian John Milton Cooper writes. While the Democrats called for "large reductions in social spending," they also kept one foot in the Progressive camp, supporting "the direct election of senators," as Goodwin writes. Parker also had a degree of sympathy for the working class, which is probably what made him a Democrat. As a judge, Parker had issued rulings that were "strongly favorable to the contentions of labor." TR straddled this issue too, calling for a "square deal to every man" and saying that he intended to "stand by the capitalist when he is right and by the laboring man when he is right."[11]

The election was a blowout victory, with Theodore Roosevelt winning 336 electoral votes and 57 percent of the popular vote, sweeping the North and the West. Only the South remained in the Democratic column. In the immediate aftermath of the election, TR made a spectacular blunder. Without fully thinking through the implications, he announced "under no circumstances will I be a candidate for or accept another nomination." He had been considering this move for quite a while to blunt charges that he was too ambitious. But he later came to rue the decision, telling a friend "he would willingly cut off his hand at the wrist" if he could take it back.[12]

The Second Term

Relieved of the charge he was an accidental president, TR now pursued a Progressive agenda aggressively. But he also continued the balancing act, placating the conservative elements in his party, in part because of their strength, in part because his own personal disposition was to find the middle course. Still, as we have seen, the business community did not trust Roosevelt. The middle way also earned him plenty of criticism from more left-leaning Progressives.[13]

Roosevelt next pursued legislation that strengthened the regulation of railroad rates, a source of conflict between large businesses that received reduced rates compared to smaller operations. Roosevelt has often been called a trust buster, but in fact he saw the need for large businesses to provide the industrial strength the United States needed in order to be a world power. What he wanted was for the federal government to regulate the large trusts in the public interest and to strengthen the hand of unions to counterbalance the excesses of large businesses. "Somehow or other we have to work out methods of controlling the big corporations without paralyzing the energies of the business community and of preventing tyranny on the part of the labor unions while cordially assisting in every proper effort made by the wageworkers to better themselves by combinations," Roosevelt said.[14]

The Hepburn Act proposed to grant the ICC the ability to set maximum railroad rates. Unsurprisingly, it faced substantial conservative opposition in the Senate. Roosevelt cleverly accepted one of the amendments proposed by the old guard to give the courts a greater role in overturning rates set by the ICC, while eschewing others that would gut the legislation. Still, "Roosevelt's willingness to cooperate and compromise exacted a price. Some Democrats and reform Republicans decried the provision for court review as a sellout," Cooper writes. Senator Robert La Follette from Wisconsin, one of TR's rivals for leadership of the Progressive movement, "was disgusted by the President's waffling," as Skowronek writes.[15]

The young novelist Upton Sinclair published *The Jungle* in early 1906. Sinclair, a committed socialist, moved to Chicago, where he analyzed the meatpacking industry. What he found shocked him as he moved around the plants, amazed "as scraps of meat that were later sold to the public were swept from the floors infested with rats and covered in human spit," Goodwin writes. "The pressure to produce profits dictated that nothing was allowed to go to waste."[16]

After reading the novel, TR sent his own inspectors to Chicago to evaluate the meatpacking industry. They confirmed what Sinclair had reported. Legislation was soon drafted to authorize federal inspection of the industry. Roosevelt overcame opposition to the bill by releasing the inspector's report of findings, which caused public outrage, and he soon signed the bill. This was followed by the passage of the Pure Food and Drug Act. The law was spurred by an investigative report published by *Collier's* Magazine, which shows that many of the drugs that were sold were fraudulent or dangerous. The act established the Food and Drug Administration to regulate both foods and medicines.[17]

It was a remarkable series of legislative accomplishments and the high-water mark in Roosevelt's dealings with Congress. "During no session of Congress since the foundation of the Government had there been so much done . . . to extend the Federal power of regulation and control over business in the country," the *New York Times* wrote.

The legislation also reflected the evolution of the administrative state as TR began to build a powerful executive branch. He appointed a commission on department methods, which helped the president build a "strong, stable and professional arm of civil administration under executive control," Skowronek writes. The commission helped to modernize the civil service system by implementing more competitive pay and retirement benefits. While patronage had not disappeared, it was beginning to be supplanted by a professional cadre of governmental workers.[18]

Likewise, TR thought that regulating industry was best left to experts in the executive branch and not Congress or the courts. Roosevelt "had little faith in the capacities of either to meet the challenges of government in an industrial society," according to Skowronek. Roosevelt believed that "government control must be exercised through administrative and not judicial officers if it is to be effective." In this, he would run into opposition from the old guard in Congress, who feared that Roosevelt was usurping the role of Congress. TR would soon find himself in a battle with Congress over an issue he cared deeply about: conservation.[19]

Conservation was another hallmark of the Progressive Era. In the 1890s the Census Bureau announced that the frontier was closed. A portion of the public became concerned with preserving wilderness from further exploitation. This view was best expressed by John Muir, the founder of the Sierra Club and a leader of the movement, a man who wanted to protect the natural environment from development.[20]

Not everyone agreed with the goals of the conservation movement, especially many in the West who wanted to exploit the resources of their newly developing region. TR tried to again strike a balance between the extremes. As a rancher in the Dakotas, he saw the "dilemma of the commons, where each individual's pursuit of self-interest . . . threatened the ruin of all," as Brands writes. Roosevelt essentially wanted part of the undeveloped western lands to be open for sustainable development, while preserving the most scenic and important sites for future generations. During his tenure in office, Roosevelt designated some of the most iconic national parks that America has to offer, such as Yosemite, Yellowstone, and the Grand Canyon. Of the Grand Canyon, he said, "Keep it for your children, your children's children and for all who come after you, as one of the great sights which every American . . . should see."[21]

The battle over conservation reached a climax in 1907 and reflected both the strengths and weaknesses of Roosevelt's leadership style. He had used executive power to protect and preserve a wide range of public lands in the West. Congress became concerned about executive overreach, both by Roosevelt and also by the head of the Division of Forestry, Gifford Pinchot, and "rescinded presidential authority to create forest reserves in all the western states," as Cooper writes. Rather than fight the amendment, Roosevelt issued a series of proclamations to preserve twenty-one more forest preserves totaling seventeen million acres before the law went into effect. It was a daring use of presidential power to sidestep congressional intent.[22]

TR was what the political scientist James David Barber characterized as an active-positive president, one with "high self-esteem" who is goal oriented and productive. "The active-positive Presidents are those who appear to have fun in the vigorous exercise of Presidential power. They seek out—even create—opportunities for action, rather than waiting for the action to come to them," Barber writes. But active-positive presidents have difficulty in seeing their own limitations; they attempt to draw too much power to themselves and often have trouble understanding the point of view of others.[23]

TR's success was partly rooted in the personal qualities he brought to the presidency. Teddy was a larger-than-life figure in American life, full of energy and confidence. The historian Jeremi Suri describes Roosevelt as "vain, fanatical, even demagogic," a man "intoxicated with power and an exaggerated sense of his own superhuman capabilities." Yet Roosevelt also sincerely cared about promoting the public interest and was "devoted to making the lives of citizens better, not just getting himself elected," according to Suri. Roosevelt once told one of his sons, "I always believe in going hard at everything." A visitor to the White House reported that after shaking hands with Roosevelt one needed "to wring the personality out of your clothes."[24]

Roosevelt's success was also a product of the times he lived in. The public was clamoring for national action to advance progressive causes and rein in large monopolistic businesses. The entire Progressive movement, as we have seen, emanated from the middle class upward through nonprofits, local service organizations, and state and local governments, and had finally reached the federal government. "At the time Roosevelt entered the White House, a new and intoxicating feeling of reform and change was pervading the nation," Burns writes.[25]

Yet Roosevelt failed to convert the Republicans into a party that continued to support active government. Perhaps the forces arrayed against him, especially the opposition of the old guard and the business community, made this impossible. While the historical cycle he found himself in was one where public purpose was paramount, the customary laissez-faire traditions had not been completely repudiated. Roosevelt's failure may have also been caused by the very success of industrialization, which had been a goal of both Hamilton and Henry

Clay. In the aftermath of the Civil War, industrialism took off, and by the early twentieth century the goal had been achieved. Many conservatives no longer supported active government since there was no longer a need to nurture and sustain industry, and the uses for active government during the Progressive Era were designed to control large businesses and level the playing field for average people, goals that were more in keeping with the Democratic Party.

Roosevelt's leadership style also contributed to his failure. "Increasingly during his years in the White House, he exhibited the kind of volatility, emotionalism, anger, and over reactiveness, and indulged in the type of self-aggrandizement through personal politicking and policy-making that had always worried prudent republicans about executive excess," Burns writes of Roosevelt. Reminiscent of Andrew Jackson, Roosevelt saw himself as the true representative of the people. While he had to work with Congress and put up with the courts, he preferred centralizing power in the presidency and ultimately in himself. His failures come into focus by examining his handpicked successor for the presidency, William Howard Taft. The rift that developed between the two men "revealed . . . how little lasting impact Roosevelt had left on the party and how tenuous were his triumphs as president," Brands writes.[26]

President William Howard Taft

Taft and Roosevelt had been friends since 1890, when each served in Washington, DC, as part of the administration of William Henry Harrison. Taft served as solicitor general, while TR was a member of the civil service commission. Perhaps it was because they were so different that they became such good friends. But ultimately Roosevelt would turn on Taft once he became president.

As president, Taft fit the passive-positive model that Barber writes about. "This is the receptive, compliant, other-directed character whose life is a reward for being agreeable and cooperative rather than personally assertive," Barber writes. For Taft, who was born in Cincinnati in 1857, this pattern was established early in life. He graduated from both high school and Yale University near the top of his class, not because of his own internal motivation but in order to please his parents. At Yale, his favorite teacher was the Social Darwinist William Graham Sumner, who taught him "that property rights demanded protection against the onslaught of radical theories and socialist ideals," as Goodwin writes. Yet he rejected at least part of Sumner's teachings and supported some progressive causes.[27]

Taft's life became focused on the law. After graduating from the Cincinnati College of Law, he opened a law practice and was appointed as a judge to the Sixth Circuit Court, where he served from 1892 to 1900. His wife Nellie, whom he had married in 1885, was the one who harbored strong political ambitions for Will Taft. She had not been happy when Taft took the judgeship, because it meant they would leave Washington, DC, and return to Cincinnati. Nellie held strong sway over Taft, who early on told her sister that "what she thought became of much more importance to me than what I thought myself."[28]

In the aftermath of the Spanish-American War, the United States had become a world power and set out to establish an empire. President McKinley sent Taft to the Philippines, which the United States had occupied after evicting the Spanish, triggering a guerrilla war against the Americans. Taft ultimately became governor-general of the Philippines in 1901, where he attempted to "construct a democracy from the top down," an approach that was doomed to failure. It would not be until after World War II that the United States finally recognized Philippine independence.[29]

Roosevelt, once he became president, kept trying to get his old friend to return to Washington, DC. He finally succeeded, and in 1904 Taft became his secretary of war. TR twice offered to nominate Taft for the Supreme Court, which is where his ambition lay, but each time his wife nixed the idea. Nellie thought he "would be shutting the door on any further political advancement" since he was "the logical candidate for president in 1908." Taft did not want to be president, but ultimately pressure from both TR and Nellie led him to run in 1908, and he defeated William Jennings Bryan. Once elected, he soon said, "I feel just a bit like a fish out of water."[30]

Barber calls Taft a "conservative progressive," which sounds like an oxymoron, but also captures the essence of his presidency. On the one side, Taft believed the United States government was limited in its power by the force of law, especially the Constitution, which established a series of enumerated powers. He also believed in the limited nature of the role of the presidency, unlike Roosevelt's expansive vision. Yet Taft also supported much of Roosevelt's progressive agenda. He saw his administration's role as implementing the legislation that TR had pioneered, and he also supported "a progressive income tax and the direct election of senators," Goodwin writes.[31]

Always a people pleaser, Taft too attempted to steer a middle course between the old guard and the progressives within the Republican Party. Yet his lack of skill as a politician and his limited view of the presidency left him with little sway over either side. As part of the Republican platform, he had insisted on a plank that recommended reforms and a lowering of the tariff. The legislation he signed into law reduced some tariffs, and as part of the process he was able to convince

Congress to pass a corporate tax and amend the Constitution to allow for an income tax, which the Supreme Court had previously found unconstitutional. Unfortunately, the tariff bill was widely seen as a victory for the old guard, and Taft as their tool. It was an inauspicious start, and it only got worse from there.[32]

Taft had promised to retain Roosevelt's cabinet, but he also needed to establish a degree of independence from Roosevelt. And so he broke his promise and began to make changes in his administration. "No appointment would have more far-reaching consequences for Taft's administration than his decision to replace Interior Secretary James Garfield (the son of the former president) with Richard Ballinger," Goodwin writes. Both Garfield and Pinchot were very close to Roosevelt, and the decision caused quite a rift, especially when Pinchot leaked information that Ballinger may have been involved in corrupt dealings while he was a land commissioner. The charges proved untrue, and so Taft fired Pinchot, who complained to Roosevelt during his return trip from Africa. It was another sign of an impending break between Taft and Roosevelt.[33]

What caused a final rift between the two was an antitrust lawsuit that the Taft administration filed in October of 1911 against the U.S. Steel Corporation. The issue had its roots in the Panic of 1907, when TR had turned to J. P. Morgan to help bail out the American economy from a speculative bubble that had burst. Roosevelt was under attack from conservative businessmen who claimed his reform measures had undermined the economy, and as a protective measure TR had turned to Morgan. The House of Morgan "proposed that the United States Steel Corporation be allowed to purchase controlling assets in the Tennessee Coal and Iron Company to prevent a collapse of the whole banking structure," Burns writes. With a wink and a nod, Roosevelt agreed.[34]

Now Taft's Justice Department was bringing a lawsuit against the very merger Roosevelt had supported. In the lawsuit, the Justice Department made it appear that TR may not have had all of the facts, and newspapers began to report that "Roosevelt Was Deceived." Roosevelt was, unsurprisingly, irate. "What I did was right," he stated and argued that his attempts to end the panic were done to save "the plain people, the common people." The split would cause Roosevelt to challenge Taft in the 1912 election.[35]

The 1912 Election

Why did Roosevelt ultimately decide to challenge his old friend Taft for the Republican nomination? There had certainly been a falling-out between the two men, yet Roosevelt hesitated to directly challenge Taft until February 1912. The historian John Milton Cooper argues that Roosevelt felt the times he served in did not allow him to join the pantheon of great American presidents. "If there is not the great occasion, you don't get the great stateman," TR said. "If Lincoln had lived in times of peace, no one would have known his name now."[36]

Roosevelt increasingly came to see himself as the embodiment of the American people, as "the agent of the people's will," as Brands frames it. As such, Roosevelt wanted the people to draft him, saying that if "a genuine popular demand" arose, he would accept the nomination of the Republican Party. TR had the support of seven governors who urged him to run, and he had them sign a public statement of support. Yet he overplayed his hand in attempting to get the support of the Republican Party. At a speech in Columbus, Ohio, on February 21, Roosevelt proposed that "when a judge decides a constitutional question . . . the people should have the right to recall that decision if they think it is wrong." It was TR's attempt to rein in the courts, which were in thrall to a laissez-faire approach to the economy during this era. Roosevelt believed that the people must be "the masters and not the servants of even the highest court in the land," the "final interpreters of the Constitution." As the *New York Times* reported, this proposal, which applied only to state courts, lost TR any chance to secure the Republican nomination through the normal channels. "Conservatives fled hysterically, charging him with undermining the integrity of the judiciary," Abrams reports.[37]

It turned into an ugly campaign for the nomination, with Roosevelt and Taft throwing invectives at each other. Since Taft had the old guard and the party machinery behind him, Roosevelt dove headlong into campaigning in the newly created presidential primary system in the states that held primaries at that time. He actually did quite well, winning in nine of the thirteen states that held them in 1912. On the Democratic side, Woodrow Wilson was also running as a Progressive. "Perhaps the greatest of Roosevelt's political achievements was that all three of the major candidates in 1912 claimed to be progressive reformers," Skowronek writes. This was not lost on TR, who said, "Wilson and Taft both fervidly announce themselves as Progressives," even though Roosevelt questioned their commitment to the cause.[38]

It all came to a head at the Republican Convention in Chicago, where 250 delegates were in dispute. TR needed to win 70 of those to secure the nomination, but the party regulars awarded most of them to Taft. Roosevelt charged the party bosses with corruption, telling his supporters, "we have the people behind us overwhelmingly . . . we are warring against bossism, against privilege social and industrial." When he bolted the Republican Party to run under the banner of the Bull Moose Party, he handed the election to Woodrow Wilson.[39]

President Woodrow Wilson

No sooner had Wilson been elected governor of New Jersey in 1910 than he began to eye the presidency. One of the great questions that Governor Wilson faced was whether he was truly a Progressive. William Jennings Bryan had begun to move the Democratic Party away from the Jeffersonian commitment to small government, but would Wilson continue in this vein? As a young PhD candidate, Wilson had written "[M]ust not government lay aside all timid scruple and boldly make itself an agency for social reform as well as for political control?" He had never been particularly enamored with Jefferson, preferring Hamilton and John Marshall as exemplars from the founding era, both of whom supported an active role for the federal government.[40]

As he began to consider running for office, Wilson flirted with the conservative Democrats, showing support for limited government and states' rights. In a speech in New York in 1904, he told a group of Democrats they should repudiate "populists and radical theorists." Arthur M. Schlesinger Jr. has written that in 1906 Wilson still opposed "nearly all forms of public intervention in the economy." One of his biographers reports that "Wilson's public and private utterances in 1907 marked his longest stretch toward conservatism." But then he suddenly shifted toward the Progressives. In his 1908 book entitled *Constitutional Government in the United States*, "Wilson again revealed that he had no use for absolutist state-rights, [and] limited government views," Cooper writes. Some of this may have been political expediency, since he saw the popularity that Roosevelt's progressivism had earned him. Wilson admitted as much, saying, "A politician, a man engaged in party contests, must be an opportunist" in order "to lure the majority to your side."[41]

But Wilson had a problem, which was how to be a Democrat while rejecting the core of the party's small-government political philosophy. Wilson began to finesse his views of Jefferson, moving away from Jefferson's reticence about small government when he ran for president. In a speech celebrating Jefferson's birthday in 1911, Wilson talked about how much had changed since the founding era, when "the opportunities of America were so obvious to every man." But now, the great trusts had taken over, limiting equality of opportunity. Government therefore needed to be on the side of the average person and "regulate business, because that is the foundation of every other relationship." He also repudiated Jefferson's view of minimal government, saying it "is one principle of Jefferson's which no longer can [be] obtain[ed] in the practical politics of America." Yet Wilson also equivocated on the role of government, at one point saying: "I do not want a government that will take care of me."[42]

Wilson's pursuit of the presidency was far from a sure thing. He struggled to secure the Democratic nomination against Speaker of the House Champ Clark from Missouri and Oscar Underwood of Alabama, the House majority leader. Wilson finally won the nomination on the forty-sixth ballot when Underwood and William Jennings Bryan threw their support to Wilson. It was Roosevelt's nightmare, since he would have much preferred to face one of the conservative Democrats. Now he and Wilson would vie for the same Progressive voters.[43]

In some ways, Wilson was fortunate in having a united Democratic Party behind him. But this was a bit of a mirage, since there were still many in the party that were supporters of "sound money, lowered tariffs, and states' rights . . . economic individualism . . . laissez-faire, and governmental economy," as Burns writes. While Wilson supported many of these, his shift in support for active government put him at odds with the conservative wing of the party. Wilson also had to deal with the South, which remained the heart of Democratic support. Wilson, as a child of the South, had a view of Black people that fit in with the party, yet cost him little in the election since neither he nor Roosevelt showed interest in the problems that Black people faced in the Jim Crow South.[44]

While Taft and the Socialist Eugene V. Debs were also in the race, everyone knew that either Roosevelt or Wilson would ultimately win. Both Roosevelt and Wilson shared many of the same Progressive views, but they came from very different philosophical perspectives, rooted in the age-old debate in American society over the importance of the group versus the needs of the individual. Roosevelt tilted more to the group and "sometimes used the word 'collectivism' to describe his arguments," Cooper writes. Wilson stressed the individual more and the need to create greater social mobility.[45]

The major policy difference between the two men involved what to do about the trusts, which encapsulates much of their underlying philosophical disputes. Wilson's campaign slogan was dubbed the New Freedom while Roosevelt's was the New Nationalism (taken from Herbert Croly). Roosevelt described the New Nationalism as one that put "the national need before sectional or personal advantage" under a powerful executive. He wanted to call the American people to do great things under the guidance of "leaders inspired by visions of unifying, uplifting national ideals," as Cooper writes. And of course, there was a good dose of the martial spirit in Roosevelt's approach. Whereas Roosevelt wanted to regulate the trusts, Wilson wanted to break them up. "Ours is a program of liberty, and theirs is a program of regulation," Wilson argued. To the extent that the trusts were broken up, then the playing field would be leveled, and average Americans could compete on an equal basis. "If out of the average men we can't get our great men, then we have destroyed the very springs of renewal in the America" in which anyone can "make the best of himself."[46]

One of Wilson's supporters and advisors was the great legal theorist Louis Brandeis. Brandeis's parents had emigrated from Bohemia in 1848, settling in Kentucky. Like Wilson, Brandeis was a Southerner, and the two men also attended Ivy League schools, with Brandeis a graduate of Harvard Law. Brandeis's view of the law was that it should sustain "a politically and economically independent citizenry," the legal scholars Joseph Fishkin and William Forbath have written. Brandeis believed that all Americans "must have a reasonable income . . . health and leisure . . . [and] some system of social insurance." For Brandeis, the key to achieving these goals was the breakup of the large trusts, which he and Wilson agreed on, and in implementing a form of industrial democracy in which the interests of the workers were protected by strong unions.[47]

Despite his skepticism of Jefferson, Wilson shared with Brandeis a belief in the importance of creating greater equality for the individual—a cornerstone of Jeffersonian thought. Both Jefferson and Wilson were optimists when it came to human nature, with a strong belief that, through education, people "could grasp what was best for themselves and ought to be able to follow their dreams and desires with little guidance," as Cooper writes. Roosevelt, who was a disciple of Hamilton, had a pessimistic view of human nature and a top-down view of leadership in which the leader's role was a means to control man's baser instincts. TR also questioned the idea that upward mobility could solve the problems of a modern industrial society. Better to push for "higher wages and safer working conditions for industrial workers" through direct government action. In a rarity for American elections, the campaign turned on large, almost philosophical ideas of freedom, equality, and the individual versus the group.[48]

Ultimately, Wilson swept into office as Taft and Roosevelt split the Republican vote. While Wilson won a landslide in the Electoral College, receiving 435 votes to 88 for Roosevelt and only 8 for Taft, he only won 42 percent of the popular vote. But Democrats also took control of both houses of Congress, giving Wilson the ability to implement his policies.

First-Term Legislative Success

During his inaugural address, Wilson returned to his New Freedom theme. He bemoaned that America had devolved into a place where every man looks out for himself. Only those who were in control of the "giant machinery" of industrialism would be in a position to do that. For everyone else, "there can be no equality of opportunity." As president, Wilson would put into practice his theory, developed over many years, that the executive and legislative branches of government should work together more closely. The president "must be the prime minister, as much concerned with the guidance of legislation, as with the just and orderly execution of the law." In pursuit of legislation that advanced the cause of Progressivism, Wilson would have his greatest accomplishments.[49]

Wilson and the Democrats began with tariff reduction, a goal of theirs since before the Civil War. He was able to defeat attempts to weaken the bill by the protectionist lobby, and overall tariff rates dropped by between 24 and 26 percent. To backfill for the lost revenue, a progressive income tax was implemented, as allowed for by the recently ratified Sixteenth Amendment to the Constitution, which Taft had pushed for.[50]

Ever since Andrew Jackson destroyed the Second Bank of the United States, there had been no central banking system in the United States. Wilson and the Democrats were able to pass legislation implementing the Federal Reserve System. Louis Brandeis helped to craft the legislation and ensure the Federal Reserve would be in the hands of the government, not the banking community. In June of 1913 Wilson went before Congress and argued that "the control of banking . . . must be vested in the Government itself, so that the banks may be the instruments, not the masters, of business . . ." The Federal Reserve Act, which passed in December of 1913, established both a centralized board filled by presidential appointment and a set of regional banks.[51]

On the antitrust issue, Wilson began to change his mind. During the campaign, as we have seen, he proposed to break up the large trusts. Yet under the guidance of Brandeis, he instead decided that Roosevelt's approach of regulation would in fact be better. Brandeis had changed his mind and now believed "that an expert regulatory commission could do a better job than courts in curbing the trusts, because it could stay abreast of constantly changing technological and business conditions," as Cooper frames it. With Wilson's backing, Congress created the Federal Trade Commission to regulate large businesses. They also passed the Clayton Act, which strengthened the hand of government in regulating trusts by banning certain types of activities and included criminal penalties for violations of the law.[52]

The Intrusion of Events

It was a remarkable series of legislative accomplishments, but it also signaled the high-water mark for the entire Progressive movement.

The cycles of history were about to move in a different and more conservative direction over the next several years, in part because the ideal of a laissez-faire approach to economics had not been discredited and had many adherents. But events also began to wear down the Progressive cause, and none were more important than the outbreak of war in Europe in 1914.

"It would be the irony of fate if my administration has to deal chiefly with foreign affairs," Wilson told a friend before he became president. In fact, a whole school of foreign policy would emerge, sometimes referred to as Wilsonian, which posited "that order must also be based on principles of democratic government and the protection of human rights," as the political scientist Walter Russell Mead writes.[53]

As he approached his reelection in 1916, Wilson vowed to keep the United States out of World War I. Meanwhile Congress continued to pass progressive legislation, including a "ban on most child labor, mandating an eight-hour day for railroad workers, and establishing an inheritance tax," as Brands writes. These measures and Wilson's pledge about the war helped him to squeak through and be reelected. Yet it was a pledge he could not keep. In early 1917, Germany announced a policy of "unrestricted submarine warfare against American shipping and the revelation of [a] plan to foment a Mexican war against the United States," historian Michael McGerr succinctly writes. The United States then entered World War I with a goal to "make the world safe for democracy."[54]

Wilson seemed to sense that the war would endanger his progressive agenda. "Every reform we have won will be lost if we go to war." Initially, the war effort increased the scope and size of government, as wars often do. Not only did the United States need to fill an army, which was done through the draft, but "the federal government intervened in all aspects of the economy," as McGerr writes. The Wilson administration established the War Industries Board, which had nearly dictatorial powers in order to obtain supplies for the armed forces. The mining engineer Herbert Hoover, who had done so much to ensure that the Belgians received food during the war, returned to the United State to become the "food czar" for domestic consumption. He soon became known as "the Autocrat of the Breakfast Table" and created slogans like "wheatless days in America make sleepless nights in Germany." No sector of American life was shielded from the reach of the federal government.[55]

If the Gilded Age represented an era of unbridled individualism, then the war years saw a dramatic shift toward centralized governmental power. The delicate balance between the importance of the individual and the group was lost during the war years, with fatal consequences for Progressivism.

Many of the measures that were undertaken had a coercive quality to them. "The liberal spirit of progressivism seemed diametrically opposed to the stern mind set required of a nation at war," according to Brands. None were more troubling than the Espionage Act of 1917 and the Sedition Act of 1918, which were reminiscent of the Alien and Sedition Acts implemented in the late 1790s by the Federalists to stifle dissent during the Quasi-War with France. The Sedition Act of 1918 "prohibited disloyal, profane, scurrilous, or abusive language about the form of government of the United States" or its armed forces. Both laws had a chilling effect on free speech and led to the arrest of the labor leader and Socialist Eugene V. Debs, who had run for president in 1912. Debs was sentenced to ten years in prison for criticizing the government's policy on the war.[56]

In the aftermath of the war, President Wilson was preoccupied with negotiating the Treaty of Versailles, which ended the war, and in implementing the League of Nations, designed to prevent future wars. Wilson did attempt to revive the Progressive agenda, cabling Congress in May 1919 of the need for the United States to implement "a new organization of industry, a genuine democratization of industry" based on "cooperation and partnership based upon a real community of interest and participation in control."[57]

But the war had led to changes in the world that made implementation of pro-government policies difficult at best. Monarchies and regimes that had survived for hundreds of years came crashing down. The Russian Revolution occurred in 1917, whose leaders killed Czar Nicholas II and his family. By November the Bolsheviks had come to power, a communist regime "that condemned capitalism, opposed private property, and had abandoned the Allies to pursue a separate peace with Germany," McGerr writes. Those who supported progressive causes were now labeled as "parlor Bolsheviks" and accused of attempting to implement communism in the United States. Even worse, a "Red Scare" swept the country, led by Attorney General Mitchell Palmer, who staged raids against supposed communists.[58]

It also didn't help that the war had unleashed inflationary pressures. Wilson had ended all price controls after the war ended, which led to an increase in the consumer price index of 105 percent by 1920 over 1916 levels. A depression began to set in. Unions had complied with the demand to keep wages down during the war, but beginning in 1919 they began to push their agenda for higher wages. The year 1919 saw a total of 2,600 strikes, including major ones by the United Mine Workers and the United Steel Workers. Racial strife also spread across the country as Black soldiers returned home from the war only to find the country they had fought for continued to deny them basic rights. The migration of Black Americans from the South to Northern cities continued apace as well. "The result was a chain of race riots," McGerr reports, "largely instigated by the white working class."[59]

To top it all off, Woodrow Wilson, while doggedly pursuing support for the League of Nations in the Senate, suffered a massive stroke in October of 1919. He would not recover his health, nor would he get the Senate to support the league. By the time the presidential election of 1920 rolled around, the country was ready for a less active role for government, and Progressivism was dead—at least for the time being.

Endnotes

1   Stephen Skowronek, *The Politics That Presidents Make: Leadership from John Adams to Bill Clinton* (Cambridge: Belknap Press, 1997), p. 34.

2   Brands, *TR*, p. 417–418; Goodwin, p. 280–281.

3   Skowronek, p. 36–41 and p. 228; Burns, p. 345.

4   Skowronek, p. 236.

5   Goodwin, p. 291 and p. 296; the quotes are from Roosevelt's address to Congress dated December 3, 1901, and were retrieved on January 6, 2022, from https://www.presidency.ucsb.edu/documents/first-annual-message-16.

6   Tim Wu, *The Curse of Bigness: Antitrust in the New Gilded Age* (New York: Columbia Global Reports, 2018), p. 24–25; Goodwin, p. 298–299 and p. 398–399.

7   Jeremi Suri, *The Impossible Presidency: The Rise and Fall of America's Highest Office* (New York: Basic Books, 2017), p. 116; Burns, p. 333.

8   Goodwin, p. 344–346.

9   Skowronek, p. 240–241.

10   Brands, *TR*, p. 504; Goodwin, p. 405–407.

11   John Milton Cooper, *Pivotal Decades: The United States, 1900–1920* (New York: W.W. Norton & Company, 1990), p. 57; Goodwin, p. 407–408 and p. 415–417.

12   Goodwin, p. 421–423.

13   Edmund Morris, *Theodore Rex* (New York: Modern Library, 2001), p. 227.

14   Brands, *TR*, p. 541–548.

15   Cooper, p. 96–97; Skowronek, p. 249.

16   Goodwin, p. 459–461.

17 Goodwin, p. 462–465.

18 Goodwin, p. 465–466; Stephen Skowronek, *Building a New American State: The Expansion of National Administrative Capacities 1877–1920* (Cambridge: Cambridge University Press, 1982), p. 183.

19 Skowronek, *New American State*, p. 254–255.

20 Chambers, p. 182–183.

21 Brands, *TR*, p. 186; Chambers, p. 183; Goodwin, p. 352.

22 Burns, p. 349; Cooper, p. 110–111.

23 James David Barber, *The Presidential Character: Predicting Performance in the White House* (Englewood Cliffs: Prentice Hall, 1992), p. 9 and p. 267.

24 Suri, p. 108–109; Ward and Burns, p. 108–109.

25 Burns, p. 345.

26 Burns, p. 352; Brands, p. 664.

27 Barber, p. 10; Goodwin, p. 21–32.

28 Goodwin, p. 95.

29 Goodwin, p. 274–276.

30 Goodwin, p. 497–500 and p. 14–15.

31 Barber, p. 196–197; Goodwin, p. 549–550.

32 Goodwin, p. 583–599.

33 Goodwin, p. 561; Cooper, *Pivotal Decades*, p. 155; Burns, p. 359.

34 Burns, p. 350.

35 Goodwin, p. 667–668.

36 Cooper, p. 171; Brands, p. 705.

37 Brands, p. 699–702; Goodwin, p. 679; Abrams, p. 79; Fishkin and Forbath, p. 194.

38 Goodwin, p. 696; Skowronek, *The Politics*, p. 258.

39 Brands, p. 713–715.

40 Cooper, *Wilson*, p. 60.

41 Arthur M. Schlesinger Jr., *The Age of Roosevelt: The Crisis of the Old Order 1919–1933* (Cambridge: Riverside Press, 1957), p. 28; Cooper, *Wilson*, p. 98 and p. 106.

42 Cooper, *Wilson*, p. 143; Berg, p. 216–217; Cooper, *Pivotal Decades*, p. 181.

43 Cooper, p. 168–175.

44 Burns, p. 373; Cooper, *Pivotal Decades,* p. 184.

45 John Milton Cooper Jr., *The Warrior and the Priest: Woodrow Wilson and Theodore Roosevelt* (Cambridge: Belknap Press, 1983), p. 215. This section of the book has been greatly influenced by Professor Cooper's analysis of Roosevelt and Wilson, especially how their debates both reflected and diverged from the debates between Hamilton and Jefferson. See especially chapter 14.

46 Cooper, *Pivotal Decades*, p. 183; Cooper, *The Warrior*, p. 214.

47 Fishkin and Forbath, p. 196.

48 Cooper, *Wilson*, p. 178–179; Cooper, *The Warrior*, p. 216.

49 Burns, p. 384; Cooper, *Pivotal Decades,* p. 190–191.

50 Cooper, *Pivotal Decades,* p. 195.

51 Cooper, *Pivotal Decades*, p. 197–198; Brands, *Wilson*, p. 35.

52 Cooper, *Pivotal Decades,* p. 200–201; Brands, *Wilson*, p. 36.

53 Brands, p. 71; Walter Russell Mead, *Special Providence: American Foreign Policy and How It Changed the World* (New York: Knopf, 2001), p. 139.

54 Brands, p. 71–72; McGerr in a *Fierce Discontent* has a very well written analysis in chapter 7 of how the war led to end of the Progressive Era, which I have summarized in this ending section. The quote is from p. 279.

55 McGerr, p. 281–284; William Leuchtenburg, *Herbert Hoover* (New York: Times Books, 2009), p. 33–37.

56 Brands, p. 84; McGerr, p. 289.

57 Schlesinger, *The Age*, p. 40.

58 McGerr, p. 305–307.

59 Cooper, *Pivotal Decades*, p. 323; McGerr, p. 303–304.

CHAPTER 9

The Age of Normalcy

The chief business of the American people is business.
—Calvin Coolidge

The 1920s saw another swing in the cycles of history, featuring a conservative backlash to the Progressive Era. People were exhausted and demanded a "return to normalcy" in the words of President Warren G. Harding in one of his campaign speeches. The Roaring Twenties, as the decade is known, revived laissez-faire economics; however, it was anything but a time of conformity, especially among young people. Politics and society were moving in the same direction, toward greater individualism and away from community concerns. As James MacGregor Burns succinctly summarizes the decade, "the Republican leaders and the business leaders . . . conducted a crowning experiment in America's capitalistic brand of conservatism."[1]

The Politics of the 1920s

"The country yearned for release from the attacks of reformers and the demands made for altruism and self-sacrifice," historian William E. Leuchtenburg writes. The nation found its man in Warren G. Harding, and soon thereafter Calvin Coolidge, who represented the future of the Republican Party. Rather than a conservative party committed to active government, in the mold dating all the way back to the Federalists, the Republicans would hereafter largely be committed to limited government and the primacy of the private marketplace.[2]

Harding was born in 1865 as the Civil War was ending. His father was a doctor and a farmer in a small town in Ohio, and he also had partial ownership of a newspaper. Warren worked on the farm and at the newspaper, and after graduating from college, he purchased his own newspaper with the help of his father, the *Marion Star*. He also launched a weekly version of the newspaper that "was solidly Republican," according to one of his biographers, John Dean (of Watergate fame).[3]

Harding may have been happy running a small-town newspaper, but that all changed when he met and married Florence Kling. She was a demanding wife, so much so that Warren called her "the Boss." Florence was incredibly ambitious and ultimately took over managing the newspaper business so that Warren could run for political office. Harding worked to get McKinley elected in 1896, and he was elected to the Ohio senate in 1899.[4]

In the early 1900s Harding was forced to leave politics to take care of Florence, who had developed nephritis, a form of kidney disease. Once Florence recovered, Harding reentered politics and sided with Taft in 1912 against Roosevelt. "Harding was not opposed to progressive ideas," Dean writes, but thought Roosevelt was motivated by a "personal lust for power" and was angry at Teddy for bolting the Republican Party.[5]

In 1914 Harding got elected to the US Senate. Two years later, he gave the keynote speech to the Republican Convention, appealing for unity between the progressive and conservative wings of the party.

It was his springboard to run for the presidency in 1920. Harding emerged from a deadlocked convention as the moderate conservative, standing for "America First" in the aftermath of the bruising battles over the League of Nations. In one speech he told his audience "America's present need is not heroics, but healing; not nostrums, but normalcy." Harding selected Massachusetts governor Calvin Coolidge as his running mate, and the two men swept to victory in the November election over James M. Cox and Franklin D. Roosevelt. "His popular majority (60.2 percent) was the largest yet recorded in the nation's history," historian Robert K. Murray writes. The Republicans also took control of Congress.[6]

By and large, Harding selected a cabinet of highly qualified men. None was more important than Andrew Mellon, who served as treasury secretary until Hoover left the White House in 1933. He was from a family of Pittsburgh bankers, and by the 1920s he was one of the richest men in the world. "Above all Mellon symbolized the unity between corporate power and the Grand Old Party," Burns writes. For commerce secretary, Herbert Hoover got the nod. He had a reputation as a great humanitarian for his work feeding people during World War I. Yet despite the overall quality of the appointments, Harding also made some terrible selections that would come back to haunt him.[7]

One of the major goals for the Harding administration was to cut taxes on the wealthy and rein in government spending as a way to end the depression that had begun in the aftermath of the war. The depression had occurred when the Federal Reserve raised interest rates to reduce inflation that had soared in the postwar years. President

Wilson had also already begun significant budget cuts as well. Farms prices had dropped in 1921 as Europe was no longer purchasing surplus American foodstuffs, unemployment soared to approximately 20 percent of the workforce, and the gross national product dropped from $89 billion in 1920 to $74 billion in 1921.[8]

The proposed tax cuts were focused on reducing excess profits tax rates and corporate tax rates. "In short, it was a tax break for the rich," according to John Dean. Cutting taxes for the rich proved more difficult. The Senate stood in the way of those portions of the tax-cut plan that most favored the wealthy. Harding was in over his head in dealing with the Senate on the matter since he had very little understanding of tax policy or economics. Ultimately, a more equitable tax-cut plan was passed with "some relief for everyone, rich and poor alike, and represented a typical product of compromise politics," historian Robert K. Murray writes. But this was only a temporary setback for Mellon, who would continue to pursue tax reductions for the rich once Coolidge became president.[9]

Harding had more success in managing the federal budget process. He was able to get the Budget and Accounting Act of 1921 passed, which established the Bureau of the Budget and the General Accounting Office. The act gave the president much greater control over the federal budgeting process. Harding hired an Illinois banker, Charles Dawes, to be the first director, "and in whirlwind performance [he] swiftly made budget control and a reduction in government spending a reality."[10]

In James David Barber's typology, Harding was a passive-positive president, a "responder, not [an] initiator" of policy proposals; in fact, he was a man with limited knowledge of policy. Harding was a good old boy, preferring to golf and play cards with his friends than to do the hard work of a president in providing leadership. He had a "hunger for love," as Barber writes. In the debate over tax policy, he could easily be swayed from one side to another. He told an old friend who visited him in the White House: "I don't know what to do or where to turn on this taxation matter. Somewhere there must be a book that tells all about it. . . . My God, this is a hell of a place for a man like me to be."[11]

Harding's real downfall would be the friends he appointed to high office who turned out to be corrupt. The extent of the corruption would not become fully known until after Harding's death on August 2, 1923, from a massive stroke or a heart attack. Before he died, Harding knew that something was amiss in his administration, telling the reporter William Allen White, "I have no trouble with my enemies . . . but my damn friends . . . keep me walking the floor nights." As became public knowledge after Harding's death, the secretary of the interior, Albert Fall, had leased government oil reserves in both California and Teapot Dome, Wyoming, in return for kickbacks. The attorney general, Harding's campaign manager and good friend Harry Daugherty, "was indicted twice for conspiring to defraud the United States," Barber writes.[12]

Silent Cal

"Silent Cal" Coolidge was sworn in as president of the United States at 2:47 a.m. on August 3, 1923, by his father. He had been in Vermont, visiting his father, who had awakened him at midnight to tell him the news. Coolidge remembered thinking, "I believe I can swing it." He promised to continue Harding's policies and to keep his cabinet, which would soon become problematic as the extent of corruption was revealed. He would ultimately fire Daugherty and support the call for a special counsel to prosecute Fall and others for Teapot Dome.

Coolidge's "air of rectitude" shielded him from the worst impacts of the scandal.[13]

Coolidge was, in some ways, the antithesis of the Roaring Twenties, which saw the Jazz Age, flappers, speakeasies, movies, radio, and the beginning of modern America. With a "disapproving grimace, the dour Coolidge seemed to many a world apart," his biographer David Greenberg writes. Born on July 4, 1872, Coolidge was from the small town of Plymouth Notch in Vermont. It represented the New England Puritan ethic of piety and hard work. Young Cal was a shy boy, but he was also ambitious, and he loved the study of history and politics. He honed his public speaking skills during high school and delivered the graduation address to his class. He attended Amherst College, where he continued to study history, and then went on to law school.[14]

In 1898 Coolidge launched his political career, getting elected to the city council in Northampton. "For the next thirty years he would remain, almost uninterrupted, a holder of public office," Greenberg writes. In 1905 he met his wife, Grace Goodhue, who was described as the "personification of charm." She helped to round him out and add "gaiety . . . style and poise" to the sometimes-austere Coolidge.[15]

Coolidge was a moderate, supporting certain progressive causes like direct election of senators and women's suffrage. He preferred slow change and denounced radicalism. In 1918 he was elected governor of Massachusetts and blended his moderate conservative ideology into support for economy in government and reductions in taxes. Yet he also signed laws "to improve working conditions, regulate landlords, fund new forests, and control outdoor advertising," according to Greenberg. Coolidge was part of a long conservative tradition, dating back to Hamilton and later the Whig Party, that believed there was an overall public interest and that "the needs of business [were] largely congruent to that of the public," as Greenberg writes.[16]

It was Coolidge's actions against labor that ultimately brought him to national attention. When the police went on strike in Boston in 1919, Coolidge called out the National Guard to restore order. The police commissioner, who had triggered the strike by firing those who had formed a union, now fired the entire police force for striking. It was an incredibly harsh action, yet Coolidge, who up to this point did not have a reputation as anti-labor, supported the commissioner. "There is no right to strike against the public safety, by anybody, anywhere, any time," Coolidge said at the time. It's little wonder that Ronald Reagan so admired Coolidge and would emulate him when Reagan fired the air traffic controllers when they went on strike in 1981. Coolidge's actions "tapped a nationwide vein of antagonism to trade unions" according to Greenberg, one that helped Coolidge gain a place on the ticket in 1920 with Harding.[17]

Good Times / Bad Times

Coolidge focused on continuing the Harding policies of reducing taxes and government spending, and paying down the national debt. The economy responded with tremendous growth during his presidency, ending the short but deep depression that occurred in 1920 and 1921. Between 1921 and 1924, the gross national product increased by 9 percent while inflation fell. Unemployment also fell from 11.7 percent to 5 percent. Overall, the economy grew by 42 percent during the 1920s. The growth of the economy matched the mantra of the Coolidge administration that "the chief business of the American people is business."[18]

Cutting taxes, as proposed by Andrew Mellon, was the centerpiece of the Coolidge agenda. In 1924, the top tax rate was reduced to 40 percent (from the 50 percent level in the 1921 law). This was followed by the "1926 Mellon bill [that] provided for across-the-board income tax cuts, zeroed out the gift tax, halved the estate tax, and slashed surtaxes on the wealthy to 20 percent," Greenberg writes. After his election as president in 1980, Ronald Reagan would emulate the Coolidge approach with his own policies for trickle-down economics.[19]

Coolidge also believed that American society should have goals that went beyond the creation of wealth. Wealth needed to be put to good use, to "the multiplication of schools, the increase of knowledge, the dissemination of intelligence, the encouragement of science, the broadening of outlook, the expansion of libraries, the widening of culture." In identifying with a wider goal for society, Coolidge placed himself in the great classical republican tradition dating back to the American founders.

Coolidge was joined in this broader vision of what an industrial society should look like by members of the business community, most prominently Henry Ford. Ford Motor Company had done much to fuel the growth of the early twentieth century. The number of cars had grown from a minuscule 4,000 cars in 1900 to 4.8 million in 1929, and "it stimulated public spending for good roads, extended the housing boom into the suburbs, and created dozens of new small businesses," historian William E. Leuchtenburg writes. Ford, for his part, created a car company that pioneered high wages for its workers and reflected the model of the enlightened businessman of the era. In 1914 he offered a wage of five dollars a day, nearly double the going wage. However, this came with a price: "the production line was speeded up, lunch breaks were cut to fifteen minutes, and trips to the toilet were limited to three minutes," according to Nathan Miller. It was through improved manufacturing processes for producing his famous Model T that Ford was able to drop prices from $850 in 1908 to $265 in the 1920s. Ford built cars for the middle class.[20]

Ford wasn't the only businessman to have a broader view of the role of the corporation beyond profit. As Leuchtenburg has written, business owners implemented a program of welfare capitalism. "They built clean, trim, well lighted factories with safety devices to forestall injury. They installed cafeterias . . . and instituted group insurance plans and introduced profit sharing." Later, in the aftermath of the New Deal and World War II, businessmen would come to embrace the role of government in promoting a sound economy. Business owners and their managers should deal "frankly with his employees, pay the highest wages, and promote the self-interest of the workingman," Paul Hoffman of Studebaker would later remark, which included "belonging to a union."[21]

The prosperity of the times "was widespread enough to change markedly the life of millions of Americans," Leuchtenburg writes. It was not just the widespread sale of cars, but the expansion of electricity that brought light into homes, eased domestic chores through electric appliances, and allowed for entertainment right in the home through the radio. Spectator sports like boxing and baseball also took off during the 1920s, as did the opening of movie theaters. There was much to admire about the Roaring Twenties.[22]

Continuing Problems

Still there were continuing problems that Calvin Coolidge ignored. He was a passive-negative president who had a "readiness to pull away from problems, to wait them out," as Barber writes. Greenberg adds that there were "too many problems left unaddressed, [that] mounted; too many causes languished unpursued. His constricted vision of his office crippled him." Yet in his approach, he reflected the times he lived in. The *New Republic* wrote, "Mr. Coolidge has not seen the vision of an America better than the America of which he is president."[23]

But ignoring problems will not make them go away. Unsurprisingly, the 1920s saw the renewed concentration of business, which was encouraged by both the Harding and Coolidge administrations. The number of annual mergers expanded rapidly and were four times higher in 1929 that in 1921. Both corporate and individual income became more concentrated. "By 1928, 5 percent of the population possessed more than one third of the disposable income in the country, up from 24 [percent] at the start of the decade," Abrams writes. By 1929, more than half of the country's population had income levels that were below what was needed to maintain a "decent standard of living," according to the Bureau of Labor Statistics.[24]

Standards of living were sustained by a substantial increase in debt for many of the American people. The rapid rise in the number of automobiles was in part due to the introduction of financing through credit. In 1919, General Motors began its own credit system with the introduction of the General Motors Acceptance Corporation. The cost for borrowing was quite high during the 1920s, with interest rates of up to 30 percent for the purchase of a new car. The level of demand, and thus economic growth, was being propped up by an unsustainable level of debt.[25]

Part of the problem for many may have been related to the struggles of organized labor. While this was the dawn of the age of welfare capitalism, at least part of the motivation for this was an attempt by businesses to eliminate unions. Employers now pushed the idea of the "open shop" in which employees were not required to join a union. Corporations also created company unions to which almost 1.4 million Americans belonged in 1926. It was the Supreme Court of the 1920s that continued a hostile legal environment for unions. Former president William Howard Taft, now the chief justice, sent "the law on labor relations reeling backward into the nineteenth century," according to Abrams, using antitrust laws against unions rather than corporations. Between 1920 and 1933, the percentage of people in unions fell from 12 to 6 percent of the workforce.[26]

The 1920s were also a time of great stress for the American farmer. Farm prices crashed in 1920 in the aftermath of the war, as European farms began to produce food once again for domestic consumption. By 1924, farms prices began to rise, but the farmers' share of national income continued to shrink, from roughly 25 percent of gross domestic product in 1900 to 12 percent in 1925. The McNary-Haugen plan proposed that farm surpluses be dumped overseas to raise prices, but the plan's success was doubtful. Numerous "leaders pointed out that such a policy would raise domestic food prices unnaturally high, impinging on the mass of the urban working population," Abrams writes. Coolidge twice vetoed the legislation, although he failed to provide any alternatives.[27]

Fundamentalism, Nativism, and Racism

Changes that had been occurring in American society starting in the aftermath of the Civil War sent rural areas in a more fundamental direction. As Richard Hofstadter has observed, "The United States was born in the country and has moved to the city." By the 1920s, many in rural America had begun to question the opinion of experts and especially the dominance that science was beginning to achieve in America. Science challenged the long-held religious beliefs of many, especially the view that the Bible was literally true.[28]

The debate between science and religion reached it apex when John Scopes was tried for teaching Darwinian evolution in Tennessee. In 1925 the legislature had made it illegal "for any teacher . . . to teach any theory that denies the story of the divine creation of man as taught in the Bible." William Jennings Bryan, the former Democratic nominee for president and the secretary of state for Wilson, prosecuted the case. Clarence Darrow, who was "the most famous defense lawyer in the country," defended Scopes. Ultimately, Scopes was found guilty and fined one hundred dollars, but the most interesting element of the trial was when Darrow called Bryan to the stand. "Bryan was revealed by Darrow's devasting probing to be a man of dense ignorance," Leuchtenburg writes. Still, both the law that Tennessee passed and the trial itself showed how rural Americans were willing to use the legislative process to stop changes they found threatening.[29]

Religious fundamentalism was not the only reaction to modernity. Politically the country took a turn toward nativism during the 1920s, rejecting all things foreign. Part of this reflected disenchantment with the war effort. Americans had begun to resent involvement in foreign wars and feared being "infected by the social diseases of the old world," including class conflict and communism. The expansion of immigration in the aftermath of the war, which was needed to fuel the growth of industry, set off a backlash, as so often happens in American history. Between 1921 and 1924, net immigration to the United States totaled over 1.7 million people. This led to the introduction of the National Origins Act of 1924, and immigration plunged by two-thirds by 1925.[30]

The 1920s also saw the rebirth of the Ku Klux Klan, a movement committed to the supremacy of the white race. In its new form, it was not just opposed to Black people but also to Jews, Catholics, and foreigners. The Klan's members in the North were largely from small-town America and were protesting the rise of cities, the control of society by urban elites, and the birth of a multi-ethnic society. The Klan tapped into "inchoate grievances of the underclass against big business and economic exploitation," Miller writes. Where the Klan rose, violence soon followed against all those they opposed.[31]

Northern membership in the Klan was at least partly fostered by the Great Migration that took place from the South during World War I and in the years afterward. As Isabel Wilkerson has written, Black people came north and west to escape the caste system of the South. With immigration cut off during the war, Black Americans were recruited to fill industrial jobs in cities like New York, Chicago, Detroit, and Philadelphia. A total of a million Black people may have moved north during the war, and ultimately close to half of all Black Americans left the South, remaking the cities of the North. Whites resented the intrusion of Black people into their midst. "Nerves were rubbed raw on both sides as the races jostled for limited housing and jobs, on the streets and in the shops of the overcrowded cities," according to Miller.[32]

Racial tensions during and in the aftermath of World War I led to significant racial strife even before the 1920s. African American veterans, who had fought in a war to save democracy, returned home to find that the benefits of democracy were denied to them. There were race riots in Houston and east Saint Louis during the war, and in 1919 there was extensive racial violence against African Americans in cities like Chicago, San Francisco, and Wilmington, Delaware. One of the most deadly incidents occurred in Tulsa, Oklahoma, in 1921. White mobs attacked and destroyed the Black neighborhood of Greenwood. It was one of the worst race riots in American history, with hundreds killed and many thousands left homeless.[33]

The problems that African Americans continued to face were fertile ground for the rise of new, more militant leadership. Booker T. Washington, born enslaved, represented an accommodationist approach to race relations. "In matters purely social we may be as separate as fingers, but as the one hand in matters essential to mutual progress." Washington did make progress in helping African Americans gain literacy and become property owners, and he also worked to end segregation and discrimination. But many in the Black community were looking for change to occur faster than Washington's approach could yield.[34]

Some looked to Marcus Garvey, the Jamaican immigrant, for leadership. In 1914, he organized the Universal Negro Improvement Association. It was a movement for Black nationalism, Black separatism, and Black pride. Garvey came to the United States in 1916, and by 1924 he was proposing that African Americans return to Africa. It was reminiscent of attempts in the early 1800s by the American Colonization Society to emancipate and colonize former enslaved people in Africa, which most Black abolitionists opposed. Garvey's proposal was not much more successful. His biographer writes that not many African Americans "seriously entertained the idea of a return to the African homeland." Still, Garvey instilled a sense "that black skin was not a badge of shame but rather a glorious symbol" of pride.[35]

Another important leader was the Harvard intellectual W. E. B. Du Bois. By the early part of the twentieth century, Du Bois had begun to reject Washington's focus on "material wellbeing" and instead wanted African Americans to focus on "higher education for intellectual and political leadership," Cooper writes. In 1909, Du Bois helped to form the National Association for the Advancement of Colored People (NAACP), and he became the editor of its magazine the *Crisis*. Like Garvey, Du Bois wanted Black people to "embrace their African heritage even as they worked and lived in the United States," as the NAACP website writes. In his role as the editor of the *Crisis*, Du Bois focused attention on the problem of lynching in the South and advocated for Congress to outlaw such killings. The NAACP would come to be known as the leading protest organization for Black Americans.[36]

Youth and Cultural Ferment

The 1920s were a decade of cultural ferment among the young, many of whom rejected the fundamentalism of the countryside. The youth were protesting the conformity, conservatism, and consumerism of the age. But the protests of the young had one overriding characteristic in common with the establishment: they were grounded in individualism.

Perhaps no two people reflected the views of the young more than F. Scott Fitzgerald and his wife, Zelda. Named for Francis Scott Key, who wrote "The Star-Spangled Banner," Fitzgerald was raised in Saint Paul, Minnesota. After returning from the war in 1919, Fitzgerald was a struggling writer who was still being supported by his parents at the age of twenty-two. He had met Zelda in 1918 in Montgomery, Alabama, while he was still in the service. Because his prospects seemed so poor, she initially refused to marry him. But then his first novel, *This Side of Paradise*, was published just before he turned twenty-three, bringing Scott both success and Zelda. "Over the next few months, his life became the concrete expression of the American dream of easy, overnight success that is a persistent theme of the Jazz Age (a term that Fitzgerald coined)," according to Miller.[37]

Like so many of their generation who were bored with the conformity of life in the 1920s and who rejected a traditional lifestyle, the Fitzgeralds moved to France. They were not alone. So too did Ernest Hemingway, John Dos Passos, and approximately thirty-two thousand other Americans. They mingled with Gertrude Stein and her companion, Alice B. Toklas, at her apartment. "You are a lost generation . . . you have no respect for anything. You drink yourselves to death," Stein told Hemingway.[38]

Stein may have been onto something. The young during the 1920s blamed their parents for the state of society and a war that was fought to save democracy but had done no such thing. Fitzgerald was, in many ways, their spokesman, depicting the world of the young, who "drank and smoked and petted in the rumble seats of roadsters in reckless defiance of what was regarded as proper behavior," as Miller frames it. Both F. Scott and Zelda lived a bohemian lifestyle—in Paris and when they returned to New York. Here are some of the descriptions that Miller provides:[39]

> Scott stripping at the theater and being thrown out by the ushers

> Zelda dancing the Charleston on tables at parties while Scott got into drunken fights with waiters

> Scott doing headstands in the lobby of the Biltmore

> Zelda sitting on the roof of a taxi while Scott straddled the hood

Zelda may have been a bit more unrestrained than most, which might have contributed to her taking an overdose of sleeping pills in 1924. But mores were changing for many women during the 1920s, with more women joining the workforce. By 1927, one in five wage earners were women, although they made much less than men and many were poorly paid. Hemlines for women's dresses and skirts were being raised from the ankle to just below the knee. Drinking among college students was widespread for both men and women despite Prohibition. "For the first time—and in a prelude to the Sixties—the nation's youth rather than their elders set the standards for American society," Miller writes.[40]

Sexual repression, which was so prevalent in traditional American society, was rejected by many of the young. "The anti-Puritan revolt . . . [was] a generalized revolt against everything that is hard, narrow and intolerant in the old American life, and which sees sexual repression as its most potent symbol of attack," one anthropologist has written. The youth of the era were self-absorbed in so many ways. No attempts were made to improve society or to work through government or nonprofit organizations to improve society. Cynicism was the hallmark of the 1920s. While the youth rejected much of traditional society, no attempts were made to bind people together in community to solve the problems of the day.[41]

🖝🖝🖝

"History doesn't repeat itself, but it does rhyme," is a quote often attributed to Mark Twain. The alternative lifestyles of the young during the 1920s reminds one of the 1960s. However, there was nothing new about the nativism and racism of the era in American history. Racism goes all the way back to the original Virginia colony and the introduction of slavery in 1619. Our founding generation feared non-British immigrants coming to the shores of America, and numerous times in our past nativism has arisen when large numbers of immigrants have come to the United States. Even after the Civil War and the constitutional amendments that banned slavery and promised equality for all, Black people were increasingly isolated from the main-stream of American life. The Populists had ejected Black Americans from the Farmers' Alliance. During the Progressive Era, despite its liberalism, Jim Crow laws continued to expand in the South; it was an era when most Black people were disenfranchised. Even those who escaped the South faced continuing discrimination in the North. "In many Northern cities Jim Crow was a culturally sanctioned reality, often enforced with violence," Putnam and Garrett write. Woodrow Wilson resegregated federal public service.[42]

Writing from the perspective of the early 2020s, it feels like our current world is once again rhyming with this part of our past. African Americans are still subject to systematic racism and predatory policing. Immigrants are unwelcome. Many in rural America feel ignored and put down by those who live in cities and on the coasts, sensing a loss of status and a fear that their existing way of life is being threatened. We have seen a recent resurgence of white supremacy, encouraged and exploited by Donald Trump, who rode the issues of white fear, racism, and nativism to the White House in 2016.

And in one other area we can see how the late 1920s compares to our own age: the economic collapse of 1929.

The Economic Storm on the Horizon

Booms and busts are a natural occurrence in a capitalist society. But predicting when one will occur is another matter. The economist Paul Samuelson once said that the stock market had predicted nine of the last five recessions. But beginning in 1927, the rapidly rising stock market would be an early indicator that the economy was on the precipice of disaster.

The stock market was on a wild upswing as Calvin Coolidge left office, to be replaced by Herbert Hoover (more on Hoover in the next chapter). Hoover had criticized Coolidge for ignoring the warning signs. "The outstanding instance was the rising boom and orgy of mad speculation which began in 1927, in respect to which [Coolidge] rejected or sidestepped all of our anxious urgings and warnings to take action." Coolidge, for his part, did not think much of Hoover either. "That man has offered me unsolicited advice for six years, all of it bad."[43]

The big run-up in the stock market at the end of the 1920s was fueled by margin buying of stocks in which a purchaser need only make a down payment of from 10 to 50 percent, with the balance of the funding coming from brokers' call loans. The stock itself served as collateral for the loan, and if the stock went down, the broker could then call the loan. Broker loans had increased rapidly, from around $1.5 billion in the early twenties to over $6 billion by the end of 1928. The "lust for the fast buck had loosed all restraints of financial prudence or even common sense," historian David M. Kennedy writes.[44]

The Federal Reserve attempted to tamp down speculation in the summer of 1929 when it raised its rediscount rate (the interest rate it charges banks) to 6 percent. But by then, it was too little too late. Call loans returned from 12 to up to 20 percent for banks, and the speculator could make as much as "500 percent on the appreciation in the value of his investment," economist John Kenneth Galbraith writes. By September of 1929, one observer noted, "Sooner or later a crash is coming, and it may be terrific." The high point of the market was in September, but the actual crash came on October 29, Black Tuesday. "By mid-November some $26 billion, roughly a third of the value of stocks recorded in September, had evaporated," according to Kennedy.[45]

The collapse of economies all over the world would not be far behind. Several countries were already falling into a recession from the Federal Reserve's interest rate increase since much of the world had become dependent on American credit. Americans also began to cut back on their borrowing and spending in the wake of the collapse of the stock market. "People felt that the ground under their feet was giving way," the economist Joseph Schumpeter would later write. As demand dried up, factories would begin to close, and banks would soon fail.[46]

One of the major problems that contributed to the Great Depression was expanding inequality, which meant that demand for products could not be sustained. While the 1920s had seen a major increase in income and wealth, most of the increase was concentrated at the top, with 0.01 percent of American families controlling income that was equal to what the bottom 42 percent earned. "Stated in absolute numbers, approximately 24,000 families had a combined income as large as that shared by more than 11.5 million poor and lower-middle class families," the historian Robert S. McElvaine points out. While productivity had increased rapidly during the 1920s, the gains were not shared equally: productivity had increased by 32 percent; wages had increased by only 8 percent. Although overall income rose by 9 percent, the top 1 percent received 75 percent of the income gain. Wealth inequality was even worse, with the top 0.5 percent owning 32 percent of all net wealth. "This represented the highest concentration of wealth at any time in American history," McElvaine writes. Given this, there simply was not enough money in the hands of enough people to sustain a mass-consumption society, which had been propped up with easy credit.[47]

Most experts agree "that the precipitous drop in American stocks on Black Tuesday . . . didn't trigger the Great Depression," Joyce

Appleby writes. In fact, by April of 1930 stocks had regained much of their value. The American Economic Association "predicted recovery by June 1930." But as we know today, that would not be the case as what is now called the Great Depression began to set in, as aggregate demand for goods and services collapsed.[48]

Endnotes

1   Burns, p. 484; see also https://en.wikipedia.org/wiki/Return_to_normalcy.

2   William Leuchtenburg, *The Perils of Prosperity: 1914–32* (Chicago: University of Chicago Press, 1958), p. 84.

3   John W. Dean, *Warren G. Harding* (New York: Times Books, 2004), p. 5–13.

4   Dean, p. 21–23.

5   Dean, p. 27–29.

6   Dean, p. 34–40; Robert K. Murray, *The Politics of Normalcy: Governmental Theory and Practice in the Harding-Coolidge Era* (New York: W.W. Norton, 1973), p. 1–2.

7   Burns, p, 486.

8   Nathan Miller, *New World Coming: The 1920s and the Making of Modern America* (Cambridge: Da Capo Press, 2004), p. 87; Dean, p. 105; information on the causes of the depression of 1920 was from "In the Shadow of the Slump: The Depression of 1920–21," retrieved April 22, 2022, from https://econreview.berkeley.edu/in-the-shadow-of-the-slump-the-depression-of-1920-1921/.

9   Dean, p. 107; Murray, p. 58.

10 Murray, p. 49.

11 Barber, p. 212.

12 Barber, p. 210 and p. 213; Leuchtenburg, p. 93.

13 David Greenberg, *Calvin Coolidge* (New York: Times Books, 2006), p. 43–44 and p. 51–52.

14 Greenberg, p. 5–21.

15 Greenberg, p. 21–22.

16 Greenberg, p. 24–33.

17 Greenberg, p. 29–31.

18 Miller, p. 149.

19 Greenberg, p. 72, p. 80, p. 128.

20 Leuchtenburg, p. 186; John Steele Gordon, *An Empire of Wealth: The Epic History of American Economic Power* (New York: Harper Perennial, 2005), p. 297–298.

21 Leuchtenburg, p. 201; Jacob Hacker and Paul Pierson, *American Amnesia: How The War on Government Led Us to Forget What Made America Prosper* (New York: Simon & Schuster, 2016), p. 141–142.

22 Leuchtenburg, p. 194–197.

23 Barber, p. 179; Greenberg, p. 14.

24 Abrams, p. 151; Miller, p. 282.

25 Kennedy, p. 22; Eric Rauchway, *The Great Depression & The New Deal: A Very Short Introduction* (Oxford: Oxford University Press, 2008), p. 13–14 .

26 Abrams, p. 153–154; Philip Dray, *There Is Power in a Union: The Epic Story of Labor in America* (New York: Doubleday, 2010), p. 411–412.

27 Leuchtenburg, p. 100–103; Abrams, p. 156–157.

28 Hofstadter, p. 23.

29 Leuchtenburg, p. 218–223.

30 Leuchtenburg, p. 204–206; Roger Daniels, *Coming to America: A History of Immigration and Ethnicity in American Life* (New York: Perennial, 2002), p. 287–288.

31 Leuchtenburg, p. 208–211; Miller p. 144.

32 For a masterful account of the Great Migration, see Isabel Wilkerson, *The Warmth of Other Suns: The Epic Story of America's Great Migration* (New York: Random House, 2010); Miller, p. 48–50.

33 Information about racial violence was retrieved on May 18, 2022, from https://www.history.com/topics/roaring-twenties/tulsa-race-massacre and https://billofrightsinstitute.org/essays/postwar-race-riots.

34 Cooper, *Pivotal*, p. 74–76.

35 E. David Cronon, *Black Moses: The Story of Marcus Garvey and the Universal Negro Improvement Association* (Madison: University of Wisconsin Press, 1969), p. 128 and p. 4.

36 Cooper, *Pivotal*, p. 77–78; the quotes from the NAACP were retrieved on May 19, 2022, from https://naacp.org/find-resources/history-explained/civil-rights-leaders/web-du-bois.

37 Miller, p. 3–10.

38 Miller, p. 199–203.

39 Miller, p. 210.

40 Miller, p. 255–259.

41 Abrams, p. 184.

42 Putnam and Garrett, p. 222.

43 David M. Kennedy, *Freedom from Fear: The American People in Depression and War 1929–1945* (New York: Oxford University Press, 1999), p. 34.

44 Kennedy, p. 36–37; John Kenneth Galbraith, *The Great Crash 1929* (London: Penguin, 1954), p. 22–23.

45 Galbraith, p. 31 and p. 76; Kennedy, p. 38.

46 Rauchway, p. 12 and p. 19.

47 Robert S. McElvaine, *The Great Depression: America, 1929–1941* (New York: Times Books, 1993), p. 38–40.

48 Kennedy, p. 40.

CHAPTER 10

Two Extraordinary Men

Progress is born of cooperation in the community—not from governmental restraints.
  —HERBERT HOOVER

It is common sense to take a method and try it. If it fails, admit it frankly, and try another. But above all, try something.
  —FRANKLIN D. ROOSEVELT

Herbert Hoover was an extraordinary man. Orphaned at a young age, he learned to be self-reliant and to rise through hard work, ultimately being elected president in 1928. But his life story, and specifically his underlying philosophy of voluntarism, doomed him during the Great Depression.

Hoover was an active-negative president who struggled to get along with people. Given this, he was a poor politician. One of his friends said of him that he lacked "the least appreciation of the poetry, the music, and the drama of politics." As an engineer, he lacked the ability to govern with his "heart no less than [his] mind," as one of his biographers wrote, and he was incredibly inflexible once he made a decision.[1]

Franklin D. Roosevelt too was an extraordinary man. He was raised in a patrician household, a part of the old-money aristocracy of New York, and a distant cousin of President Theodore Roosevelt, whom he modeled himself after. Polio would change Roosevelt, helping to make him empathetic to the less fortunate, and to understand the need to rely on others. More than anything, polio made FDR a pragmatist, which would help him to deal with the Great Depression.

Franklin D. Roosevelt was an active-positive president, one of "those who appear to have fun in the vigorous exercise of Presidential power," Barber writes. He was an eternal optimist. Having conquered polio (even though he would never walk again), he believed he could conquer anything. That optimism would help the country to survive during the depths of the Great Depression. One of the hallmarks of Roosevelt's life was a willingness to experiment with new ideas and ways of doing things. To the active-positive president, "the future is not set . . . it is not to be mastered by some mechanical application of 'principles,' but by imaginative experimentation," according to Barber. This, more than anything else, described the difference in leadership style between these two extraordinary men.[2]

Herbert Hoover

Herbert Hoover was born in Iowa in 1874 to a Quaker family. His father was a successful businessman who became a city council member in their hometown of West Branch. His mother was known for her piety. His Quaker upbringing helped to mold young Bertie, as he was known, and to inculcate a view of the world that included self-reliance along with a duty to "good works" and "trust in a community of neighbors to sustain the needy," as his biographer William E. Leuchtenburg writes.[3]

Orphaned at the age of eleven, Bertie had to learn self-reliance by direct experience, living with his uncle John in Oregon. Hoover would ultimately end up at a new university in California, Stanford, where he was admitted provisionally because he had little by way of formal education. It was at Stanford that he found his great loves: geological engineering and his future wife, Lou. After graduating, he was hired as a mining engineer and sent to Australia in 1896, where he began a very successful career and made his fortune. In between assignments, Hoover returned to the United States in 1899 and married Lou, and the two set off for his next job in China. Travel would help to open Herbert Hoover's worldview, to see firsthand the problems of the poor in so many parts of the world.[4]

Success in business was not enough for Hoover, who wanted to leave a more lasting mark on society. He told his friends that "just making money wasn't enough." By 1909 he was back at Stanford, where he met the sociologist Thorstein Veblen and began to develop a more progressive mind set. He became a supporter of an eight-hour workday and saw the need for organized labor. He supported Theodore Roosevelt in the election of 1912.[5]

Just as World War I broke out, Hoover went to London to work on the Panama-Pacific International Exposition. It was during the war that Hoover made his reputation as a great humanitarian. He organized an effort to help Americans get back to their country. He was then asked by the American government to assist with the dire situation in Belgium. "The Belgians faced mass starvation within two weeks" when Hoover was called on to help. Hoover agreed to head the Commission for Relief in Belgium, where he performed a secular miracle. Early on, he put his own money on the line to ensure that food was available to the starving Belgians. By the time the war ended, over five million tons of food had been delivered. Hoover drew another lesson from his work feeding the starving Belgians—that it was voluntary action that saved the day, and "that one should rely not on government but on civic-minded individuals" to solve even the most daunting challenges. This opinion ignored the fact that 80 percent of the funding for the relief effort came from governments.[6]

Hoover's approach to humanitarianism was oddly impersonal. As Joan Hoff Wilson, one of his biographers, writes, Hoover "never referred privately or publicly to the human suffering of any of the war victims." It was as if feeding people was another engineering problem. Hoover could also be quite abrasive in how he treated governmental officials that he thought stood in the way of achieving his goals. The US ambassador to Belgium, Brand Whitlock, said that Hoover was "always trying to force, blackmail, to frighten people into doing things his way. . . . What a bully!" It was this side of his personality, which showed a cold callousness toward people, that would cause him so much trouble in dealing with the Great Depression.[7]

The other personality characteristic that would impact Hoover during the Great Depression was inflexibility. Hoover had a well-developed philosophy of public life, as described in his book, *American Individualism*, which was published in 1922. His philosophy combined individualism with voluntarism. It was in many ways a remarkable work that combined the two great strands we have been evaluating throughout this book: classical liberalism, with its focus on the importance of the individual; and classical republicanism, grounded in the need for a community response to resolve common problems. Hoover, through his work during the war, had become committed to "the use of voluntarily decentralized groups to carry out nationally coordinated programs," as Hoff Wilson frames it. It was an "attempt to reconcile individualism and cooperation through voluntarism."[8]

Hoover's development of an overarching political philosophy put him in good company with the founding generation, including men like Madison, Jefferson, and Hamilton. Lincoln too had developed a fine-tuned approach to public life during the 1850s. Yet the difference between each of these men and Hoover was that when political realities changed, they were flexible enough to change their philosophy. Madison had been one of the main architects of the newly strengthened central government under the Constitution but went into opposition when he opposed the policies his friend Hamilton began to implement. Jefferson was a strict constructionist when it came to the Constitution, yet he abandoned this view when it endangered the Louisiana Purchase. Lincoln began the Civil War with a goal to preserve the Union, but ultimately decided the war provided an opportunity for a new birth of freedom when he issued the Emancipation Proclamation and freed the Black people being enslaved in the states that had seceded.

Hoover's abrasive personality would also continue to haunt him. As commerce secretary, Hoover became an empire builder. "His singular incursions into other jurisdictions—State, Interior, Treasury, Agriculture, Labor—elicited the well circulated quip that Hoover was Secretary of Commerce and Under Secretary of all other departments." This, of course, caused friction, not only with fellow cabinet members but also with President Coolidge.[9]

Yet his policy positions could not be easily pegged. As we have seen, Hoover was a progressive on a number of issues, including taxes. He wanted to tax the rich at a higher rate than the middle class and thought that the poor should pay no income tax at all. He favored conservation measures. He thought that government had a role to play in fighting economic downturns, but that this should occur by leading voluntary action. "I am a strong believer in the Government intervening to induce active co-operation in the community itself." But the one thing he did not support was action by the government to directly assist individuals. He warned against "government doles and other fallacious remedies," which were "not consonant with the spirit of the American people . . ." Hoover's underlying philosophy would ultimately contribute to his downfall.[10]

Franklin D. Roosevelt

For those who think that being a great president can be accomplished without being a great politician, the case studies of Hoover and Roosevelt reveal this is a specious claim.

Franklin Delano Roosevelt was a natural politician in the best sense of the word; Herbert Hoover was a great technician but a poor politician.

The word *politician* carries both negative and positive descriptions. A quick survey of the internet reveals the following types of descriptions for a politician:

Attributes of a Politician

Negative	Positive
Unscrupulous	Astute
Shrewd	Complex
Cunning	Masterful
Pompous	Reputable
Ruthless	Enlightened

FDR no doubt had some of each of these characteristics, which is what made him a great politician and ultimately a great president, often rated as one of the top three, along with Lincoln and Washington. Machiavelli famously wrote that a prince must "imitate the fox and the lion, for the lion cannot protect himself from traps, and the fox cannot defend himself from the wolves." James MacGregor Burns was so enamored with how FDR reflected these two qualities that he titled one of his books *Roosevelt: The Lion and the Fox*. It is an apt description of the man.

Franklin D. Roosevelt was born in January 1882, the only child of James Roosevelt and Sara Delano. He was fifty-three, she twenty-six when they married. James's first wife had died, and he already had one son from his first marriage, who was the same age as Sara. Obviously, the Roosevelts had a long and distinguished lineage in America, but so too did the Delanos, whose first ancestor came on the *Mayflower*. Sara always considered Franklin more a Delano than a Roosevelt. She was tall, well traveled, and a bit intimidating, a woman who may have needed an older man to stand up to her.[11]

Franklin was the center of his parents' world, and they bred into him the optimism and self-confidence that would define his personality. Sara was determined to raise him as a Delano, "which meant to raise him as she had been raised under the benign discipline of her father," FDR biographer Jean Edward Smith writes. Sara was the most important person in his life from a parenting perspective, while his father was more like a friend. They traveled, hunted, fished, and sailed together. "Went fishing yesterday afternoon with papa, we caught a dozen minnows," he wrote to his mother when he was six.[12]

Roosevelt spent most of his early life in the company of his parents and other adults, and he traveled widely in Europe, much as his cousin Theodore had. It gave him "an uncommon intuitive capacity and interpersonal intelligence," which allowed Franklin "to read the intentions and desires of his parents," Goodwin writes. But it also meant that he had little experience in getting along with other children. In 1896 his parents sent him to Groton, two years after the other students had started. "The other boys had formed their friendships. They knew things he didn't; he felt left out," Eleanor would later find out from Franklin. It was young Roosevelt's first chance to develop his skill at adapting to uncomfortable circumstances, and he never divulged his true feeling to his parents, telling them, "He was getting on very well with the fellows." He would eventually decide to get into a bit of trouble to better fit in. "I managed to get three or four black marks this week," he proudly wrote his parents in his second year at Groton.[13]

FDR learned early in life the need to conceal certain thoughts and feelings. It was an outgrowth of being raised by an overbearing mother who made him the center of her universe but also tried to dominate his life. He would make some of his most important decisions on his own and only let her know afterward. This gave an inscrutable element to Roosevelt's personality, causing many to feel they never completely knew his inner core. One of his advisors would later say, "you . . . keep your cards close up against your belly." Another said that "there was another Roosevelt behind the one we saw and talked with." Roosevelt recognized this in himself, once saying: "Never let your left hand know what your right is doing."[14]

Tragedy struck Roosevelt during his freshman year at Harvard when his father, who had fallen ill with heart disease during his time at Groton, died. "Suddenly Franklin was forced to take stock of his position, desires, and ambitions," Goodwin writes. He was a mediocre student but found his true calling working on the *Harvard Crimson*, telling his mother, "I am working about 6 hours a day" on the paper. In the future, he would always refer to himself as a newspaperman. His leadership skills began to develop from his work on the *Crimson*. While he sometimes came across as cocky and conceited to some, others found him "quick witted" and "a very good companion." One of his biographers has written that "at Groton, Roosevelt learned to get along with his contemporaries; at Harvard he learned to lead them."[15]

It is worth spending some time on Franklin D. Roosevelt's relationship with his wife, Eleanor. Of all the decisions Roosevelt hid from his mother, none was more important than his decision to marry Eleanor. She was the daughter of Teddy's brother Elliot. Eleanor lost her mother when she was eight, and then Elliot died two years later of alcoholism. At this point in her life, Eleanor felt lost, but she was able to regain her footing when she attended boarding school in England under the tutelage of Marie Souvestre.[16]

Franklin found Eleanor "irresistible" in the words of historian Robert Dallek. She was very bright and her "social consciousness . . . far exceeded his," according to Goodwin. Sara made them wait a year to marry, believing they were too young, since he was only twenty-one and she eighteen. Sara also dominated their early years of marriage, purchasing two houses in New York with a common entrance. "Granny's ace in hole . . . was the fact that she held the purse strings in the family," James Roosevelt, the second child of Franklin and Eleanor, later explained.[17]

Eleanor proved to be a great partner for FDR's political career, although he was unfaithful to her. They ultimately stayed together after Franklin's affair with Lucy Mercer when Sara threatened to cut him off from his inheritance should they divorce. Their relationship would never be the same again and would become more of a partnership than a deeply affectionate marriage. "Eleanor apparently also refused to have future intimacy with her husband," Dallek writes.[18]

With Eleanor's support, Franklin's political ascent had begun, following in the footsteps of his cousin Theodore. He went from the state senate in New York to undersecretary of the Navy when Wilson became president, and became the vice presidential candidate in 1920 on the Democratic ticket. But there was something missing in the young Franklin. He was a bit too arrogant, a bit too much of the patrician. Frances Perkins, who would go on to work for FDR in both Albany and Washington, DC, remembered how "disagreeable" young Roosevelt was. "He had a youthful lack of humility, a streak of self-righteousness," about him. Others described him as a "dilettante," "a damn fool," and a "stage dandy." It was polio, the greatest challenge of his life, that would not only change him personally but also spark his great ability to adapt to changing circumstances.[19]

The Challenge of Polio

In 1921, when FDR was thirty-nine, he contracted polio. It changed him physically, from a young and athletic man to one who would never walk again without the aid of braces and crutches. It also gave him "a new humility of spirit, a concern for the pain and suffering of others," as Goodwin frames it. Roosevelt would need to learn to depend on other people, especially his wife, who helped him over the traumatic period of the disease when he could not even sit up. Sara wanted Franklin to retire from politics and lead the life of a rich country squire, but Eleanor knew better—that this would crush his spirit. Eleanor would say that Franklin's illness caused her to "stand on my own two feet." Both Eleanor and Louis Howe, his campaign manager, also became his surrogates in the political world, keeping his name alive and delivering speeches on his behalf during his recovery.[20]

Roosevelt applied his penchant for trial and error to polio. In 1924 he visited the Warm Springs facility in Georgia and found the eighty-eight-degree waters restorative. He actually hoped he could learn to walk again, but instead he learned to live more fully with polio. Warm Springs was a ramshackle resort when FDR arrived, and the owners discouraged other polio victims from using the facility. FDR decided to buy the place, despite opposition from both his mother and his wife, and undertook a complete rebuilding of the resort.[21]

Franklin D. Roosevelt soon became an advocate for the other polio patients who came to the facility, and they began to call him Dr. Roosevelt. He worked with many of them, applying lessons he had learned from other health care professionals. Working with his secretary, Missy LeHand, he prepared "a series of charts showing the human musculature and indicating which muscles were affected by polio and therefore needed special exercise," H. W. Brands writes. FDR's time at Warm Springs not only allowed him to help others but to empathize with those who were less fortunate than himself. In return, people also began to identify with Roosevelt. As Brands writes, "candidates for president needed to display a common touch if they hoped to win the people's confidence." FDR would have that quality and then some when he returned to politics in 1928, winning the governorship of New York.[22]

The Great Depression

As we saw in the last chapter, no one could foresee the depths the economy would fall into during the Great Depression. Herbert

Hoover, with his background as a progressive, began to take steps immediately to counter the stock market crash of 1929. He did this despite the opposition it engendered among the old guard in the Republican Party, who believed in an orthodox economic theory "that government should refrain from interfering with the natural course of recovery," historian David M. Kennedy writes. Andrew Mellon, still in his role as treasury secretary, advised Hoover to "liquidate labor, liquidate stocks, liquidate the farmers, liquidate real estate."[23]

Classical economic theory had followed Say's Law, developed by the French economist Jean-Baptist Say in 1803. The essence of the theory was that supply and demand would balance out during an economic downturn. Men like Andrew Mellon thought that depressions played a significant role in purging "the rottenness out the system." As John Kenneth Galbraith has written, the classical economists argued that a downturn "extruded poisons that had been accumulating in the economic system." "This ruling doctrine—that in the long run, the Great Depression would turn out to have been good medicine for the economy . . . [was] completely bats, simply insane," DeLong writes. The solution, according to John Maynard Keynes, was for the government to borrow money and put people to work, thereby creating demand.[24]

Hoover went part way, but not all of the way, toward a Keynesian solution. He began to implement his favored approach of voluntary cooperation as outlined in *American Individualism*. It was an unfortunate title, since in fact Hoover was looking for a middle way between "the laissez-faire of the 18th century" and the collectivism that socialism and communism represented. Hoover believed in "the ideal of service" and in voluntary groups to carry out "nationally coordinated programs," historian Joan Hoff Wilson writes. Unfortunately for the

American people, Hoover's voluntarism would prove no match for the Great Depression, and his inflexibility would cost both the country and him a great deal.[25]

In November of 1929, Hoover brought together the leaders of American industry, who agreed to maintain wages and expand spending on construction projects. Hoover announced that the Federal Reserve would reduce interest rates and expand the money supply. He also requested that the states and localities expand or speed up their own public works projects to stimulate the economy, and he requested that Congress spend $140 million on their own public projects. All of this was keeping with Hoover's approach of voluntarism, using the government to set a broad direction and then have it implemented largely in the private sector and at the state and local level.[26]

Yet these actions failed to stem the hemorrhaging economy. "By the spring of 1930 breadlines were familiar sights on city sidewalks," Leuchtenburg writes. Unemployment reached almost 9 percent in 1930, business failures were climbing rapidly, and the gross national product fell by 13 percent. Yet Hoover refused to take any direct action or provide relief to the unemployed. "Curiously, he was convinced that federal relief would debauch the poor, but handouts from private agencies . . . would not," according to Leuchtenburg.[27]

The Republicans lost seats in Congress during the midterm elections in November 1930 as the crisis worsened. Banks also began to fail, with six hundred closing their doors in the last two months of 1930. Hoover's response was to recommend that the federal budget be balanced, exactly the wrong medicine for a sick patient, when economic stimulus was needed. But perhaps worst of all for Hoover was the perception that he didn't care about the common man. This was not true, and in private he suffered over the plight of those who were out of work. But in public, he said that "local communities . . .

have assumed the duty of relieving individual distress" and there was "minimum actual suffering." Part of the perception that Hoover was uncaring was because of his worsening relations with the press. Always thin-skinned, he now withdrew from the public due to criticism of his policies. "This inability to relate in person or via radio to the plight of those stricken by economic disaster was not a new Hoover characteristic," Wilson writes. He had always had trouble dealing with people. Now, those who were left as vagrants on the streets—due in part to his policies—began to refer to their "miserable shantytowns" as Hoovervilles.[28]

By the end of 1930, Hoover said that "the major forces of the depression now lie outside the United States." While there was truth to his statement, it also kept Hoover from having to admit "that his cooperative policies based on the only true 'laws of progress' were not effective," according to Wilson.[29]

But, in fact, the continent had continued to struggle in the aftermath of the war, and by the middle of 1931 Europe also fell into depression. Germany's problems continued under the weight of onerous reparations. Adolf Hitler and the Nazi Party "exploited festering resentments over reparations and the deeply depressed state of the German economy to score ominous gains in Parliamentary elections," in September of 1930, Kennedy writes. The American crash further restrained credit and trade in Europe, as did the Smoot-Hawley Act, which raised tariffs in the United States right before the stock market crash.[30]

To help stabilize Europe, Hoover responded with perhaps his most courageous policy proposals to date. The United States would place a one-year moratorium on the payment of European war debts, and in return the Europeans would do the same for German reparations. Unfortunately, the European situation had already begun to spin out of control. In September of 1931, Great Britain went off the gold standard. Gold was the centerpiece of the international monetary system at the time and "most economists and statesmen reverenced gold with a mystical devotion that resembled religious faith," according to Kennedy.[31]

To keep gold from flowing out of the United States, the Federal Reserve began to raise interest rates, further reducing liquidity in the financial system. Herbert Hoover, for his part, increasingly focused on balancing the federal budget, saying: "The primary duty of the government [was] to hold expenditures within our income." It was exactly the wrong set of policies during an economic downturn, akin to removing oil from an automobile and expecting it to run properly. In Hoover's defense, his attempt to balance the budget was a part of standard economic theory of the time, before John Maynard Keynes, the British economist, had fully developed his theory that governments should borrow and spend during an economic downturn to stimulate demand.[32]

The Depression continued to worsen. Unemployment soared, from 8.7 percent in 1930 to almost 16 percent in 1931. "Desperate men selling apples appeared on urban street corners, breadlines stretched block after block, community soup kitchens ladled out thin porridge, and 'Hoovervilles' . . . were springing up" everywhere, historian Jean Edward Smith writes. It is hard to overstate the desperation that was beginning to set in in the country. Yet Hoover, who had done so much to relieve hunger in Europe during the war, refused to take direct action to aid those who suffered. Hoover truly believed that direct federal action would make Americans dependent on government. One of his advisors perhaps summed it up when he said: "My sober and considered judgement is that . . . Federal aid would be a disservice to the unemployed."[33]

Meanwhile, Franklin D. Roosevelt had returned to politics in 1928, encouraged by Al Smith to run for governor of New York. Smith was the Democratic candidate for president in 1928, and he wanted FDR to run for governor to protect New York's electoral votes for him. Roosevelt was the underdog in the race, and he campaigned nonstop, often giving the appearance that he could still walk. "Franklin had hit upon the technique of gripping someone's arm with one hand and propelling himself forward with a cane in the other," Dallek writes. It was indicative of FDR's dogged determination to prevail in the face of overwhelming odds, and he emerged victorious by a very slim margin. Smith had also assumed that if he lost the presidency, he would be the true power behind the new governor. He was not the first or the last person to underestimate Franklin D. Roosevelt, who had put so much effort into overcoming polio that he was not about to allow the former governor to control him.[34]

With the onset of the Great Depression, FDR became the overwhelming favorite for the Democratic nomination in 1932. Unlike Hoover, Roosevelt had no qualms about using the resources of the government to directly aid those in need. In October 1931, he proposed to the New York legislature that they appropriate $20 million to provide work for people and money for "food against starvation and with clothing and shelter against suffering." In his speech proposing a form of unemployment insurance, FDR asserted "that modern society, acting through its government, owed the definite obligation to prevent the starvation or dire want of any of its fellow men and women." Roosevelt structured his proposal in such a way that Hoover could not attack it as "a public dole," as Dallek has framed it. Still, Roosevelt had begun to redefine the role of government, which would eventually usher in the welfare state as part of the New Deal.[35]

In 1932 Herbert Hoover finally began to move away from voluntary action as the sole means to resolve the Great Depression. He was being pushed from the left, from Democrats—as well as the remaining progressive Republicans, and even some conservative Democrats. As early as 1930 Senator Robert F. Wagner of New York proposed a bill for further public works spending and unemployment insurance, but Congress refused to approve unemployment insurance and Hoover vetoed the public works bill as too expensive. But as the situation worsened, Hoover was forced to confront the reality of the desperation unleashed by the Great Depression.[36]

In January 1932 Hoover supported and Congress passed legislation that established the Reconstruction Finance Corporation (RFC). The RFC was given $500 million and the ability to borrow up to $1.5 billion to support American businesses. "However grudgingly, Hoover had now unmistakably compromised his belief in voluntarism and embraced direct government action," Kennedy writes. But still, the aid was focused on businesses, not on the unemployed. This was not lost on Wagner, who asked: "But is there any reason why we should not likewise extend a helping hand to that forlorn American . . . who had been without wages since 1929?" He soon worked with the conservative Democrat John Nance Garner of Texas to put together a bill that would increase the lending authority of the RFC for loans to states for local relief. Fearful of the dole, Hoover vetoed the bill in July 1932, although he was ultimately forced to accept a compromise that included the funding.[37]

Perhaps no one has summarized the dilemma of Herbert Hoover as the 1932 election approached better than Arthur M. Schlesinger Jr.: "In the end, Hoover, dragged despairingly along by events, decided that where he finally dug in constituted the limits of the permissible. . . . He had himself done unprecedented things to show the potentialities of national action; but anyone who went a step beyond transgressed the invisible line and menaced the American way of life. His was the tragedy of a man of high ideals whose intelligence froze into inflexibility and whose dedication was smitten by self-righteousness."[38]

The 1932 Election

The Great Depression continued to worsen during 1932. Unemployment affected over 12 million Americans by the end of the year, almost 24 percent of the workforce. In large industrial cities like Chicago and Detroit, unemployment approached 50 percent. It wasn't just the unemployed who felt the impact, but so did those who were employed, who were forced to work for less pay or worked only part-time. Compensation for employees fell by 39 percent, corporations lost over $2 billion, and the income of small businesses fell by 64 percent. The financial system was a disaster, with 5,100 banks failing by 1932, which equaled one in five banks.[39]

With all the misery that had impacted the American people, were they on the verge of a revolution? Some certainly thought so. Two large-city mayors, Anton Cermak of Chicago and Fiorello La Guardia of New York City, saw major trouble on the horizon. Cermak warned that the federal government either needed to send relief or federal troops. La Guardia warned that we would either have reform "or we are going to have chaos and disorder." A Kentucky miner said, "I am going to murder, rob for my children because I won't let my children starve . . ."[40]

But as the historian Lawrence W. Levine has written, "the remarkable thing about the American people before reform did come was not their action but their inaction, not their demands, but their passivity, not their revolutionary spirit but their traditionalism." Americans were experiencing both trauma and fear in the aftermath of the onset of the Great Depression. Individualism was ingrained in the culture of the United States, as we have seen throughout this book, and many people blamed themselves for the calamity they were going through. "Americans had long been taught that human beings were ultimately responsible for themselves . . . that unemployment was an indication of indolence and failure."[41]

As the Great Depression continued to worsen during 1932, the mood of the country began to shift. "For the first time, a bitterness was beginning to rise against the rich and respectable," Schlesinger writes. Levine argues that "had there been no eventual social and economic reform of significance, there would have been upheaval of some kind." The 1932 election would be the opportunity for the American people to weigh in on their unhappiness and to set a new course. FDR would provide that opportunity to the voter.[42]

☞ ☞ ☞

Governor Roosevelt officially entered the race for the presidency in January of 1932. Al Smith soon followed in February. The two men had once been close, but ever since Roosevelt had refused to allow Smith to be the power behind the throne, the two had grown apart.

There were also other favorite sons in the race, including John Nance Garner of Texas, who won primaries in both Texas and California. Garner was supported by the newspaper magnate William Randolph Hearst. Roosevelt continued to amass delegates as the convention loomed on the horizon, but he lacked the two-thirds majority required for the nomination.[43]

In a speech FDR gave in April of 1932, he talked about the need for better planning that put its "faith once more in the forgotten man at the bottom of the economic pyramid." Then in May he called for the need for "bold, persistent experimentation." But the fox in Roosevelt wanted to avoid any real specificity, at least publicly. He felt that the election was going to be a referendum on Hoover, and "that settling on decisive economic actions during the campaign was a formula for political defeat," Dallek points out. His best chance to be elected was "to spark hope and belief that he could do better" than Hoover, according to Dallek. Planning for what he would do if elected occurred in private, and FDR called together three college professors to help him with this task. The three, Raymond A. Moley, Rexford G. Tugwell, and Adolf A. Berle Jr., would become what was known as the Brain Trust.[44]

FDR's supporters arrived at the Democratic Convention in Chicago in late June with the majority of delegates, and he was able to clinch the nomination when Garner was placed on the ticket as vice president. Garner then released his delegates to vote for Roosevelt. This not only helped wrap up the nomination but also strengthened Roosevelt's position in the South. Roosevelt was in the process of "reconciling the urban and rural wings of the Democratic Party," Dallek writes. FDR would also get substantial support from women and Black voters in the North. As Roosevelt closed out the party's nomination, the band played his new theme song, "Happy Days Are Here Again," meant to capture "the robust optimism that Roosevelt exuded," according to Smith.[45]

Roosevelt wanted to show that he was going to change direction from the way things had been done in the past. He announced he would fly to Chicago to speak to the convention and accept the nomination, a departure from past practice. Historically, party leaders came to the nominee in the aftermath of the convention to tell him he was nominated. FDR called this an "absurd tradition." It was during his speech to the convention that he said, "I pledge you, I pledge myself, to a new deal for the American people. Let us all here assembled constitute ourselves prophets of a new order." Those two words, *new deal*, would come to define Roosevelt's program of action, even though at the time no one knew it, least of all Roosevelt.[46]

❧ ❧ ❧

Meanwhile, Hoover made a major blunder in the summer of 1932 that would haunt him throughout the rest of the campaign. A group of men who had fought during World War I arrived in Washington, DC, requesting that the bonus that was promised them, which was to be paid years later, instead be paid now. They became known as the Bonus Army. While the House passed legislation to pay them, both Hoover and the Senate opposed the early payment. When the Washington, DC, police attempted to evict the Bonus Army from the building they occupied, violence ensued, with two people killed. "Hoover—insensitive to how his action might appear—ordered the U.S. Army to rout the squatters and to confine the rest of the bonus marchers in the Flats," Leuchtenburg writes. General Douglas McArthur exceeded his orders and proceeded to evict the Bonus Army from the Anacostia Flats as well. The American public was outraged. One newspaper wrote that it was "a pitiful spectacle" for the American government to be "chasing unarmed men, women and children with army tanks." FDR would soon remark, "This elects me."[47]

While his advisors urged Roosevelt to avoid any active campaigning, he instead went off on an extensive trip to the West and Midwest in September. Pundits at the time and later historians have taken Roosevelt to task for a campaign both devoid of specifics and containing contradictory messages. There is truth to this, with FDR offering policies that stretched from massive aid to a balanced budget.[48]

Yet there was an underlying logic to Roosevelt's approach that tied him to the Democratic Party of Jefferson and Jackson. FDR planned to govern in a way that would advance the interests of the average person, the "forgotten man," as he framed it. FDR would use activist government to promote the interests of the many over the few to achieve greater equality. Some quotes from his speeches during the campaign help to exhibit this:

> "This nation cannot endure if it is half boom and half broke."

> The purpose of his farm policy was "the restoration of agriculture to economic equality with other industries within the United States."

> "We must have . . . national planning in agriculture."

> The problem of railroads was "the entire absence of national planning."

> He called hydroelectric power "the great possession that belongs to all of us."[49]

Perhaps Roosevelt's most philosophical speech was the one he gave to the Commonwealth Club in San Francisco on September 23, 1932. In it, he talked about how much American society had changed with the closing of the frontier as a safety valve. "At the very worst there was always the possibility of climbing into a covered wagon and moving west where the untilled prairies afforded a haven for men to whom the East did not provide a place." But the Industrial Revolution had changed society, and "opportunity would no longer be equal" without the hand of government to regulate industry, as Theodore Roosevelt had done. But even with those regulations, "we are steering a steady course toward economic oligarchy." The "task now is . . . distributing wealth and products more equitably, of adapting existing economic organizations to the service of the people." Roosevelt declared that "the task of government" was to develop "an economic declaration of rights," not dissimilar to what he would later declare as the Four Freedoms.[50]

A few weeks later in Detroit, Roosevelt gave a speech on "social justice, through social action." He talked about two approaches to prosperity, one being "if we make the rich richer, somehow they will let a part of their prosperity trickle down to the rest of us." The second was to "make the average of mankind comfortable and secure, [then] their prosperity will rise upward." FDR then went on to talk about measures that had already been implemented to reduce poverty, such as investment in public health and the implementation of workers' compensation laws, and how more needed to be done, including implementing unemployment insurance and "old age insurance and old age pensions," which would eventually become the Social Security system.[51]

While FDR may have been vague on specifics, he was clear that he intended to use the power of the federal government to assist those in need during the Great Depression. Herbert Hoover understood where Roosevelt was intending to go with the New Deal, and in the final six weeks of the campaign defended himself and attacked the Democratic nominee. Hoover called Roosevelt "a chameleon in plaid" because of FDR's vague policy statements. "Hoover was sure that the New Deal was bringing communism to America," historian Eric Rauchway writes. At one point Hoover compared Roosevelt and the Democrats with "the same philosophy of government which has poisoned all of Europe . . . the fumes of the witch's caldron which boiled in Russia," referring to communist revolution in that country. He told people that the "so called new deals would destroy the foundations of the American system of life."[52]

"There is little doubt that Hoover was at his defensive worst by the summer of 1932," Hoff Wilson writes. Hoover also continued to display a tin ear when it came to the suffering of so many Americans. "Nobody is starving. The hobos, for example, are better fed than they have ever been," he told one journalist. His public appearances in the fall caused quite a stir in many locations. In Detroit, men yelled, "Hang Hoover!" In New York, people cried, "We want bread." Hoover's unpopularity followed him everywhere, even to his home state of California, where he received a telegram that read: "Vote for Roosevelt and make it unanimous."[53]

☙ ☙ ☙

The election wasn't close. FDR won forty-two of the forty-eight states and amassed a popular vote total of 22.8 million to Hoover's 15.8 million. Congress went overwhelmingly Democratic.

Near the end of the campaign, during a speech at Madison Square Garden in New York, Hoover had said: "This election is not a mere shift from the ins to the outs. It means deciding the direction our Nation will take over a century to come." On this, Hoover could not know how correct he was.[54]

While debates over the role of government had been central to the American experience since the very beginning, the liberal and conservative parties had now switched places. The Democratic Party since the time of Jefferson had supported limited government. But starting with Bryan, and running through Wilson, the party had begun to move toward support for active government. Roosevelt completed the transformation. The Republicans were the conservative party, inheritors of the tradition of active government to promote economic development. But in the aftermath of the election loss of 1932, they became what they had flirted with for some time, the antigovernment party.

These trends would become more apparent in the battle between Hoover and Roosevelt during the interregnum and during the first one hundred days of the new administration. "The conflict between them, and the tradition of liberalism and conservatism they established, remain central to US politics today," Rauchway writes. "The election did not decide the outcome of this contest, but only began it."[55]

Endnotes

1 Barber, p. 58.

2 Barber, p. 267.

3 William Leuchtenburg, *Herbert Hoover* (New York: Times Books, 2009), p. 1–3.

4 Leuchtenburg, *Hoover*, p. 4–18.

5 Joan Hoff Wilson, *Herbert Hoover: Forgotten Progressive* (Prospect Heights: Waveland Press, 1992), p. 24; Leuchtenburg, *Hoover*, p. 19–20.

6   Leuchtenburg, *Hoover*, p. 24–31; Wilson, p. 46.

7   Leuchtenburg, *Hoover*, p. 27; Wilson, p. 46.

8   Wilson, p. 55–58.

9   Leuchtenburg, *Hoover*, p. 63–64.

10   Leuchtenburg, *Hoover*, p. 60–61 and p. 65.

11   Jean Edward Smith, *FDR* (New York: Random House, 2007), p. 15.

12   Smith, p. 19; Doris Kearns Goodwin, *Leadership in Turbulent Times* (New York: Simon & Schuster, 2018), p. 43–44.

13   Goodwin, *Leadership*, p. 48–49; Robert Dallek, *Franklin D. Roosevelt: A Political Life* (New York: Viking, 2017), p. 21–23.

14   Goodwin, *Leadership*, p. 51; Dallek, p. 128 and p. 197.

15   Goodwin, *Leadership*, p. 50–51; Smith, p. 33.

16   Dallek, p. 33.

17   Dallek, p. 34–35; Goodwin, *Leadership*, p. 54.

18   Dallek, p. 68–69.

19   Goodwin, *Leadership*, p. 58; Smith, p. 79–80.

20   Goodwin, *Leadership*, p, 164–165; Dallek, p. 81.

21   Goodwin, *Leadership*, p. 164.

22   H. W. Brands, *Traitor to His Class: The Privileged Life and Radical Presidency of Franklin Delano Roosevelt* (New York: Doubleday, 2008), p. 174–182.

23   Kennedy, p. 51.

24   DeLong, p. 205–206 and p. 216; Galbraith, *The Age*, p. 218.

25   Kennedy, p. 46–47; Leuchtenburg, *Hoover*, p. 66–67; Wilson, p. 55–57.

26   Kennedy, p. 52–54.

27   Leuchtenburg, *Hoover*, p. 106–109; Lester V. Chandler, *America's Greatest Depression 1929–1941* (New York: Harper & Row, 1970), p. 4–5.

28   Leuchtenburg, *Hoover*, p. 112–113; Wilson, p. 140.

29   Wilson, p. 148–149.

30   Kennedy, p. 70–72.

31   Leuchtenburg, *Hoover*, p. 126; Kennedy, p. 75.

[32] Leuchtenburg, *Hoover*, p. 113 and p. 127; Kennedy, p. 78–79.

[33] Smith, p. 250; Leuchtenburg, *Hoover*, p. 130.

[34] Dallek, p. 94–102.

[35] Smith, p. 250–251; Dallek, p. 107.

[36] Arthur M. Schlesinger Jr., *The Age of Roosevelt, The Crisis of the Old Order: 1919–1933* (Cambridge: Riverside Press, 1957), p. 225.

[37] Schlesinger, *Age*, p. 240; Kennedy, p. 91.

[38] Schlesinger, *Age*, p. 246–247.

[39] Chandler, p. 5–8; Kennedy, p. 87.

[40] Lawrence W. Levine, *The Unpredictable Past: Explorations in American Cultural History* (Oxford: Oxford University Press, 1993), p. 208; Kennedy, p. 88.

[41] Levine, p. 210–214.

[42] Schlesinger, *Age*, p. 252 and p. 268–269; Levine, p. 208.

[43] Smith, p. 258–262.

[44] Dallek, p. 113–117.

[45] Dallek, p. 120 and p. 10; Smith, p. 268–269; for more information on the role of women and Black voters, see Eric Rauchway, *Winter War: Hoover, Roosevelt, and the First Clash Over the New Deal* (New York: Basic Books, 2018), chapters 4 and 5.

[46] Dallek, p. 122–123; James MacGregor Burns, *Roosevelt: The Lion and the Fox* (New York: Harcourt, 1956), p. 140.

[47] Leuchtenburg, *Hoover*, p. 135–136; Kennedy, p. 92.

[48] See Dallek, p. 126–127; Burns, *Roosevelt*, p. 142–143; Kennedy, p. 101–102.

[49] From Brands, *Traitor*, p. 255–256.

[50] Roosevelt's speech to the Commonwealth Club was retrieved on June 13, 2022, from https://www.americanrhetoric.com/speeches/fdrcommonwealth.htm.

[51] Roosevelt's speech in Detroit was retrieved on June 20, 2022, from https://www.presidency.ucsb.edu/documents/campaign-address-detroit-michigan.

[52] Rauchway, *Winter War*, p. 10–11; Smith, p. 286–287.

[53] Leuchtenburg, *Hoover*, p. 140–141; Hoff Wilson, p. 163.

[54] Leuchtenburg, *Hoover*, p. 141.

[55] Rauchway, p. 18.

CHAPTER 11

Two Hundred-Plus Days

The only thing we have to fear is fear itself.
—FRANKLIN D. ROOSEVELT, FIRST INAUGURAL ADDRESS

The contours of the modern political system began to solidify in the months leading up to Roosevelt's swearing in as president. Hoover's opposition to FDR's election and to the New Deal would begin to embed conservative opposition to active government ever further into Republican Party politics. Roosevelt, in his first one hundred days in office, would utilize aggressive governmental power to fight the Great Depression. While it would take American entry into World War II to end the Depression, Roosevelt would establish the Democrats as the party of active government. The great flip, years in the making, had finally happened.

The Interregnum

Prior to ratification of the Twentieth Amendment to the Constitution in 1933, a new president's term of office did not begin until March 4 of the year following the election. Congress had an even longer waiting period, not meeting for the first time until the December of the year following the election. Under the Twentieth Amendment, the dates were moved up to January 20 for the president and January 3 for Congress. But when Roosevelt was first elected, the Twentieth Amendment had not yet been ratified. FDR's election helped to speed the amendment through the states.[1]

Roosevelt was an incredibly optimistic man who brimmed with self-confidence. It was one of the keys to his success as president. Eleanor thought that his "striking self-confidence" was rooted in his religious beliefs. But on the night of his election, he told his son Jimmy that he was afraid. When Jimmy asked him what he was afraid of, he replied: "I'm just afraid I may not have the strength to do this job . . . I am going to pray that God will help me, that he will give me the strength and the guidance to do this job and do it right."[2]

Even such an extraordinary man as Roosevelt had his doubts, as well he should have. The Great Depression was already bad enough when he was elected in November, and it continued to worsen during the winter of 1932–33. If Hoover had been worried about FDR ushering in a period of radicalism that could lead to communism, Roosevelt worried about fascism if he did not act decisively. FDR had watched McArthur during the attack on the Bonus Army the previous summer and had called him the most dangerous man in America. "There's a potential Mussolini for you. Right here in America." In February of 1933, Walter Lippmann had gone to see Roosevelt, telling him, "The situation is critical, Franklin. You may have no alternative but to assume dictatorial powers." But Roosevelt rejected such pleas. He intended to preserve both American democracy and the underlying elements of capitalism, while making "America more humane and less vulnerable to future economic downturns," according to Dallek.[3]

But it would be a different form of capitalism. One of the members of Roosevelt's Brain Trust, Raymond A. Moley, described FDR's political principles as follows: "He believed that government not only could, but should, achieve the subordination of private interests to collective interests, substitute co-operation for the mad scramble of selfish individualism." Moley went on to say that Roosevelt had "a very keen awareness that political democracy could not exist side by side with economic plutocracy," a point of view consistent with the original founder of the Democratic Party, Thomas Jefferson. Support for greater economic equality for the common person tied Roosevelt and Jefferson together, even if Jefferson advanced that cause through a belief in limited government. The New Deal would forevermore change the nature of capitalism, smoothing out its rough edges and making it more humane by introducing a welfare state that provided a social safety net for individuals in society.[4]

This need for social reform went hand in hand with an attempt to change the dynamics of the political parties. "I'll be in the White House for eight years. When those years are over, there'll be a Progressive party," he told Rex G. Tugwell, another member of the Brain Trust. Even though he was not sure that it would still be called the Democratic Party at the end of his presidency, he hoped to assemble progressives into one party. FDR would lead the Democrats to be the party of active government, and he would ultimately label this party as liberal. Hoover, for his part, would lead the Republicans to be the party opposed to active government, contrary to the history of conservatives, dating back to Hamilton, who believed in active government to promote economic development. As we have seen, these trends had been emerging since the end of the Civil War.[5]

"These three purposes—social reform, political realignment, and economic recovery—flowed and counterflowed through the entire history of the New Deal," Kennedy writes. FDR's first and most important challenge would be to revive the economy. Roosevelt knew that if he failed at reviving the economy, which would prove difficult, he could not succeed. During his first one hundred days, the Roosevelt administration focused on economic revival. Reform would take shape in what historians have called the Second New Deal. After his inauguration, a person came to Roosevelt and told him, "Mr. President, if your program succeeds, you'll be the greatest president in American history. If it fails, you will be the worst one." Roosevelt replied, "If it fails, I'll be the last one." But before he could implement his plans, he needed to become president and avoid any commitments that Hoover was attempting to get him to agree to—all set in the context of massive bank failures.[6]

Two problems arose during the interregnum that would test FDR's ability to keep from being trapped in Hoover's policy preferences. The first was international debt; the second, the continuing crisis of the banks. Hoover's deferral of debt payments from Britain and France was set to expire on December 15, and both countries wanted to skip the payments that were due. Hoover reached out to Roosevelt to elicit his input on what should be done. "It had all the appearance of a magnificent gesture of statesmanship," Kennedy writes. "It also contained sinister political implications." Since skipping the debt payments would be very unpopular with the American people, Hoover hoped "to get this debt matter off my doorstep and put it on Roosevelt's."[7]

FDR could hardly ignore the president's request, and so he agreed to meet with Hoover in Washington, DC, on November 22 on his way to Warm Springs. It was a cold and awkward meeting, with Hoover dominating the proceedings and showing his wide-ranging grasp of the debt issue. Hoover kept his head down for most of his monologue, occasionally looking up at Moley, who had accompanied Roosevelt. FDR nodded his head at various points. As Moley pointed out, a Roosevelt head nod "did not at all mean that he agreed with what had been said," just that he understood the points that Hoover was making. As to be expected, FDR had no intention of allowing Hoover to back him into a corner on the debt issue, and after the meeting he issued a statement that said: "Responsibility . . . rests upon those now vested with executive and legislative authority." Hoover, for his part, continued to look down upon FDR, saying he had spent time "educating a very ignorant . . . well-meaning young man."[8]

For Roosevelt, there were multiple reasons to avoid being trapped by Hoover, the most important being that he lacked executive authority. Each man also had their own theory for the causes of the Great Depression. As we have seen, Hoover blamed the international situation, in part because this absolved him of the failure of his policies. "Roosevelt, by contrast, professed to find the sources of the Depression in the United States, in structural deficiencies and institutional inadequacies that a vigorous and far-reaching reform program might remedy," Kennedy writes. For FDR to cooperate with Hoover on the debt issue would be an admission that the causes of the Depression were indeed international, and could undercut his plan to undertake vigorous government action in response to the crisis.[9]

❧ ❧ ❧

The New Deal almost ended before it began when a gunman tried to assassinate the president-elect on February 15, 1933, in Miami. The shooter, a disgruntled Italian immigrant named Giuseppe Zangara, apparently hated all rich and powerful elites. He missed his target and instead shot the mayor of Chicago, Tony Cermak. Roosevelt did not panic and insisted that Cermak be taken to the hospital in his car. When Cermak died a few weeks later, Zangara was tried and executed. Moley reported that after the incident "Roosevelt was simply himself—easy, confident poised" and that his response "brought a surge of national confidence in him as had none of his other actions since the election." But for a woman grabbing Zangara's arm as he shot, the New Deal may have died with Roosevelt while the conservative John Nance Garner was elevated to the presidency, "which would lend force to reactionary politics within the United States," as Rauchway writes.[10]

While the nation may have had an increased sense of confidence in Roosevelt due to the incident, the same could not be said of Hoover. Banks had continued to fail in record numbers. "Told that some banks were unsound, depositors lost their nerve and demanded their money from their own bank, whether it was actually troubled or not," Rauchway writes. Depositors converted their dollars to gold, draining the Federal Reserve of its reserves of gold. Some of this gold was shipped out of the country to places considered safer. Yet Hoover refused to order a national bank holiday, believing at this point it was better to allow weak banks to fail to purge the system.[11]

In February, Hoover delivered a handwritten letter to FDR, claiming that the Great Depression had worsened because of his election and the potential for radical action on his part through the New Deal. There was perhaps some truth to this, since uncertainty often leads to panic. But the opposite was also true—that Hoover's unwillingness to act to stem the banking crisis also fed into a sense of crisis. As Eric Rauchway has written, the differences between the two men would reflect the approach of liberals and conservatives in the future. Liberals were willing to intervene in the economy as required to save the system, while conservatives took a hands-off approach "even if it meant risking systemic collapse."[12]

In the letter, Hoover wanted FDR to promise not to do any of the following: "no tampering or inflation of the currency; that the budget will be unquestionably balanced; that the Government credit will be maintained." He also warned against "abandonment of the gold standard, political experimentation or even dictatorship," as Kennedy writes. The letter reflected Hoover's continuing commitment to old ways of thinking about the economy that were simply not valid during the Great Depression. "Austerity and orthodoxy and laissez-faire were . . . deadly destructive mistakes," DeLong writes. Hoover's letter to Roosevelt was in fact a trap, which Hoover freely admitted. "I realize that if these declarations be made by the President-elect . . . it means the abandonment of 90% of the so-called new deal." Roosevelt thought that the letter was "cheeky" and waited two weeks before he bothered to answer it.[13]

"Both sides, in fact, were stepping a dangerous political dance around the gathering economic crisis," according to Kennedy. Yet if forced to choose which man was more at fault for the impasse, this writer would place the blame on Hoover. Perhaps this is personal bias, given I have always found Roosevelt to be both a fascinating historical figure and one of the greatest presidents the country has ever had. Given this, my rationale is grounded in the fact that Hoover never made a good faith effort to gain FDR's support. He only offered up policy prescriptions he knew Roosevelt would reject, the same type of policies that the electorate had also just rejected in a landslide win for the president-elect. Hoover also showed a great deal of animus toward Roosevelt, at one point saying, "I never will be photographed with him. I have too much respect for myself." Finally, Hoover had the power of the presidency and could have acted to stem the foreign debt and bank crisis had he chosen to do so, since he was the president. He did not.[14]

By the time Roosevelt arrived in Washington, DC, for his inaugural, most of the nation's banks were closed because of bank holidays declared at the state level. The Federal Reserve had concluded that a bank holiday was the only answer, since the New York Federal Reserve Bank's gold reserves had fallen below the amount they were legally required to hold. Confronting the recommendation of the Federal Reserve and the fact that "by the early evening of Friday, March 3, banks in thirty-two of forty-eight states were closed," Hoover finally agreed. But once again, he wanted FDR to support the action in order to provide cover should Democrats in Congress attack him.[15]

Hoover approached Roosevelt on March 3 at the White House for his support of the bank closures. Eleanor had accompanied Franklin for the get-together with the Hoovers. Hoover asked Roosevelt to meet with him privately after the tea. Eleanor reported what happened next. "They forgot to close the door and I could hear everything they said. Mr. Hoover said to Mr. Roosevelt, 'Will you join in a joint proclamation closing all of the banks?' Then she heard her husband say, 'Like hell I will! If you haven't the guts to do it yourself, I'll wait until I'm president to do it.'" The incident made Roosevelt "visibly angry" as one of his aides reported, since he felt that he was "treated like a schoolboy." Publicly FDR responded that he "was wholly agreeable to his closing all the banks by Proclamation," but that "as a private citizen," he could not "join him in such a Proclamation."[16]

One Hundred Days

Saturday, March 4, dawned cold and gray, fitting the national mood. Roosevelt began the day with a prayer service at St. John's Episcopal

Church across from the White House. He was joined by family and friends, with his old schoolmaster, Endicott Peabody, in attendance. Roosevelt lingered after the service on his knees in private prayer and contemplation.[17]

At 11:00 a.m. Franklin and Eleanor arrived at the White House. Hoover and Roosevelt then drove to the Capitol at the head of a seven-car procession, neither man speaking much to the other. When Chief Justice Charles Evans Hughes began the swearing in, FDR repeated the oath rather than saying simply "I do." It was symbolic of the changes Roosevelt hoped to implement. He then began his first inaugural address, which lasted fifteen minutes.[18]

Roosevelt had been thinking about the contents of the inaugural address for at least six months, much of which he wrote himself. Robert Jackson, secretary of the Democratic Party, later related that Roosevelt told him that "his most important task was to revive the confidence of the people in their government." In what over time would prove the most durable section of the speech, Roosevelt said, "This great Nation will endure as it has endured, will revive and will prosper. So, first of all, let me assert my firm belief that the only thing we have to fear is fear itself—nameless, unreasoning, unjustified terror which paralyzes needed efforts to convert retreat into advance." The speech was sprinkled with references to the "interdependence" of the people of the country. "We now realize as we have never realized before our interdependence on each other"—a clear reference that the days of rampant individualism must end. But on the day of the speech, the line that drew the most applause had to do with what would happen should Congress fail to respond: "I shall ask the Congress for . . . broad Executive power to wage war against the emergency." Yet in keeping with his commitment to the democratic process, he never mentioned the word *dictatorship*. His biographer Jean Edward Smith has written that "the effect of the speech was electrifying." Now words would need to be put into action, to "adopt decisive and unorthodox measures," as FDR told Jackson.[19]

Roosevelt, upon entering his office for the first time, found himself alone, with an empty desk, not even a phone or buzzer to call for assistance. He "gave a mighty shout" and two of his assistants soon joined him. A member of his Brain Trust, Rex G. Tugwell, thought that FDR saw the incident as "a parable of the national helplessness."[20]

Roosevelt was far from helpless. Both his legal team and Hoover's outgoing administration knew that the Trading with the Enemy Act, passed during World War I, was still in effect and could be used to declare a nationwide bank holiday and to stop the flow of gold from leaving the US. Although there was some legal dispute over use of the law for this purpose, it was the same authority Hoover had refused to use without Roosevelt's endorsement. Declaring a bank holiday under the provisions of the act, which would go into effect on Monday, March 6, would buy time to develop a more comprehensive plan and get congressional buy-in when they reconvened in the emergency session Roosevelt had called for, which would not open until the following Thursday.[21]

Under incredible time pressure, Roosevelt's financial team, led by William Woodin, worked with Hoover's people to develop a plan for the failing banks. Woodin was "a Republican industrialist, director of the Federal Reserve Bank of New York, and a trustee of the Warm Springs Foundation," according to Brands. He was also a good friend of FDR. Woodin had been selected as treasury secretary over Senator Carter Glass, who was a hard-money man who favored staying on the gold standard.[22]

It was a rare display of bipartisanship as the two sides worked together in drafting legislative language for the bank bill to be presented to the upcoming Congress. As Raymond A. Moley, now the assistant secretary of state, framed it, we had "forgotten to be Republicans or Democrats . . . just a bunch of men trying to save the banking system." Some Progressives wanted Roosevelt to nationalize the entire banking system, but FDR's goal was not to eliminate but to reform capitalism. He also knew that if he was to succeed, he would need the support of the bankers.[23]

It was during his first week in office that Roosevelt began to hold regular press conferences with the Washington, DC, press corp. Roosevelt put on quite a show at these events, revealing "his command of policy options" and breaking "down complicated questions . . . into pieces the ordinary reporter could understand and use," Brands writes. Roosevelt's communications skills were first-rate and may have been part of the success he would see, compared to Hoover, regarding positive press coverage and the ability to sway public opinion. Roosevelt had some ground rules for the press conferences, including that he could not be quoted directly "unless Press Secretary Steve Early provided the quotation in writing," Smith relates. It was at his first press conference on March 8 that Roosevelt revealed that the US would soon go off the gold standard.[24]

The bank bill that was placed before Congress passed in less than eight hours. The bank holiday was blessed by Congress, and the government would now have the responsibility to oversee banks. Strong banks would begin to reopen the following week, others as soon as the Treasury Department was satisfied those banks were solvent. As a way to increase the amount of money in circulation, the Federal Reserve issued notes that would circulate as money but not be convertible into gold, a precursor to going off the gold standard.[25]

Roosevelt relied on his communication skills to sell his policies to the country. On Sunday evening, March 12, FDR held his first fireside chat. In plain language, the president explained banking to the American people, telling them "it is safer to keep your money in a reopened bank than under the mattress." Americans soon responded, as "deposits and gold began to flow back into the banking system," Kennedy writes. Raymond A. Moley would later assert: "Capitalism was saved in eight days."[26]

There was a zigzag quality about the early days of the New Deal. After saving the banks, Roosevelt lurched rightward, urging Congress to balance the budget by cutting pensions for veterans and reducing salaries for government workers. The proposal was not popular within his own party, yet FDR was able to push it through Congress with the help of Republicans. Robert Dallek argues that Roosevelt believed "that initial policies that echoed traditional means and ends would do more to advance subsequent progressive actions than bold strokes at the outset." This was also before John Maynard Keynes had developed his theory that downturns in the economy should be fought through government borrowing and spending as a way to stimulate demand.[27]

☞ ☞ ☞

Roosevelt next moved leftward. He believed he needed to do something to reinflate the economy, put people back to work, and stabilize the farm economy. FDR explained that "the continued lack of adequate purchasing power on the part of the farmer [was] one of the most important reasons for the Depression." Income on American farms had dropped by close to 60 percent since the start of the Great Depression. The proposed legislation, known as the Agricultural Adjustment Act (AAA), included a provision that would pay farmers to reduce production, which would be paid for with "a tax on processors of agricultural commodities." The intent was to engineer an increase in farm prices by reducing supply. It was accompanied by the creation of the Farm Credit Administration to allow farmers to refinance their mortgages and end foreclosures. The Senate had been warned by the president of the American Farm Bureau Federation that "unless something is done for the American farmer we will have a revolution in the countryside within twelve months." FDR and Congress responded.[28]

The negotiations that took place over the farm bill between the president and Congress ultimately freed Roosevelt's hand in regard to the gold standard. One of the amendments that FDR agreed to was intended to foster inflation by a variety of means, including using silver or greenbacks and reducing the rate at which dollars could be exchanged for gold. Roosevelt used the amendment as his authority to formally take the United States off the gold standard. There were many critics of moving away from the gold standard, and also support from an unusual source, J. P. Morgan. "The day after Roosevelt's announcement, stock prices soared on record volume," Smith writes.[29]

Next up was the Civilian Conservation Corps (CCC), Roosevelt's personal idea. It combined his interest in conservation with an effort to put young men back to work building trails in national parks and constructing public facilities. It would prove to be one of the most popular New Deal programs, leaving an enduring legacy of "the prevention of floods and the erosion of our agricultural fields, the prevention of forest fires, the diversification of farming and the distribution of industry," as Roosevelt himself would later describe it. Over its nine-year span, the CCC put almost three million young men to work.[30]

Legislation for the CCC was quickly followed by the Federal Emergency Relief Administration (FERA), designed to assist state governments in funding unemployment insurance to those out of work. This was a major break with the past, where direct federal aid to the unemployed was seen as being on the dole. "At the end of its first year, FERA had assisted seventeen million people and disbursed $1.5 billion," Smith writes. Still, FDR had his own concerns about the dole, fearing the impact that direct relief payments would have on the self-respect of Americans, who were used to relying on their own efforts to support themselves. Unemployment assistance would soon be supplemented by the Civil Works Administration (CWA) in November of 1933, designed to put more people to work "digging ditches, laying pipes, and building and repairing roads, schools, playgrounds, athletic fields, hospitals, airports and municipal structures." It was a program that lasted only eight months before FDR pulled the plug, deciding it was too expensive and fearing it would create a perception that "we are going to have permanent Depression in this country."[31]

Yet by 1935, FDR realized that there was "a long-term . . . deficit in the ability of the private economy to provide employment for all who sought it," according to Kennedy. The result was the Emergency Relief Appropriation Act, or the "Big Bill." It included $5 billion for relief projects throughout the country. The Works Progress Administration (WPA) was created based on the legislation, which was a follow-up to the short-lived CWA of 1933. The WPA "hired millions, and put them to work building hospitals, schools, playgrounds, and airports," Rauchway writes. Some of the more famous projects made possible by the WPA included La Guardia Airport in New York, Dealey Plaza in Dallas (where Kennedy was shot), and the Camp David retreat in the mountains of Maryland. As Rauchway wrote in

2021, "evidence of the New Deal is everywhere even now, nearly a hundred years since it started."[32]

A public works bill was also passed in June of 1933 that provided for $3.3 billion in spending on public projects. Along those same lines was the establishment of the Tennessee Valley Authority (TVA), designed to improve conditions in the rural South, which suffered from poverty and underinvestment. "Income in the region was less than half the national average. Only two out of every hundred farms had electricity," Smith writes. The TVA would help bring jobs and economic development to a seven-state area that had been ignored since the end of the Civil War.[33]

"The capstone of the one hundred days was the passage by Congress of the National Industrial Recovery Act on the last day of the session," Smith writes. The legislation had been FDR's response to a smaller-scale bill that had been proposed in Congress to limit the working hours of employees in order to create more jobs. FDR thought the bill was unconstitutional, and so instead proposed a much broader bill that would expand national planning for industry. The National Industrial Recovery Act (NIRA) allowed unions to collectively bargain and established the National Recovery Administration (NRA), which would encourage industries to work together to spur economic growth. "Production in whole industries would be controlled, and prices and wages would be raised, by government-sanctioned industrial compacts," according to Kennedy. Antitrust laws would be waived.[34]

FDR hoped the legislation would end the Depression, and initially it had a positive impact on employment, helping to add two million jobs. It also "established the principle of maximum hours and minimum wages on a national basis [and] made collective bargaining a national policy and thereby transformed the position of organized labor," Schlesinger has written. But the NRA was also an example of planning run amok, of trying to micromanage a capitalist economy. As we have seen throughout this book, Americans are looking for the right balance between the needs of the individual and the needs of the society. The legislation that established the NRA pushed the balance off course, promoting "excessive centralization and the dictatorial spirit," Walter Lippmann observed at the time. Still, it gave hope to many at the depths of the Great Depression and provided "an essential continuity in the midst of crisis [and] helped preserve American unity," according to Schlesinger.[35]

Why Was FDR So Successful?

Roosevelt proposed fifteen policies to deal with the Great Depression during the one hundred days, all of which were incorporated into law. It was an unheard-of record of success in an American political system designed to slow and at times completely stop change. Why was FDR so successful?

First, the times demanded action. There was the sense that had Roosevelt not acted quickly and decisively to provide relief to the people, the American System itself may have imploded, as happened in other countries during this period. In Germany, Adolf Hitler had become chancellor "after massive unemployment had seeded despair into millions of German households," Kennedy writes. The plight of Americans was not much different, with unemployment reaching 25 percent and men roaming the country in search of work. In Italy, Mussolini had established a fascist government, while Stalin and the USSR offered communism as an alternative. When Roosevelt came to power, "the people had seen stagnation go dangerously far. They wanted experiment, activity, trial and error, anything that would convey a sense of movement and novelty," Richard Hofstadter has written.[36]

Yet FDR's success cannot solely be attributed to the times. As Hofstadter has written, some of Roosevelt's critics believed "his successes were purely accidental." If this were true, then why did Hoover, facing the same circumstances, fail so miserably? As we saw in the last chapter, part of Roosevelt's success was found in his supreme sense of self-confidence and his willingness to try new solutions, while retaining a commitment to the overall American Creed. "Only a leader with an experimental temper could have made the New Deal possible," according to Hofstadter.[37]

Roosevelt's success can be found, at least in part, in his being a master politician in the very best sense of the word. For those who believe that the government would be better off in the hands of a nonpolitician—a businessman—the example of Hoover and Roosevelt is quite instructive. FDR liked people, and this was obvious in the way in which he responded to the public, Congress, and other elected officials. As Hofstadter has written, FDR was "warm, personal, concrete, and impulsive." Roosevelt was able to convince people that he really cared because he was genuine in his empathy. He also acted—telling the people in very general terms what he planned to do, and then he did it.

Roosevelt the politician knew how to deal with Congress. He knew when to hold steady and when to compromise to get his way. "He knew how to stroke the members, how to play to their vanity, and how to accommodate their needs," Smith has observed. This could be seen in the legislation that ultimately created the NRA, when Roosevelt helped craft a much larger law than what had originally been proposed in Congress. FDR also brought along the nation's governors with his early legislative efforts, especially the bank bill.[38]

Even more importantly, FDR had an instinctive sensibility for how to move public opinion in his direction. "When Hoover bumbled that it was necessary only to restore confidence, the nation laughed bitterly. When Roosevelt said: 'The only thing we have to fear is fear itself'... the nation was thrilled," Hofstadter has written. His fireside chats were masterful examples of how a politician can help to mold public opinion. In the aftermath of his first fireside chat, the public regained confidence in the banking system and began to redeposit their money. (After FDR died in 1945, a man who was waiting at Union Station for his funeral train to arrive was asked: "Why are you here? Did you know Franklin Roosevelt?" The man replied: "No, but he knew me.") Roosevelt also knew how to make an ally of the press. "His personal charm helped him gain the affection of an enormous variety of political and other leaders [and] . . . enabled him to keep the most diverse forces united, at least for a time, behind his programs," according to Burns.[39]

Roosevelt also knew how to make the right kinds of enemies. The journalist and public intellectual, Ezra Klein, said on one of his podcasts that "you have to convince people first and foremost that you're on their side. People judge you . . . by the enemies you choose" and the fights you take on. Klein was talking about Donald Trump, but he could just as well have had Roosevelt in mind, who placed himself on the side of the common man through his rhetoric regarding the wealthy. In his first inaugural address, FDR attacked the "unscrupulous money changers." He then went on to save the banking system. In 1935, under pressure from critics on the left, Roosevelt proposed major increases in income tax rates on the wealthy through the Wealth Tax Act. "Our revenue laws have operated in many ways to the unfair advantage of the few, and they have done little to prevent an unjust concentration of wealth and economic power," Roosevelt said.

Kennedy writes that "the hatred of the rich toward Roosevelt began to congeal into icy contempt [to this] traitor to his class." A story is told that when Roosevelt died, people in the ultrarich community of Bloomfield Hills, outside Detroit, danced around a bonfire.[40]

Yet Roosevelt also instinctively knew his limitations in bending public or legislative opinion. When the Glass-Steagall Act was passed near the end of the one hundred days, Roosevelt initially opposed the provision for deposit insurance. "It won't work, the weakest banks will pull down the strong." Yet he accepted the provision, congratulating Senator Glass on the bill and joking "that the bill had more lives than a cat," Goodwin writes. The Federal Deposit Insurance Corporation would be one of the most important and long-lasting reforms of the hundred days, a measure that provided "monetary stability" to the banking system.[41]

Much of the criticism that can be leveled at FDR involves instances in which he refused to take actions the public or his fellow politicians would not accept. African Americans were helped by many New Deal programs, getting jobs with the CCC and the WPA, and they would gradually shift their votes to Roosevelt and the Democrats and away from the party of Lincoln. Yet one of the most glaring of FDR's failings was his lack of support for an anti-lynching bill, which had sat in Congress since 1934. When it was brought up for debate again in 1937, 70 percent of the public supported it. It passed the House, but then ran into the inevitable filibuster in the Senate from Southern leaders. FDR refused to put the weight of his office behind ending the filibuster. "If I come out for the anti-lynching bill now, they [Southern senators] will block every bill I ask Congress for," Roosevelt argued. "During the twelve years FDR was president not one piece of civil rights legislation became law," Smith writes. Similar criticisms could be raised about FDR's acquiescing to the isolationism of the American people in the years leading up to World War II, and Roosevelt's willingness after the war began to intern Japanese Americans in concentration camps.[42]

During an interview about his biography of Roosevelt, the historian Robert Dallek said, "He didn't end the depression. He did something more important. He humanized the American industrial system." In many ways, the New Deal is the culmination of the transformation of liberals and conservatives in their attitudes toward government. As we have seen throughout this book, the impact that the Industrial Revolution had on both sides caused them to ultimately switch sides in their support or opposition to active government.[43]

In the run-up to his reelection in 1936, FDR began to redefine the New Deal. Whereas the first New Deal was about relief and economic recovery, the Second New Deal dealt with structural inequities in the American political and economic system and the development of a welfare state that leveled the playing field and promoted greater equality and democracy. Beginning in 1935, Roosevelt moved to the left, in part to forestall challenges from his critics, including Huey Long and his "Share-the-Wealth" proposals. Roosevelt's proposal for higher taxes on the wealthy was part of this effort. In 1935, FDR proposed a wealth tax that would include higher taxes on the wealthy, on inheritances, and on corporations. Roosevelt pointed out that the tax system had "done little to prevent an unjust concentration of wealth and economic power." But FDR's proposal for a fairer tax system was more of a campaign statement for his reelection efforts in 1936, and he did not complain when Congress watered down his proposals. Yet over the course of the 1930s, the tax system did become more progressive.[44]

One of the most successful elements in creating a more equal society during the New Deal was the sanctioning of unions. In 1935, Senator Robert F. Wagner's National Labor Relations Act (NLRA) became law. "Wagner was almost alone among liberal Democrats in placing a high value on trade unions," Schlesinger writes. Wagner recognized that in order to sustain demand, average workers would need to receive a larger share of national income. "When employees are denied the freedom to act in concert . . . they cannot participate in our national endeavor to coordinate production and purchasing power," he said during the debate on the NLRA. He worried that without a strong law on collective bargaining, the gap "between wages and profits" would continue to expand, leading to further "economic decline."[45]

FDR was a rather lukewarm supporter of collective bargaining, but he eventually supported the bill after the Supreme Court struck down the NRA, including those provisions that dealt with unions. The Wagner Act was part of what the economist John Kenneth Galbraith has called "the support of countervailing power." Rather than using the power of government to directly control capitalism, unions could be used as a check on business. The Wagner Act "helped initiate a historic organizing drive that rearranged the balance of power between American capital and labor," Kennedy writes. Union membership would gradually increase from 10 percent of workers in 1929 to 35 percent by 1945. A study by four economists in 2021 concluded, "we find consistent evidence that unions reduce inequality," explaining a significant share of the dramatic fall in inequality between the mid-1930s and the late 1940s.[46]

If sanctioning unions was Wagner's major contribution, then the most important policy proposal put forward by FDR was the creation of the Social Security system. Progressives had been considering such a system for quite some time, and Roosevelt had supported it since the 1920s. In early 1935 he submitted a proposed bill that had been put together primarily by his labor secretary, Frances Perkins, the first woman to fill a cabinet position. FDR had told her he wanted a system that would be "so simple that everybody will understand it," one that would provide a social insurance system from "cradle to grave." The result was a bill that provided not only for unemployment and disability insurance, but old-age pensions as well. The legislation elicited strong opposition from the business community and the wealthy, who called it the first step toward "ultimate socialistic control of life and industry." The bill sailed through Congress, and even most Republicans feared opposing the president on such a popular bill.[47]

FDR too had his own concerns that Social Security could be viewed as a handout, as part of the dreaded dole. He understood that Americans, who were so steeped in the importance of individualism, were hesitant to accept anything that was unearned. For this reason, he fought hard to ensure that the Social Security system would largely be funded through contributions from individuals and businesses and not overly rely on general taxes. "We put those payroll contributions there so as to give the contributors a legal, moral, and political right to collect their pensions and unemployment benefits. With those taxes, no damn politician can ever scrap my social security program," Roosevelt remarked.[48]

But Roosevelt had to pay a heavy price in order to elicit the support of Southern Democrats for Social Security. In the legislation proposed by the White House, both farm laborers and domestic help were included in the Social Security Act. Southern congressmen and senators voted to exclude them as a way to keep the benefits of the program from reaching the majority of Black people in the South. "As a consequence, southerners could vote for the bill that brought much needed funding to their poverty-stricken region while protecting the character of its racial arrangements," historian Ira Katznelson writes.[49]

Roosevelt had to defend the New Deal against the Supreme Court. The court was composed of four very strong conservatives who were committed to a laissez-faire political philosophy more in line with the old order of the Gilded Age. There were three liberal members, and two swing votes, including Chief Justice Hughes. All but one had been appointed by Republican presidents. In 1934 and 1935, the court struck down two of the core laws of the New Deal, the NRA and the AAA, based on a very narrow reading of the commerce clause. Roosevelt commented that "we have been relegated to the horse-and-buggy definition of interstate commerce." The attack on the New Deal programs by the court was not without cause, since the legislation was drafted quickly in the heart of the Depression, but rather than providing a limited rationale, the court issued opinions "so broad that it struck at all national efforts to maintain fair industrial and labor standards," Supreme Court historian Bernard Schwartz writes.[50]

Roosevelt felt that the Supreme Court had overstepped its boundaries and that the entire New Deal could now be endangered. Roosevelt viewed the court as just one of the branches of the government that could interpret the Constitution. This view, known as departmentalism, went all the way back to the time of Jefferson and Madison. "Each of the three departments has equally the right to decide for itself what is the duty under the constitution," Jefferson wrote. To do otherwise would replace judicial review with judicial supremacy.

Roosevelt believed that the Constitution was "a layman's document, not a lawyer's contract." He went on to argue that "whenever legalistic interpretation had clashed with contemporary sense on great questions of broad national policy, ultimately the people and the Congress have had their way."[51]

In February of 1937, FDR announced what would become known as his court-packing scheme. He proposed that he be allowed to add one additional Supreme Court justice for every member of the court over the age of seventy that refused to retire. It was, in the words of Kennedy, "a calculated risk, and not unreasonable." But Roosevelt, in a major blunder, had developed his scheme in private and had failed to bring along either the public or Congress. He tried to sell his plan based on efficiency, that many of the judges were too old to keep up with the demands of the job. This was patently false, and both Congress and the public saw through it.[52]

Yet if FDR's court-packing plan failed to change the composition of the court, it did change the outcome of future cases. In March of 1937, the court heard a case that dealt with minimum wage laws. A year earlier, the court had struck down a minimum wage law in New York. Yet in early 1937, Justice Owen Roberts flipped his position from opposition a year earlier to support, "a switch in time that saved nine" as it became dubbed. While the court-packing scheme could not have impacted Roberts's decision, since he had changed his mind in late December of 1936, the pressure from FDR and other political actors had begun to weigh on the court. "If laissez-faire jurisprudence gave way to judicial pragmatism, it simply reflected a similar movement that had taken place in the country as a whole," Schwartz writes. Soon thereafter, the major components of the New Deal, including the Wagner Act and the Social Security Act, were found to be constitutional by the court. In the case on Social Security, the court found that Congress should "shape . . . the concept of welfare" to meet the needs of the nation and found that the "concept of the general welfare . . . is not static [but] changes with the times." Even the Supreme Court cannot stand too far outside the boundaries of public opinion.[53]

Since the beginning of the Progressive Era, wealth inequality had begun to narrow, although the 1920s saw a reversal in this pattern. The reduction in inequality is referred to by different names by different analysts. The economists Peter H. Lindert and Jeffrey G. Williamson call it the "Greatest Leveling of All Time," the title of chapter 8 in their book *Unequal Gains*. The political scientist Robert D. Putnam and Shaylyn Romney Garrett call it the "Great Convergence." The New Deal "unleashed the full force of the Great Convergence," they write, due to a variety of policies and programs, including progressive taxation, strengthened unions, and the development of a social safety net.[54]

But despite the great progress that the New Deal made in creating a more equal society, it would take American entry into World War II to finally end the Great Depression. Roosevelt would tell reporters in 1943 that "he no longer like[d] the term 'New Deal,'" that "Dr. New Deal" had come to save the country from one set of ills, but now that it faced new perils, "his partner . . . Dr. Win-the-War," would take over. This did not mean that Roosevelt had abandoned the New Deal, but rather that the war had to be the new priority. "It seems pretty clear that we must plan for . . . an expanded economy, which will result in more security, more employment, more recreation, in education, in more health, in better housing for all of our citizens, so that the conditions of 1932 and the beginning of 1933 won't come back again." The New Deal would continue to dominate American political life until the 1970s, when the cycles of history would once again shift.[55]

Endnotes

1   Akhil Reed Amar, *America's Constitution: A Biography* (New York: Random House, 2005), p. 428–429.

2   Brands, *Traitor*, p. 268.

3   Dallek, p. 133–134.

4   Kennedy, p. 115–116.

5   Brands, p. 272.

6   Kennedy, p. 117; Jonathan Alter, *The Defining Moment: FDR's Hundred Days and the Triumph of Hope* (New York: Simon & Schuster, 2006), p. 6.

7   Kennedy, p. 105; Rauchway, *Winter War*, p. 55.

8   Rauchway, *Winter War*, p. 63–69; Kennedy, p. 109.

9   Kennedy, p. 106–107.

10 Dallek, p. 131–132; Rauchway, *Winter War*, p. 9.

11 Rauchway, *Winter War*, p. 197; Kennedy, p. 109.

12 Rauchway, *Winter War*, p. 206.

13 Rauchway, *Winter War*, p. 216; Kennedy, p. 109; Schlesinger, *Crisis*, p. 476–478.; DeLong, p. 222.

14 Franklin D. Roosevelt is almost always ranked in the top three on the list of best presidents. See for example the ranking included at https://en.wikipedia.org/wiki/ Historical_rankings_of_presidents_of_the_United_States; Rauchway, *Crisis*, p. 178.

15 Kennedy, p. 110–111; Schlesinger, *Crisis*, p. 478; Alter, p. 190–191, including the quote about the number of banks that were closed; Rauchway, *Winter War*, p. 222–223.

16 Alter, p. 198–200; Rauchway, *Winter War*, p. 223.

17 Jean Edward Smith, p. 300; Alter, p. 212.

18 Smith, p. 301–302.

19 Rauchway, *Winter War*, p. 228; Alter, p. 207 and p. 218; Smith, p. 302–303; the words

of the Inaugural Address were retrieved on July 21, 2022, from https://avalon.law.yale.edu/20th_century/froos1.asp.

20 Arthur M. Schlesinger, *The Age of Roosevelt: The Coming of the New Deal* (Boston: Houghton Mifflin, 1965), p. 2–3.

21 Schlesinger, *The Coming*, p. 4.

22 Brands, *Traitor*, p. 292.

23 Schlesinger, *The Coming*, p. 5.

24 Brands, *Traitor*, p. 298–300; Smith, p. 309.

25 Brands, *Traitor*, p. 303–304; Smith, p. 311.

26 Kennedy, p. 136–137.

27 Dallek, p. 141–142; Smith, p. 314–315.

28 Kennedy, p. 140-141; Dallek, p. 144.

29 Kennedy, p. 143; Smith, p. 328–329.

30 Kennedy, p. 144; Dallek, p. 148 .

31 Smith, p. 322-323; Dallek, p. 153–154.

32 Kennedy, p. 249; Rauchway, *The Great Depression*, p. 67; Eric Rauchway, *Why the New Deal Matters* (New Haven: Yale University Press, 2021), p. 4.

33 Smith, p. 324–325; Kennedy, p. 148. The seven states were Tennessee, Alabama, Mississippi, Kentucky, Georgia, North Carolina, and Virginia.

34 Smith, p. 157; Kennedy, p. 151.

35 Kennedy, p. 151; Schlesinger, *The Coming*, p. 121 and p. 174–175.

36 Kennedy, p 104; Richard Hofstadter, *The American Political Tradition* (New York: Knopf, 1948), p. 316.

37 Hofstadter, p. 317.

38 Smith, p. 306–307.

39 Hofstadter, p. 316; James MacGregor Burns, *Leadership* (New York: Harper & Row, 1978), p. 281.

40 For the Ezra Klein quote, see https://www.nytimes.com/2022/07/26/opinion/ezra-klein-podcast-sean-illing.html; Kennedy, p. 275–276; the information about people dancing around a bonfire comes from a podcast, Fate of Fact by Jon Meacham, which can be found at https://podcasts.apple.com/us/podcast/first-blood/id1617076670?i=1000555820351.

41 Goodwin, *Leadership*, p. 303–304.

42 Smith, p. 399–401.

43 For the Dallek quote, see the interview from 2017 found at https://www.aspeninstitute.org/blog-posts/remembering-made-fdr-great/.

44 Kennedy, p. 275–276; Dallek, p. 224; for the increasing progressivity of taxes during the 1930s, see Putnam and Garrett, Figure 2.13 on p. 56.

45 Schlesinger, p. 402; Wagner's speech on the National Labor Relations Act was retrieved on August 31, 2022, from http://web.mit.edu/21h.102/www/Primary source collections/The New Deal/Wagner, National Labor Relations Act.htm.

46 Dallek, p. 222; Kennedy, p. 291; Rauchway, *The Great Depression*, p. 87 and p. 95; Putnam and Garrett, p. 51; Henry S. Farber, Daniel Herbst, Ilyana Kuziemko, Suresh Naidu (2021), "Unions and Inequality over the Twentieth Century: New Evidence from Survey Data," *The Quarterly Journal of Economics*, vol. 136, issue 3, August 2021, retrieved August 31, 2022, from https://academic.oup.com/qje/article/136/3/1325/6219103.

47 Smith, p. 350–352; Brands, *Traitor*, p. 412–416.

48 Brands, *Traitor*, p. 416.

49 Ira Katznelson, *Fear Itself: The New Deal and the Origins of Our Time* (New York: Liveright Publishing, 2013), p. 260.

50 Bernard Schwartz, *A History of the Supreme Court* (New York: Oxford University Press, 1993), p. 232.

51 Larry D. Kramer, *The People Themselves: Popular Constitutionalism and Judicial Review*, (Oxford: Oxford University Press, 2004), p. 106 and p. 217.

52 Kennedy, p. 325–331; Smith, p. 383.

53 Schwartz, p. 234; Kennedy, p. 336; Joseph Fishkin and William E. Forbath, *The Anti-Oligarchy Constitution: Reconstructing the Economic Foundations of American Democracy* (Cambridge: Harvard University Press, 2022). p. 304.

54 Putnam and Garrett, p. 39.

55 Rauchway, *The Great Depression*, p. 126; Dallek, p. 543.

Jefferson's Legacy

What is past is prologue.
—WILLIAM SHAKESPEARE, *THE TEMPEST*

"What is past is prologue," Antonio said to Sebastian in *The Tempest*, indicating that they had been brought to their current situation by all that had gone before them. To a certain extent, American politics can also be seen in this light, especially in a nation that is bound together in part by its Founding Fathers.

None of the founders are more important than Jefferson and Hamilton in terms of the impact they have had on American politics. John Ferling, in his biography of the two men, argues that "their opposing views are like the twin strands of DNA in the American body politic." Both men's standing has fluctuated over time, with Jefferson ascendant after his victory in 1800, culminating when Lincoln at Gettysburg dated the founding of the United States to the Declaration of Independence. Jefferson's standing then slipped after the Civil War, given his status as a Southern enslaver. Theodore Roosevelt was a great admirer of Hamilton, calling him "the most brilliant American statesmen who ever lived." Woodrow Wilson would ultimately take Jefferson as his idol, as we have seen.[1]

All presidents want to be affiliated with the founding in one way or another, and Franklin D. Roosevelt was no different. As a Democrat, he claimed Jefferson, who was the original founder of the party. Fortunately for FDR, one can find in Jefferson's writings "pretty much what he or she is looking for," as Joseph J. Ellis has written. Since FDR was in the process of repudiating one of the central tenets of Jefferson—the belief in limited government and states' rights—Roosevelt would have to find other supporting strands from the Sage of Monticello.[2]

FDR and Jefferson

April 13,1943, was cloudy and windy in the nation's capital. The United States was in the third year of a war against Nazi Germany and imperial Japan that would decide the fate of democracy. Perhaps it was fitting that on the two hundredth anniversary of Thomas Jefferson's birth Franklin D. Roosevelt would dedicate the Jefferson Memorial in the middle of World War II, since no other founder was "so closely or emotionally linked to the spirit of democracy and individual freedom" as Jefferson, in the words of historian Andrew Burstein. Perhaps also fitting were the words that were chosen to wrap around the memorial: "I Have Sworn upon the Altar of God Eternal Hostility against Every Form of Tyranny over the Mind of Man."[3]

In 1933, while working on his first inaugural address, Roosevelt had told one of his advisors that Thomas Jefferson was "the best" president. The two men shared a great deal. They were both born to privilege, attended the best schools, and had known little by way of depravation in their early life. Both had created large coalitions within the Democratic Party that would sweep to victory and establish a new political order that would "shape American politics in ways that endure" beyond a single electoral cycle, as the historian Gary Gerstle frames it.[4]

"The Democrats were determined to build Jefferson a memorial in the nation's capital as splendid as Washington's and Lincoln's," Merrill D. Peterson writes. "The president constantly had his hand in this project." Roosevelt had already pushed for the Jefferson stamp and the Jefferson nickel. In 1934, Congress established a Thomas Jefferson Memorial Commission. The architect selected was John Russell Pope, who had already designed the National Archives Building (in front of the building is the statue *Future*, the base of which is inscribed with the words "What is past is prologue.") Pope created several alternatives for the memorial, including one that was modeled after the Rotunda that Jefferson had designed at the University of Virginia. A subcommittee led by Pope met FDR, who personally selected the Rotunda design, what Jefferson had once called "the perfect model" of "spherical architecture."[5]

Now FDR was dedicating the memorial to Jefferson. He needed to explain in his address how Jefferson would have reacted to the current war in which the United States was fighting against the fascist and expansionist powers. He did this by paying tribute to Jefferson's support for freedom. He opened his speech with the following words: "Today, in the midst of a great war for freedom, we dedicate a shrine to freedom. To Thomas Jefferson, Apostle of Freedom, we are paying a debt long overdue." It was a transformative moment for the memory of Jefferson, who now joined Washington and Lincoln in the pantheon of American leadership. At this moment Jefferson ceased to be a partisan figure "and became instead the presiding presence who transcended all political conflict and parties," as Joseph J. Ellis writes. Politicians from both sides of the ideological spectrum would hereafter claim Jefferson as their own.[6]

Yet more perplexing from our perspective is how Roosevelt tied together the governmental activism of the New Deal with Jefferson's preference for small and decentralized government. The historian Thomas T. McAvoy wrote the following in 1945 shortly after Roosevelt's death, which still rings true today:

> *The Jeffersonian revolution and the New Deal of 1933 and 1936 both sought that form of democratic government which seemed most likely to preserve the liberty of the common man. Jefferson saw in the centralized government of the Federalists an enemy of real democracy. Roosevelt saw in the same type of government the only agency of protecting the rights of the people.*[7]

Roosevelt had been building a bridge to Jefferson over the issue of equality for the common man for quite some time. In 1924, he had written his one and only book review for Claude Bowers's book entitled *Jefferson and Hamilton: The Struggle for Democracy in America*. In FDR's review, he equated the 1920s to the 1790s as a period where the "moneyed class" held sway over the "working masses." Eight years later, in April of 1932, FDR gave a speech at the Jefferson Day dinner in Saint Paul, Minnesota. While he recognized the "great financial genius of Alexander Hamilton," he took him to task for being an elitist. He quoted his distant cousin Theodore: "This government is not and never shall be governed by a plutocracy." Using the words of Woodrow Wilson, FDR said that if Jefferson "would return to the councils of the party, he would find that while economic changes of a century have changed the necessary methods of government action, the principles of that action are still wholly his own." And what were those principles, as Wilson laid them out? They were that government should be "the great umpire standing by to see that the game was honorably and fairly played . . . and to open the field free to every sportsmanlike contestant."[8]

In FDR's speech to the Commonwealth Club in San Francisco in September of 1932, he once again returned to his theme of Hamilton and Jefferson, placing these two men "at the heart of everything," as one historian frames it. Hamilton "believed that the safety of the republic lay in the autocratic strength of its government . . . guided by a small group of public-spirited citizens." Jefferson saw government as "a means to an end, not an end in itself" and believed that the end was to represent all people, not just an elite. "Hamilton spoke for big money, Jefferson for all who did not possess a direct connection to the powerful," Burstein writes. "The function of government must be to favor no small group at the expense of its duty to protect the rights of personal freedom and of private property of all its citizens," according to Roosevelt.[9]

New Dealers picked (some would say *cherry-picked*) those elements of Jefferson's writings that helped support their case. One was Jefferson's belief that "the earth belongs to the living" and that the current generation should not be bound by what their ancestors believed. In an 1816 letter, Jefferson had written that "laws and institutions must go hand in hand with the progress of the human mind . . . institutions must advance also, and keep pace with the times. We might as well require a man to wear still the coat which fitted him when a boy, as civilized society to remain under the regimen of their barbarous ancestors." The historian Dumas Malone, who ultimately wrote a six-part biography of Jefferson, said in 1933 that Jefferson's flexible mind "would bestow his apostolic blessing on Franklin D. Roosevelt, as the new President buckles on his Hamiltonian sword." He considered Jefferson and Roosevelt men who chased the "economic royalists" and the "corrupt monarchists" from the temple.[10]

But Roosevelt went beyond this to link himself to Jefferson and classical liberalism. In doing this, he turned the definition of classical liberalism on its head. He did this in two ways. The first was to redefine freedom itself. Whereas historically freedom was viewed as being free from government restrain, FDR tied freedom to economic security in the modern world, one in which active government was needed to ensure freedom. In his acceptance speech for the 1936 Democratic nomination, Roosevelt talked about how political equality "was meaningless in the face of economic inequality. . . . For too many of us throughout the land, life was no longer free, liberty no longer real; men could no longer follow the pursuit of happiness."[11]

Obviously, FDR was tying himself to Jefferson with his reference to how the Declaration of Independence was being violated. But it went beyond this. As we saw in chapter 2, Jefferson and his adherents in the Democratic-Republican Party of the 1790s were concerned that industrialization would create major inequalities and place workers under the power of business owners. To them, the only way a republic could survive was in a society without major inequalities of wealth, one in which property was widely disbursed. Working for wages was seen as a problem because such workers were dependent on others. "Dependence begets subservience and venality, suffocates the germ of virtue, and prepares fit tools for the designs of ambition," Jefferson had written in protest against industrialization. "Let our workshops remain in Europe." He also supported redistribution if this was needed to reduce inequality. Speaking of France prior to the revolution, Jefferson wrote to Madison in 1785 that "the consequences of this enormous inequality producing so much misery to the bulk of mankind, legislators cannot invent too many devises for subdividing property."[12]

The fear that wage laborers were a dependent class that could not be relied on to sustain a republic continued through the age of Jackson to the Civil War. Whigs and Democrats "shared the long-standing republican conviction that economic independence is essential to citizenship," the political scientist Michael J. Sandel has argued. The debate continued in the 1850s between the North and South over free versus slave labor. Southerners charged that Northern wage labor was, in fact, worse than slave labor. "The free laborer . . . was little more than the 'slave of the community'" Foner writes of the Southern point of view. One Southern senator described slave labor as "hired for life and well compensated" while paid laborers in the North were "hired by the day, not cared for, and scantily compensated." Lincoln provided the rejoinder from the free labor side, insisting that equality of opportunity in the North for free labor would open doors and allow a person to become a future business owner. "The man who labored for another last year, this year labors for himself, and next year he will hire others to labor for him."[13]

But the American economy by the dawn of the twentieth century was no longer what it had been in the days prior to the Civil War. The farm-based economy had been transformed during the Gilded Age, and now more people were wage workers in a society that was increasingly industrial and urbanized. This had led to proposals, first by Populists led by William Jennings Bryan, and then by Progressives like Theodore Roosevelt and Woodrow Wilson, to use the power of the government to help average Americans. In many ways, Roosevelt was taking the next logical step in this process. To fight the Great Depression and create a more equitable society, Roosevelt had turned to the use of an active government committed to providing economic security to the American people. Society had begun to recognize that economic security was "a political condition of personal freedom," as the writer Irwin Edman framed it in 1941.[14]

In that same 1936 speech in which Roosevelt accepted the Democratic nomination, he clearly tied the New Deal with the historic struggle to ensure that wage workers were truly free. Industrialization had caused new problems that endangered the "political and economic freedom for which Washington and Jefferson planned and fought," FDR proclaimed. "For out of this modern civilization economic royalists carved new dynasties . . . all undreamed of by the Fathers." Out of concentrated economic power, "the privileged . . . reached out for control of government itself." This meant that average working people had lost control over major portions of their lives, such as hours of work and the wages they received, which were "imposed by this new industrial dictatorship." The only way to deal with such "economic tyranny" was for the people to appeal to "the organized power of government" to ensure "equal opportunity in the marketplace."[15]

The second thing that Roosevelt did was to redefine liberalism itself. Rather than classical liberalism, which stood for limited government and the protection of the rights of the individual, he began to equate the Democratic Party and the New Deal with an updated version of liberalism. In a radio address before the midterm elections of 1938, Roosevelt linked both Theodore Roosevelt and Woodrow Wilson with "liberal government." He also called the policies that had been implemented in New York State while he was governor "a magnificent liberal program." "The voters throughout the country should remember that need for continuous liberal government when they vote next Tuesday," Roosevelt said. "FDR made liberalism the defining label of his New Deal politics and the exclusive property of the Democratic Party," Gerstle writes.[16]

Roosevelt's speech on the Four Freedoms, which he gave on January 6, 1941, as part of the State of the Union address to Congress, was the culmination of his redefinition of liberalism. The Four Freedoms were part of FDR's effort to awaken the American people and Congress to the dangers of fascism and communism, to explain the danger these ideologies posed. As we saw in the introduction, the Four Freedoms were meant to provide for the "foundations of a healthy and strong democracy" not only in the United States but also around the world. The most controversial of the Four Freedoms was freedom from want. By 1944, Roosevelt would push for an economic bill of rights designed to ensure that Americans never suffered from want again. Freedom from want blended both liberty and equality, combining the importance of the individual with the need for a strong community of support. "There can be no real freedom for the common man without enlightened social policies," Roosevelt declared late in 1941.[17]

Gary Gerstle provides a very useful summary of this marriage of classical and modern liberalism when he discusses the moral principle that the "public good ought to take precedence over private rights." He goes on to write:

> . . . *the goal of government action—and a central part of the pursuit of the public good—ought to be to enhance every individual's opportunities for personal fulfillment. Classical liberalism had long made the full flowering of each person's individuality a centerpiece of its agenda. New Dealers did not abandon this age-old liberal goal; they simply argued that government intervention in markets and, to a certain extent in private life had become necessary to position people to enjoy the full ambit of their freedom.*[18]

The Republicans and Jefferson

Hoover was embittered in the aftermath of the 1932 election. He truly believed by the summer of 1932 that his policies were working and that the worst of the Great Depression was behind the United States. "Like the deposed chief of state of a government in exile, he churned out reams of print to demonstrate that the principles he had followed were the right ones," Leuchtenburg writes. He criticized the New Deal as a "move to gigantic socialism" that had "a pronounced odor of totalitarian government." He feared that the individual "is solely the pawn of the state" under the changes that Roosevelt and the Democrats had implemented.[19]

Although Hoover had been a progressive throughout the 1920s and during his early presidency, he turned hard to the right in his postpresidential life. In 1936 he proclaimed: "Either we shall have a society based upon liberty and the initiative of the individual, or we shall have a planned society that means dictation. . . . There is no halfway ground." He seemed to have completely forgotten his own valiant attempts to use governmental intervention to confront the Great Depression and had become a great adherent of laissez-faire. Yet he stood outside of the mainstream of much of the Republican Party during these years, complaining of their "partial adherence to the planned economy and other features of the New Deal." As Joan Hoff Wilson writes, "Hoover found himself consistently uninfluential between 1933 and 1952."[20]

Each of the Republican presidential candidates during the elections from 1936 to 1952 tended to accept major features of the New Deal. Alf Landon, the Republican nominee in 1936, had been a Progressive supporter of Theodore Roosevelt. Landon favored a "social security law that was under state control," Dallek writes. Wendell Willkie had been from a Democratic family and had only become a Republican in 1940 when he was the Republican nominee. "Willkie supported virtually all of the accomplishments of the New Deal except the TVA," Smith writes. Dwight D. Eisenhower, who was first elected president in 1952 as a Republican, secured the New Deal order during the 1950s.[21]

Yet if the presidential candidates and Republican Party leaders of this period abandoned Hoover, there was an underlying right-wing movement that was critical of FDR and the New Deal and stood for the older version of classical liberalism. Many of the opponents of the New Deal took on the mantle of protecting free enterprise from the interference of government. Their members included "combinations of small businesses represented by the National Association of Manufacturers, the larger firms united in the U.S. Chamber of Commerce, moderate Republicans, conservative Democrats, reactionary newspaper publishers, libertarians, and many others," historian Lawrence B. Glickman writes.

By 1934 they formed the American Liberty League to "teach the duty of government to encourage private enterprise and protect the ownership and use of property," as Schlesinger writes. When Roosevelt was asked about the principles of the Liberty League, he said he too supported those goals, but that they were incomplete, comparing them to only "two or three of the Ten Commandments." As Schlesinger frames it, FDR thought that "the League said nothing about the need for teaching respect for the right of individuals against those who sought to enrich themselves at the expense of their fellow citizens, nor about the duty of government to find jobs for all who wished to work."[22]

In response to FDR absconding with the term *liberal*, Hoover himself refused to call himself a conservative. He was, instead, a true liberal before it had been "polluted and raped of all its real meaning," by FDR. Liberalism stood for freedom from governmental interference and "unfettered economic opportunity for the enterprising individual," as Foner frames it. This battle over the label of *liberal* would go on for some time. Both the anti-statist Austrian economist Friedrich A. Hayek and one of his disciples, Milton Friedman, considered themselves to be classical liberals opposed to the New Deal. Yet ultimately those opposed to the New Deal and its version of liberalism would come to be called conservatives. They would be in the political wilderness but would find a leader to their liking in Ronald Reagan.[23]

FDR and the New Deal certainly did not end the cycles of history. When Ronald Reagan was elected president in 1980, he began the process of unraveling the New Deal order. His mantra was "government is not the solution to our problem; government is the problem." Little wonder that Reagan would reclaim Thomas Jefferson and place him in the center of his conservative revolution.

Reagan had not always been an antigovernment conservative. As a young actor in Hollywood, he had been an FDR liberal. Roosevelt and Reagan shared certain characteristics. They were both supreme optimists, much as Thomas Jefferson was. Both men had a core to them that nobody quite knew. Reagan's second wife, Nancy, wrote in 1989 that "there's a wall around him." His closest advisors felt much the same way. "Nobody around him understood him," one of his biographers has written.[24]

It was during the postwar years that Ronald Reagan began to change regarding New Deal–style liberalism. While serving as the president of the Screen Actors Guild in the early 1950s, he was an anti-communist liberal. During a hearing in Washington, DC, regarding communist influence in Hollywood, "Reagan argued for maintaining democratic procedure and against outlawing the Communist Party," Jacob Weisberg writes. Reagan quoted Jefferson that "if the American people know all of the facts, they will never make a mistake." He would soon change his mind and urge the banning of the Communist Party. By 1952, Reagan had become a "Democrat for Eisenhower."[25]

In 1954 Reagan became the host of the television show *General Electric Theater*. As part of the job, Reagan traveled around the country, touring General Electric plants in various cities. It was during these trips, taken mostly by train, that Reagan began to read a variety of conservative books, including Hayek's *Road to Serfdom*. Over an eight-year period, Reagan moved from FDR liberal to free market conservative. Reagan described this time as his "postgraduate course in political science."[26]

His second wife, Nancy Davis, may have had some influence over Reagan during this period. Her stepfather, Loyal Davis, "was a rich and distinguished brain surgeon . . . and an adamant political reactionary filled with livid detestation for that apostate, Franklin Roosevelt," according to Barber. Loyal Davis was also good friends with Barry Goldwater, and in time, Reagan would become a Goldwater supporter.[27]

Unlike FDR, who had concluded that activist government was needed to ensure the freedom of the common man, Reagan had become convinced that government was a threat to liberty. In a speech in 1957, Reagan said: "It's just that there is something inherent in government which makes it, when it isn't controlled, continue to grow. . . . Remember that every government service, every offer of government financed security, is paid for in the loss of personal freedom." Hoover could not have said it better. Reagan was initially viewed as an extremist, but he would ride his antigovernment philosophy all the way to the White House.[28]

Jefferson's vision of small government naturally appealed to Reagan. He had been collecting quotes from the founders for many years, especially "on the dangers of consolidated government," according to Burstein. "If we can prevent the govt. from wasting the labor of the people under the pretense of caring for them, they will be happy" was a favorite saying of Reagan's. One of Reagan's supporters said that "in Ronald Reagan, this country has probably the most Jeffersonian president since Martin Van Buren."[29]

Reagan's most extensive tribute to Jefferson came in 1987, when he invoked the memory of the long-dead founder to support his "America's Economic Bill of Rights," which included a requirement to balance the budget. It was an interesting proposal given that Reagan substantially increased the budget deficit and national debt during his eight years in office. "It's time to finish the job Jefferson began and to protect our people and their livelihoods with restrictions of government that will ensure the fundamental economic freedom of the people," Reagan proclaimed. He also warned that "our overly centralized government poses a threat to our liberty" and then quoted Jefferson from his first inaugural to the effect that government should "not take from the mouth of labor the bread it has earned."[30]

As Burstein has observed, "if FDR's adaptation of Jeffersonianism can be called 'loose construction' of Jefferson, we can label Reagan's 'strict construction.'" Yet that "strict construction" left a great deal to be desired. While Reagan certainly channeled Jefferson's mistrust of large government, he did it to support the wealthy. Jefferson would have been aghast at the rise of income and wealth inequality during the Reagan presidency and its aftermath. One of the axioms that Roosevelt correctly picked up on about Jefferson was his support of the common man.[31]

It should come as no surprise that the Reagan Revolution led to the widening of both income and wealth inequality after the New Deal order had led to a decline in inequality. Whereas the top 1 percent controlled 22 percent of wealth in the 1970s, by 2014 they controlled 40 percent of wealth. Income distribution saw similar trends, with the top 1 percent controlling 10.5 percent of national income in 1976, which doubled to 20 percent by 2014. "Inequality has also increased among those in the lower 90 or 99 percent of income ranks, and real incomes at the bottom have barely risen," the economists Lindert and Williamson write. Little wonder that the Economic Policy Institute released a study in 2018 entitled *The New Gilded Age*, showing that these trends have worsened since 2015.[32]

There were numerous reasons for this, including the decline of unions, the impact of across-the-board tax cuts, the deregulation of the finance industry, and the expansion of free trade. But there is no doubt that the pendulum shift toward a more conservative politics played a role. As Lindert and Williamson write: "the rightward shift in economic policy, like the rise in inequality, was centered on countries that voted for Margaret Thatcher and Ronald Reagan, stopping their long twentieth century trend toward regulation, union power, the welfare state, and the New Deal." It was the age-old problem that we have examined in this book, that of finding the right balance between the good of the individual and the good of the broader society. "The collective norm that 'we are all in this together' was replaced by a libertarian norm that we're not," Putnam and Garrett argue.[33]

Yet Reagan could never completely overturn the New Deal, nor did he really try. Instead, the policies he followed helped to stack the deck to ensure that income would flow to the top of the income scale. But the idea of the New Deal remained, that the relationship between individual Americans and their government had changed. No longer would people be subjected to the whims of the private marketplace and the booms and busts of capitalism alone. Government would be on the side of the people and provide a safety net as needed. Programs like unemployment insurance, Social Security, Medicare, Medicaid, and the Affordable Care Act (a later program implemented during the Obama administration) would provide a floor underneath the individual.

The government would also be responsible for maintaining what economists call the *macroeconomy*. The World Bank defines *macroeconomics* as the field that "focuses on the performance of economies—changes in economic output, inflation, interest, foreign exchange rates, and the balance of payments. Poverty reduction, social equity, and sustainable growth are only possible with sound monetary and fiscal policy." During the Great Depression the British economist John Maynard Keynes argued that governments must borrow and spend public money "during the trough of business cycles," which puts "money in the hands of consumers" and stimulates the economy. While Keynesianism has its critics, most of whom are on the conservative side, that logic continues to influence economic policy today. In 2009, the Obama administration proposed, and Congress approved, a stimulus package to help offset the impacts of the 2008 financial collapse. In response to the pandemic in 2020, Congress and the Trump administration approved two massive stimulus bills, which were followed in 2021 by the Biden administration's Build Back Better legislation.[34]

Over the long sweep of American history, we have traced how liberals and conservatives have swapped positions over the role of active government. It was initially the conservatives who pushed for a powerful central government, in part to transform the United States into an industrial society. The result of their efforts would likely have surprised them beyond their wildest hopes. The American economy became very Hamiltonian, with the Industrial Revolution leading to significant growth and expanding prosperity. It also transformed the United States into a world power. The Industrial Revolution led to the creation of large-scale businesses, massive fortunes, and a prosperity that was not widely shared. It fell to the inheritors of Jefferson to adjust their worldview to deal with the world Hamilton had helped create. Starting with William Jennings Bryan and running through Wilson and FDR, Democrats turned to active government to control industrialization and give the average person a chance to advance. The inheritors of Hamilton rejected the active government he advanced in order to protect the world he helped create. It is the world we still live in.

Gary Gerstle, in his book entitled *The Rise and Fall of the Neoliberal Order*, has documented how both the New Deal order and the Reagan Revolution have ended. "Stagflation precipitated the fall of the New Deal order in the 1970s; the Great Recession of 2008–09 triggered the fracturing of the neoliberal [or neoconservative] order in the 2010s," he writes. What will come next, no one knows. Roosevelt had wondered in his book review where the next Jefferson would come from. Today, as the neoconservative order has unraveled, one wonders where the next Roosevelt will come from.[35]

Endnotes

1   John Ferling, *Jefferson and Hamilton: The Rivalry That Forged a Nation* (New York: Bloomsbury Press, 2013), p. x–xii.

2   Not everyone agrees that Jefferson was the founder of the Democratic Party. See for example Michael Kazin, *What It Took to Win: A History of the Democratic Party* (New York: Farrar, Straus and Giroux, 2022). Joseph J. Ellis, *American Dialogue: The Founders and Us* (New York: Knopf, 2018), p. 114. Ellis was speaking of all of the founders in his actual quote, whereas I have applied this to Jefferson. Yet as Ellis knows, of all of the founders, Jefferson's words can be used to support numerous positions.

3   For a description of the day of the dedication, see the article "Jefferson Memorial Dedication Drew Dignitaries," retrieved August 12, 2022, from https://www.nps.gov/articles/jeffersondedication.htm; Andrew Burstein, *Democracy's Muse: How Thomas Jefferson Became an FDR Liberal, A Reagan Republican, and a Tea Party Fanatic, All While Being Dead* (Charlottesville: University of Virginia Press, 2015), p. xii and p. 13.

4   Alter, p. 208; Thomas T. McAvoy, "Roosevelt: A Modern Jefferson," *The Review of Politics*, July 1945, retrieved from www.jstor.org/stable/1404178; Gary Gerstle, *The Rise and Fall of the Neoliberal Order: America and World in the Free Market Era* (New York: Oxford University Press, 2022), p. 2.

5   Merrill D. Peterson, *The Jefferson Image in the American Mind* (Thomas Jefferson Memorial Foundation and the University of Virginia Press: Charlottesville, 1968), p. 361–362; Burstein, p. 14.

6   Joseph J. Ellis, *American Sphinx: The Character of Thomas Jefferson* (New York: Alfred A. Knopf, 1996), p. 9.

7   McAvoy, p. 276.

8   Peterson, p. 355; FDR's speech at the Jefferson Day dinner was retrieved August 17, 2022, from https://www.presidency.ucsb.edu/documents/address-jefferson-day-dinner-st-paul-minnesota.

9   Burstein, p. 9; Roosevelt's speech to the Commonwealth Club was retrieved on June 13, 2022, from https://www.americanrhetoric.com/speeches/fdrcommonwealth.htm.

10 Koch and Peden, p. 674; Peterson, p. 356–357.

11 Foner, *American Freedom*, p. 196; for a portion of the text of that speech, including a recording of this key section, see https://shec.ashp.cuny.edu/items/show/2023.

12 Koch and Peden, p. 280 and p. 386.

13 Sandel, p. 169; Foner, *American Freedom*, p. 63; McPherson, p. 28; Joseph Fishkin and William E. Forbath, *The Anti-Oligarchy Constitution: Reconstructing the Economic Foundations of American Democracy* (Cambridge: Harvard University Press, 2022), p. 92.

14 Census data shows that while 53 percent of Americans were engaged in agriculture in 1870, by 1930 that figure had dropped to 21 percent. See table XXI at the following website: https://www2.census.gov/prod2/decennial/documents/00312147ch2.pdf; the quote is from Foner, *American Freedom*, p. 196; see also Abrams, p. 13.

15 John Gabriel Hunt, ed., *The Essential Franklin Delano Roosevelt* (Avenal: Portland House, 1995), p. 114–119.

16 For FDR's radio address, see https://www.presidency.ucsb.edu/documents/radio-address-the-election-liberals retrieved August 25, 2022; Gerstle, p. 82.

17 Foner, *American Freedom*, p. 225.

18 Gerstle, p. 26.

19 Leuchtenburg, *Hoover*, p. 150–151; Wilson, p. 212.

20 Leuchtenburg, *Hoover*, p. 151; Wilson, p. 220–221.

21 Dallek, p. 253–254; Smith, p. 452–453; Gerstle, p. 29.

22 Schlesinger, *The Coming*, p. 486–487.

23 Foner, *American Freedom*, p. 204–205; Gerstle, p. 84–85; Lawrence Glickman, "Everyone Was a Liberal," retrieved August 29, 2022, from https://aeon.co/essays/everyone-was-a-liberal-now-no-one-wants-to-be.

24 Jacob Weisberg, *Ronald Reagan* (New York: Times Books, 2016), p. 4–5.

25 Weisberg, p. 26–27.

26 Weisberg, p. 34.

27 Barber, p. 241–243.

28 Weisberg, p. 34.

29 Burstein, p. 171–173.

30 Burstein, p. 175–177.

31 Burstein, p. 178.

32 Putnam and Garrett, p. 34–37; Williams and Lindert, p. 239–240; Estelle Sommeiller and Mark Price, "The New Gilded Age: Income Inequality in the U.S. by State, Metropolitan area, and County," retrieved September 19, 2022, from https://www.epi.org/publication/the-new-gilded-age-income-inequality-in-the-u-s-by-state-metropolitan-area-and-county/.

33 Williams and Lindert, p. 240; Putnam and Garrett, p. 46.

34 See the World Bank definition of macroeconomics at https://www.worldbank.org/en/topic/macroeconomics; the quote is from Gerstle, p. 22.

35 Gerstle, p. 2.

Glossary of Terms for American Political Parties

The evolution of American political parties is confusing, largely because names recur for political parties that are not related to each other. This glossary is intended to help the reader as they attempt to untangle these relationships. The following table shows the chronological evolutions of the main political parties. Please note that the dates shown are estimates, since for many of these parties there is no one date when they began or ended. Similarly, the descriptions provided are general; the parties' platforms and agendas are described more fully in the balance of the book.

Chronology of Major Political Parties

Conservative	Liberal
Federalist (1789–1820)	Republican (1792–1825)
National Republican (1824-1833	Democrat (1825–Present)
Whig (1833–1854)	
Republican (1854-Present	

There are also a number of other parties mentioned in the book that did not survive in the long term but which the reader will encounter. These include the following:

> Know-Nothing Party

> Free Soil Party

> Greenback Party

> Liberal Republican Party

> People's Party (Populist Party)

> Progressive Party

> Grand Old Party

> Socialist Party

> Workingmen's Party

> Bull Moose Party

Major Parties

Federalist: The term *Federalist* applies both to those who supported ratification of the Constitution and to those who formed a political party during the 1790s. The Federalist Party largely dominated government during the first ten years of the new nation and supported an activist government to advance economic development and foster industry in the United States. Many members of the Federalist Party were skeptical of too much democracy. Alexander Hamilton was a leading member of the party. George Washington intended to stay above the political disputes of the day, although he largely supported the policies that Hamilton and the Federalists supported. The party began to fade in the aftermath of the War of 1812.

Republican (Jefferson): The original Republican Party formed in opposition to the Federalists. Thomas Jefferson, in a discussion with George Washington in 1792, warned that Hamilton intended to "prepare the way for a change from the present republican form of government to that of monarchy . . ." Jefferson's Republicans are sometimes called the Democratic-Republicans, although it does not appear they used that term. They wanted the United States to remain largely agrarian and supported a greater role for the common person in politics. They began to dominate politics in the aftermath of the 1800 election, in which Jefferson was elected president.[1]

National Republican: By the time that James Monroe was elected president in 1816, the Republicans were the remaining national political party. However, this masked clear factional differences between the members of the party. In 1824, when John Quincy Adams emerged as president from a vote in the House of Representatives, he and Henry Clay began to refer to themselves as National Republicans. The National Republicans had more in common with the Federalists than they did the Republicans, since they supported an activist federal government, economic development, and the creation of industry.[2]

Democrat: Those Republicans who had supported Andrew Jackson in the election of 1824 began to call themselves Democrats. They continued to support many of the earlier policies of the Republicans, such as limited government and states' rights, although they were also staunch unionists. While I have listed them as liberal, there were definitely very conservative elements of the party, including many plantation owners who had enslaved Black people. By the time of Franklin Roosevelt in the early 1930s, the party began to appear as we see it today, as an advocate for activist government in order to ensure equality for all. Conservative elements, especially from the South, remained in the party until the aftermath of Nixon's Southern strategy in 1968, when they gradually moved to the Republican Party.

Whig: Henry Clay formed the Whig Party out of the National Republicans in 1833. The party was created in response to perceived abuses of executive power by President Andrew Jackson. Clay adopted the name because the Whigs stood against "royal power and stood foursquare for freedom and independence" during the American Revolution. The Whig Party shared with the Federalists and the National Republicans support for an active federal government in order to create economic development and foster industrialization.[3]

Republican: The Republican Party also began in 1854 as an anti-slavery party. Although they are listed as conservative, they were originally a radical party committed to ending the expansion of slavery in the United States. The party also supported the active governmental policies of the earlier Federalists, Whigs, and National Republicans. They initially merged former Whigs and Democrats into a strong antislavery party based in the North. In the aftermath of Reconstruction, the party began to be dominated by a pro-business, antigovernment faction that would eventually become the dominate group in the party.

Endnotes

1   Gordon Wood, *Empire of Liberty: A History of the Early Republic, 1789–1815* (Oxford: Oxford University Press, 2009), p. 154.

2   Daniel Walker Howe, *What Hath God Wrought: The Transformation of America, 1815–1848* (Oxford: Oxford University Press, 2007), p. 210.

3   Robert V. Remini, *Henry Clay: Statesmen of the Union* (New York: W. W. Norton & Company, 1991), p. 458–459.

The letter *t* after a page number
indicates a table.

A

abolitionist movement, 54, 72–75, 160,
161–62
active government. *See* government,
active (overview)
Adams, John, 10–12, 15, 29–30, 49, 57
Adams, John Quincy, 30, 49, 54–55,
57, 64, 72
Addams, Jane, 159–61
Addams, John, 159
African Americans. *See* Black people
Agricultural Adjustment Act (AAA),
273–74
Alabama, 59
Alien and Sedition Acts, 61
AMA (American Medical Association),
163
Amalgamated Association of Iron and
Steel Workers, 112
American Anti-Slavery Society (AASS),
72
American Bar Association (ABA), 163
American Colonization Society, 71–72
American Farm Bureau Federation, 274
American Federation of Labor (AFL),
121

American Indians, removal of, 54
American Individualism (Hoover), 238
American Liberty League, 300–301
American Medical Association (AMA),
163
American Railroad Union, 121
American Revolution, government and
society. *See also* classical liberalism
(Lockean liberalism); classical
republicanism (communitarianism)
classical liberalism and
republicanism, 9–12
colonial world, 1–5
Constitution, 17–25
equality, 12–15
equality and slavery, 15–17
financing of, 83
impact of, 5–9
Antebellum period, economy and
government
banking and inequality, 64–66
free labor and slave labor, 71–75
infrastructure, 62–64
liberalism/republicanism and the
parties, 68–71
Market Revolution, 58–60
sale of public land, 66–68
tariffs, 60–62
Union collapses, 75–77

Index

conservatives
  equality and, 15
  no longer supported active
    government, 192
  top-down leadership, 70–71
Constitution. *See also* Articles of
  Confederation
  debate on government's role, 1
  drafting of, 30
  Eighteenth Amendment (1918),
    161
  elected officials, 22–23
  elitist drive for, 23
  Fifteenth Amendment (1870), 99
  Fourteenth Amendment (1868), 99
  impact on government and society,
    17–25
  infrastructure, 62–63
  money, 83
  Nineteenth Amendment (1920),
    162
  Sixteenth Amendment (1913),
    204–5
  Thirteenth Amendment (1865),
    97–98
  Twentieth Amendment (1933),
    262–63
Constitutional Convention, 23–24
Constitutional Government in the United States (Wilson), 200
Constitution of the Confederate States,
  89–90
Continental Congress, 7, 8
Cooke, Jay, 82–83
Coolidge, Calvin, 212, 214, 216–18,
  230, 239
corruption
  fear of in founding era, 11–12, 35–36
  in transcontinental railroad, 127
cotton production, 59
council-manager system (Dayton
  founding), 163–64

Cox, James M., 214
Coxe, Tench, 32
Coxey, Jacob, 143
Crédit Mobilier, 127
Crisis magazine, 225–26
Crocker, Charles, 88
Crocker, Edwin, 88
Croly, David, 168
Croly, Herbert, 168–70
Croly, Jane, 168
Cumberland Road, 63
Czolgosz, Leon, 176

D

Darrow, Clarence, 223
Daugherty, Harry, 216
Davis, Jefferson, 93, 94
Davis, Loyal, 302
Davis, Nancy (Nancy Reagan), 302
Dawes, Charles, 215
Debs, Eugene V., 121, 151, 202, 207
debt, international
  Hoover seeks FDR's advice on,
    265–66
Declaration of Independence, 30
Delano, Sara (Sara Roosevelt), 241,
  243–44
democracy
  direct vs. representative, 39–40
  growth of in Antebellum period,
    53–58
  power in, 135–40
Democratic-Republicans (Jeffersonian).
  See Republicans/Republican Party
  (Jeffersonian)
Democrats/Democratic Party
  (Jacksonian)
  artificial inequality, 66–67
  Bryan and, 144–47
  chronology of political parties,
    309*t*, 311–12
  election of 1824, 54

liberty
  government protection of, 9–10
  positive versus negative, 55
Lincoln, Abraham
  changing purpose of Civil War, 94–98
  Gettysburg Address, 12, 80, 135
  habeas corpus, 93–94
  ranking of, 129*t*
  rise of, 76–77
  transcontinental railroad, 87–89
  wage labor, 296
Lippmann, Walter, 263
Locke, John, xviii–xix, xx
Lodge, Henry Cabot, 173–74
Long, Huey, 281
Lovejoy, Owen, 86

M
Machiavelli, 241
Macon, Nathaniel, 48
macroeconomy, 305
Madison, James
  on confederacies, 19
  on democracy, 20–23
  drafting of Constitution, 30
  economics (Madisonian platform),
    44–47
  on Federalists, 39
  on government, xvii, 23
  infrastructure, 63
  on national debt, 33–35
  on slavery, 16
Madisonian Platform, 44–47
Mao Zedong, 135
market economy, 41*t*, 58–60, 64–66
Market Revolution. *See* market
  economy
Marx, Karl, 116
Marxism/Marxists, 116, 117, 119–20,
  159
Maryland, 3
Mason, George, 16

Massachusetts, 16, 19
Massachusetts colony, 7
Maysville Road, 64
McArthur, Douglas, 255–56, 263
McClellan, George, 95
McClure, Samuel S., 167
McClure's Magazine, 167
McCosh, James, 177
McKinley, Ida (Ida Saxton), 149
McKinley, William, 148–50, 151–53,
  175–76, 184, 195
McKinley Tariff Act, 141, 149–50
McNary-Haugen plan, 222
meatpacking industry, 190
medicine as profession, 162–63
Mellon, Andrew, 214, 215, 218–19, 246
Mellon bill, 219
Mercer, Lucy, 243
Mexican-American War, 73–74
middle class, rise of, 120, 148, 157–58
military draft, 91–92
Mississippi, 165
Missouri Compromise (1820), 75, 87
Moley, Raymond A., 254, 263–64, 266,
  272
Monroe, James, 64
Morgan, John Pierpont, 108–9, 157,
  186, 274
Morrill, Justin Smith, 85, 87
Muir, John, 191
Mussolini, Benito, 277

N
Nation, Carrie, 160–61
National Archives Building, 292
National Association for the
  Advancement of Colored People
  (NAACP), 225–26
National Banking Act (1863), 84
National Industrial Recovery Act
  (NIRA), 276–77
National Labor Relations Act (NLRA)